Traits of Writing

The Complete Guide
for **Middle School**

RUTH CULHAM

SCHOLASTIC

New York • Toronto • London • Auckland • Sydney
Mexico City • New Delhi • Hong Kong • Buenos Aires

For Sam, always

CREDITS:

Pages 91–92: Excerpt from *How Angel Peterson Got His Name and Other Outrageous Tales About Extreme Sports* by Gary Paulsen. Copyright © 2003 by Gary Paulsen. Used by permission of Random House Children's Books, a division of Random House, Inc.

Page 97: Excerpt from "Making Writing Instruction a Priority in America's Middle and High Schools," April 2007, published by the Alliance for Excellent Education.

Pages 124 and 242: Excerpt from *Winterdance: The Fine Madness of Running the Iditarod* by Gary Paulsen. Copyright © 1994 by Gary Paulsen. Reprinted by permission of Houghton Mifflin Harcourt Publishing Company. All rights reserved.

Page 136: Excerpts from *Beyond the Game: The Collected Sportswriting of Gary Smith*. Copyright © 2001 by Gary Smith. Used by permission of Grove/Atlantic.

Page 137: From "Baseball for Life" by Sara Corbett. Published in *New York Times Play Magazine*.

Page 141: Peanuts cartoon copyright © by Unied Feature Syndicate, Inc. Reprited by permission. All rights reserved.

Page 164: Excerpt from *My Life in Dog Years* by Gary Paulsen. Copyright © 1998 by Gary Paulsen. Used by permission of Dell Publishing, a division of Random House, Inc.

Page 248: From *Bat Loves the Night* by Nicola Davies. Copyright © 2001 by Nicola Davies. Published by Candlewick Press.

Page 249: "Waiting on the World to Change" by John Mayer. Published by Hal Leonard Corporation.

Page 261: AP Images/*Post Register*, Robert Bower

Every effort has been made to find the authors and publishers of previously published material in this book and to obtain permission to print it.

Editor: Raymond Coutu
Cover and Interior Designer: Maria Lilja
Copy Editor: Carol Ghiglieri
Photographer: Bridey Monterossi
ISBN-10: 0-545-01363-1
ISBN-13: 978-0-545-01363-5
Copyright © 2010 by Ruth Culham.
All rights reserved. Printed in the U.S.A.

2 3 4 5 6 7 8 9 10   23   14 13 12 11 10 09

Contents

Acknowledgments

For years, this project haunted me. I desperately wanted to write about teaching middle school, but was terrified I'd have nothing new to say. Thanks to so many people, though, I found my voice while drafting these pages.

Linda Brock, eighth-grade English teacher at Delta Woods Middle School, Blue Springs, Missouri, never faltered in supplying student papers and support. Thank you from me and every teacher who finds inspiration and courage to teach writing because of your generosity.

I extend thanks, too, to Melanie and Ryann, the two talented, Cheez-It-obsessed students featured in the prologue and epilogue, and to their moms, Jennifer Landon and Beth Lowther, who trusted me with their greatest treasures. Meeting them was, without question, the highlight of this project.

Here's to the middle school students and their teachers across the country whose fine work and wise insights about the traits pepper these pages. This is a better book for your contributions. A special thank-you to Kelly Knudsen and to April Harmon of Blue Springs, Missouri, for helping Emilee, Ashton, Preston, and Jared create the presentation posters. And to Peter and Sarah Hillebrand, whose mom slipped me your remarkable papers.

I'm grateful to Julie Redding and the staff at Palmyra Middle School in New York, to Jennifer (J.J.) Kochn, sixth-grade teacher in Shelby Township, Michigan, and her artist class, and to Becca Gilman of Mt. Lake Middle School in Newman Lake, Washington. The teachers and administrators at the Beaufort School District in South Carolina welcomed me with open arms, sharpened pencils, and taught me so much, and I continue to learn from them.

There would be no book without the love, support, and encouragement of colleagues and confidantes. Linda Rief and Laura Robb, visionary thinkers and writers, have put middle school literacy on the map for legions of educators. My deepest gratitude also goes out to David L. Harrison for not only writing the brilliant poem at the start of Chapter 8, but also knowing when to nudge me to soldier on and when to tell me to call it a day.

Sharon Northern was enormously helpful as she navigated my moods and quirks through this process, and Bridey, Rhett, Jean, Ann, Janet, Mary Sue, Denise, Chico, and all my other dear friends continue to try to fill a gaping hole in my heart.

To Don, my writing mentor and beloved uncle. Because of you I fell in love with words. I miss you already.

Thank you to Scholastic for adopting me and this work, especially to members of the Teaching Resources team: Virginia Dooley, Eileen Hillebrand, Susan Kolwicz, Joanna Davis-Swing, Jaime Lucero, Maria Lilja, Carol Ghiglieri, Kevin Taylor, and, retired but always in my heart, Terry Cooper.

And to Ray Coutu. No writer could have a better editor. No person could have a better friend.

Foreword
By Linda Rief

Several years ago, I saw photographs in a magazine of two signs advertising puppies for sale. One sign was created from an old piece of barn board that was gray with age and had obviously suffered a multitude of uses and misuses, judging from the number of nails that were holding it together. The black painted letters rose and fell like scratch marks in sand. They said:

MUST SELL
FRESH LITTER OF MUTTS
OUT OF CONTROL
555-1090
DON'T CALL Before 6 pm

The other sign, which appeared next to the first one, was printed on a clean, white board and was written in easy-to-read black block letters that said:

Puppies for Sale

Beautiful mixed litter,
full of energy.
555-1090
Please call after 6 PM.

I tore the page out of the magazine, laminated it, hung it on my classroom wall, and wrote underneath it: "Writing—it's all in the words you choose and how you present them."

It's unlikely that the first sign would persuade any potential buyers. The second sign, however, most likely would, because it was carefully crafted to reach readers and tempt them to pick up the phone. This is what good writers do. They know that the words they choose contribute to the clarity of their ideas. They know that the presentation of those ideas impacts readers—either stopping them completely or pushing them to read on and, perhaps, react.

Our students need to know that when they have something important to say in writing, and they want that writing to be understood, craft matters. Good writers revise and edit their work. Good teachers show their students how to revise and edit their work. In this book, Ruth Culham shows all of us how to use the traits to help students do what good writers do.

In the voice of a teacher who spent 19 years in the classroom and who still knows the value of listening to students, Ruth begins and ends the book by letting Melanie and Ryann, two middle school students with "energy, vision, desire, and willingness," tell the story of how the traits help them revise and edit their work until it says clearly and exactly what they want it to. In between, she lets other students tell their stories—students at every point on the developmental spectrum.

Ruth does not bury us in educational jargon and research findings, but she does give us enough to frame and ground our thinking about the difficult task of teaching writing. She validates and supports us in our complex work by letting us know, in clear, concise terms, what the experts say.

Ruth also shows us explicitly how to use the traits to guide our writing instruction. She offers mini-lessons, activities, and assessment tools that nurture the voices of every student and provide the structure we need to help that student become the strongest writer he or she can be.

Why does this matter so much? Because writing matters. It empowers students to figure out what they know and want to know. It nurtures their voices and provokes their own thinking and the thinking of others.

By reflecting on and applying the traits of writing, students become the strongest writers/thinkers they can be—articulate, responsible citizens of a democratic society. Have I said what I want to say, clearly and simply? Is this well organized in developing my ideas? Have I used the sharpest, tightest, most vivid language? Does my lead capture readers and give them a clear direction to where I want to take them? Is my voice clear throughout the piece? Does my writing make the reader think or feel or learn something? These are the kinds of transformative questions Ruth encourages students to ask themselves as they revise and edit.

Of course, for all that to happen, our students have to care enough about their writing. They have to be given opportunities to find topics that matter to them. If that happens, they will revise and edit.

Ruth says, "The writing lives of your middle school students depend on us getting it right." Ruth, like Melanie and Ryann, has the energy, vision, desire, and willingness we all need as teachers of adolescents. With deep respect for students and teachers, she shows us important and practical things we can do to help our students become the strongest writers they can be. We work so hard every day to help them develop the competence and confidence they need to enrich their lives and succeed in their complicated world. Ruth, indeed, helps us "get it right."

Through her carefully crafted lessons, her thoughtfully chosen examples of student work, her energetic voice, and her passion for teaching and learning, Ruth Culham proves, "Writing—it's all in the words you choose and how you present them."

Linda Rief is a teacher at Oyster River Middle School in Durham, New Hampshire. She is the author of *Seeking Diversity: Language Arts With Adolescents* (Heinemann), *100 Quickwrites* (Scholastic), and *Inside the Writer's-Reader's Notebook* (Heinemann).

Prologue

Not too long ago, I was in an eighth-grade classroom, working with a production team to create a professional development video. The students were intrigued by the equipment being set up around them—lights, microphones, cameras, dollies, gels, reflectors, and scrims. During a break, I eavesdropped on a most interesting conversation.

"It's called a 'C47,' " Perry, one of the camera guys, said.

"What? Why on earth would you call a clothespin that?" asked Melanie, one of two students waiting to be interviewed for the video.

"Yeah, that's pretty weird," chimed in Ryann.

"The 1940s was the heyday of filmmaking," Perry explained. "Much of the equipment we use today was developed back then. What looks to you like a simple clothespin enabled cameramen to attach gels and remove scrims from lights without burning their fingers. Cameramen didn't use real clothespins since only equipment from the catalog was allowed on the set. So the equipment manufacturer developed a new item, a 'C47.' Most people think the name comes from the section and page of that original catalog: section C, page 47. The name stuck, and the C47 is still in widespread use in the video and movie industry today."

Perry's account fascinated the girls. They looked around at the camera crew's equipment with heightened interest. "What other video things have funny names like that?" asked Melanie.

In the next half hour, the girls created a list of video-related terms for their writer's notebooks. They added *sticks* (tripod), *craft services* (food), *juicers* (electricians), *apple box* (footrest), and *Elvis side* (the shiny side of a reflective board used for directing light). But their favorite term, by far, was *baby*, a small, high-watt light. At break time, the director would shout, "Kill the baby," meaning turn off the light. Melanie and Ryann were positively gleeful over that one.

The more terms the girls collected and shared, the more interested in video production everyone in the class became. Linda Brock, their English/language arts teacher, seized the moment and promised students that once the video was "in the can," they would study the video words and their origins for a week instead of ordinary words. Nice.

Even though I spent 19 years as a middle school teacher, I frequently ask myself what makes a middle school writing classroom work. I know successful teaching is a series of flexible moving parts. I know it's one part inspiration and a bigger part organization. I know that every middle school teacher struggles to achieve more good days than bad. And I knew I was watching a great day in action as we filmed.

Imagine my surprise when, about a month later, I got this letter from Melanie and Ryann:

Hey Ms. Culham,

We still laugh about the stuff we did during filming. Melanie and I have our C47s attached to our pencils. We also still have our papers of definitions. Mine is hanging in my room. Thanks for teaching us those cool words. Have you writen any books? You should make a fictional book about a CSI case and make Melanie and me the kid detective. That would be a good book. I would read it!!!!!

I could't a lot of the 8th graders to read it. You'd be famous and so will we. Sorry about the paper color change. We ran out of the cool tye dye paper. How often do you come back to this place? We hope you will write back! If you're too busy, we can wait. We're already passing notes with an 8 year old. (Mrs. Brock's youngest daughter) Have fun on your trip.

Sincerely,
Ryann & Melanie.

P.S. I improved my handwriting just for you

I love that Ryann was still using the terms like *C47*. But then look: She completely moves away from the topic of video production, seeming to say, "Yes, words about filming are cool, but I'd make a cool CSI detective in a book you'd write and I'd read. And by the way, other kids would read it. And we're writing to our teacher's daughter. Have fun traveling and did you notice my neat handwriting?" This is a quintessential example of the way middle school students think. They typically have so many thoughts that it's almost impossible to contain them in one place. (Small wonder middle school teachers often report that the trait of organization is particularly challenging!) Following Ryann's thinking here is not impossible, but you have to focus.

I wrote Melanie and Ryann back and challenged *them* to write the book, offering to provide feedback. Within a week they responded.

One of the things I've found interesting about Melanie and Ryann as writers is how they jumped from studying video terms to writing a detective novel, with hardly a breath in between. In an e-mail message, they told me they were inspired to write their book after thinking about how words we use change depending on our purposes for using them. This reminded me that learning is not always linear, nor is it always transparent, which presents challenges for those of us trying to assess where students are and where we need to take them.

After a few weeks, a draft of the first chapter arrived.

Chapter 1   Mango and Tang

Mango wound up her arm and swung with all her might. Her hand made contact with the back of Tang's head. Tang jerked up opening her eyes. "Dang, what was that for?" asked Tang rubbing her head. "You fell asleep and Mr. Magget asked you a question." Mango answered whispering and gesturing towards the front of the room. Tang stared at the board, hopefully trying to get information for the question she was supposed to be answering.

"Ms. Taylor, we're waiting." said Mr. Magget directing all eyes on Tang. She searched frantically through her mind and all she came up with was, "Um, False?"

Everyone laughed. "Ms. Taylor, if you fall asleep one more time, you'll spent the day with Mr. Grizzly in the principal's office." Tang looked at Mango for sympathy. Mango looked at her wide eyed and shrugged. Tang slumped in her seat and rested her head in her hands hopefully hiding her face from all those eyes staring and mocking her.

Isn't that a great final line? It captures the deepest fear of practically all middle school students: public ridicule. Melanie and Ryann nailed it. With the draft came this voice-filled e-mail:

> This is what we think should be the first chapter. Do you think it's long enough to be a chapter? Is it any good? Mrs. Brock can send you the rough drafts but me and Melanie will type it up and send it to you this way. Hope you like it. Do you think you can make grammatical editing? Is that even a word?
>
> Ryann and Melonhead
>
> P.S. that is our signature mark. Oh Yeah!! Mwahahahahaha.

And so the writing went: a few e-mails followed a longer draft, on which I weighed in with some heavy suggestions for revision. After a few days of silence, I received an enthusiastic e-mail response, with a second draft attached:

> Thanks for the advice and the help. We're not very good at writing books, let alone essays. I had a dream the first night you responded. It was a dream about the book. It was like I was really in the book!! I wrote everything I saw in my dream and found an awesome way to finish up the first chapter. I'll send it a little later because it's a lot and right now it's kinda late. Do you think the second chapter is a good place to find the first clue to bring us into the case? Or is it too early? Wait till you see who finds out about their secret life! I'm going to print the story and confer with my writing buddy.
>
> Ryann
>
> P.S. For some reason, people at school are starting to call me and Melanie Thing 1 and Thing 2.

Here's a taste of their second draft:

> Chapter 1: Mango and Tang
>
> Mango wound up her arm and swung with all her might. Her hand made contact with the back of Tang's head. Tang jerked up opening her eyes. "Dang, what was that for?" asked Tang rubbing her head. "You fell asleep and Mr. Maggot asked you a question," Mango answered whispering and gesturing towards the front of the room. Tang stared at the board, hopefully trying to get information for the question she was supposed to be answering. All it said was Proclamation of 1763. She was never very good with social studies.
>
> "Ms. Taylor, were waiting." said Mr. Maggot, directing all eye on Tang. She searched frantically through her mind and all she came up with was, "Um, F-False?"
>
> Every one laughed. "Ms. Taylor, if you fall asleep one more time, you will the day with Mr. Grizzly in the principal's office." Tang looked at Mango for sympathy. Mango looked at her wide eyed and shrugged. Tang slumped in her seat and rested her head in her hands hopefully hiding her face from all those eyes staring and mocking her...

Melanie and Ryann are writers. They have energy, vision, desire, and a willingness to revise. With coaching from their teacher and me, their ideas began to take shape and their draft improved dramatically. We corresponded a couple more times, their voices growing even stronger with each new message. But, as the school year progressed and our lives got busier, our correspondence began to trickle off.

Midwinter, I wrote Linda to see if Melanie and Ryann had written any new chapters. Her answer reminded me of the ephemeral nature of middle schoolers. "I'm not really sure," Linda replied. "The girls are totally into poetry right now."

If the girls never finish their novel, it's not the biggest problem in the world. The biggest problem would have been never starting, never wanting to try, never thinking that writing a book is possible when you are 13 years old. And there are way too many students in our middle schools who have that problem.

What I Know Works in Middle School

Melanie, Ryann, and Linda's story confirms what I know in my heart works in the middle school writing classroom:

The teacher must model how to learn.

By inviting in the film crew, Linda took a risk because she opened up her classroom to thousands of viewers: nameless, faceless teachers who might applaud or criticize her teaching. Even though she was anxious about the project initially, she welcomed the experience—and allowed her students to observe her angst and, ultimately, her pride. The same principle applies to writing: If we want our students to write, we have to show them we are writers ourselves, which means opening ourselves up to scrutiny.

Learning should be infectious.

Using the video crew's vocabulary as inspiration for word study was a great idea. Linda saw her students' interest and capitalized on it by revising her lesson plans accordingly to foster a fascination with language, not just an understanding of terms. Who knows where this might lead?

Students must be active.

Engaging in lively activities, working in small groups, sitting on the floor, listening to music, using the computer, and talking about works in progress kept Linda's students moving and, therefore, learning.

Students will work hard if we give them rigorous, relevant tasks.

Melanie and Ryann took a giant step forward by coming up with their own project and using all the skills they had learned over the years to accomplish it. What they wrote matters less than the fact that they chose to write with such passion and determination.

Students deserve honest, detailed feedback.

As Melanie and Ryann got more serious about their writing, Linda and I got more serious about our feedback. They appreciated our suggestions for making their writing smoother, clearer, and more interesting, and, like any serious writers, didn't always agree or follow them. But the girls trusted us to tell them the truth because they knew our feedback, as difficult as it sometimes was to convey, would help to propel their work forward.

These are just a few ways to help middle school writers succeed. There are many more, which I cover in the chapters that follow. As you read those chapters, keep Melanie and Ryann in mind, along with the millions of other middle school students who need us. The secrets of writing, once locked away in the writing teacher's vault, must be revealed and explored. How else will we sort out what works from what doesn't? You know this already. Otherwise, you wouldn't be reading this book. The writing lives of your middle school students depend on our getting it right.

What We've Learned About the Teaching of Writing

Research on writing conducted over the past fifty years provides an abundance of information about what works in middle school and what doesn't. As a result, our greatest challenge may not be understanding best practices, but implementing those practices in classrooms where writing skills vary, time is precious, and the demand for high test scores can smother even the most creative teaching.

Take heart. Teaching writing well is not impossible. In this book, I share meaningful and practical ideas for using what we have learned about teaching writing in middle school. My aim is to validate what you already know and give you new ways to support students. I also point out obstacles to watch out for and ways around them so you don't sacrifice the integrity of your teaching or the writing lives of your students.

Part One contains a research review and discussion of the big issues that drive teaching and learning in middle school.

In Chapter 1, I discuss challenges and opportunities. Taking a cue from current writing research, I address issues that often confound middle school teachers and offer suggestions that, I hope, will provide perspective. This chapter also covers the state writing assessment, how it's scored and how it typically influences instruction.

In Chapter 2, I look at the evolution of the writing traits and the writing process and explain why understanding both is critical to teaching writing. You will learn how the traits—ideas, organization, voice, word choice, sentence fluency, conventions, and presentation—grew out of the writing process movement to become a highly successful model of instruction.

In Chapter 3, I talk about the role of the traits within the writing process, dividing the traits into two categories: those that support revision (ideas, organization, voice, word choice, and sentence fluency) and those that support editing (conventions and presentation). You'll find practical, ready-to-implement ideas for setting up your classroom with instructional and organizational systems that work. I also focus on applying modes of writing (narrative, expository, and persuasive) and formats of writing.

Part Two provides an in-depth examination of the five revision traits, in a chapter devoted to each one. Those chapters are organized into two sections: (1) how to assess papers accurately and reliably, using a new trait-specific scoring guide designed for middle school teachers, and (2) how to teach students using lessons and activities that focus on the key qualities of the trait.

Part Three focuses on the two editing traits. Like the chapters devoted to the revision traits, the chapters in this part contain an assessment component and an instruction component organized around the trait's key qualities.

Teaching Writing in Middle School Today:

Challenges and Opportunities

While standing in line at the grocery store one evening years ago, I noticed that two people ahead of me were paying with the same type of debit card as mine: Portland Teachers Credit Union. The cashier asked, "Oh, are you teachers?" Both responded, "Yes," and a cheery conversation followed.

"What grade?"

"Fourth," the first woman happily responded.

"Second," chimed in the second.

The cashier smiled warmly and commented to the fourth-grade teacher, "A wonderful age. It must be a joy to do such important work." Turning to the second-grade teacher she added, "Oh, I bet you have fun every day."

When I handed my debit card to her, I fully expected chitchat along the same lines. "Oh, another teacher. What a coincidence. What grade do *you* teach?" the cashier asked.

"Seventh," I answered proudly.

She broke eye contact, suddenly more interested in scanning my items than talking, and muttered with pity in her voice, "Oh, that's too bad." She felt sorry for me. It probably never occurred to her that teaching middle school was a deliberate choice. And I want to make that clear: I *chose* middle school. In 19 years of classroom teaching, I always believed middle school was where I belonged—an unpredictable and wild ride at times, but richly rewarding. I didn't want to teach other grades, although circumstances sometimes forced me to temporarily. And now, as I sit here years later writing a book for middle school teachers, it feels like coming home.

This book is about teaching middle school writers as accomplished as Melanie and Ryann, the students featured in the prologue, as well as students who struggle. I hope traveling through this text is a satisfying journey, worthy of the students it describes and respectful of the teachers it's designed to serve. It is a challenging time to teach writing in middle school because the stakes have never been higher. So having the best ideas and the right tools to create strong writers has never been more important.

Recent Research on Writing

Writing instruction has come of age. For many years, reading instruction dominated the research literature on literacy. However, recent books and reports such as *Because Writing Matters* from the National Writing Project (2003), *The Neglected "R"* from the National Commission on Writing (2003), *Writing Next* from the Alliance for Excellent Education (Graham & Perin, 2007), and the summary report from the National Assessment of Educational Progress (NAEP) (2007) document the importance of writing and the most effective ways to teach it. The consensus is that we have made strides, but we have a long way to go to create classrooms that meet the needs of today's students. Providing some troubling statistics, these publications concur that many secondary writing classes are failing students in key areas. The following recommendations stem from them.

> **"** Writing today is not a frill for the few, but an essential skill for the many. **"**
>
> —The National Commission on Writing, 2003

We need to give students complex, relevant writing tasks that require analysis and synthesis.

Findings confirm that a steady stream of work sheets and prompts still dominate despite the fact that we know using them does not lead to thoughtful, complex prose. Instead, it serves to reinforce the notion that writing is a simple task whose purpose is to satisfy the teacher (Graham & Perin, 2007; National Commission on Writing, 2003). Sadly, this is not new information. A decade earlier, educational researcher George Hillocks, Jr., concluded, "Exercises in declarative knowledge likely had negative effects on writing quality because, in many instances, they supplanted opportunities for students to actually engage in writing" (1986, p. 225).

If middle school students are to learn to think, reason, and communicate, they should be encouraged to use writing as a means to discover what matters. They must "struggle with details, wrestle with the facts, and rework raw information and dimly understood concepts" (National Commission on Writing, 2003, p. 9). This does not happen through repetitive, skill-and-drill exercises and endless prompts. It happens when teachers understand that writing is thinking on paper and when they provide rich, diverse opportunities for students to practice that thinking.

We need to provide students with the tools they need to perform beyond a basic level.

The NAEP puts students on a continuum of writing levels from "below basic" to "basic" to "proficient" to "advanced." The 2007 report notes steady gains over the past 15 years in the number of eighth graders moving from below basic to basic. The report also shows, however, that students have not moved significantly from basic to proficient. Further, it points out only one writer in a hundred achieved the distinction of advanced.

Why is student progress stalling out? It may have something to do with the fact that so many of us don't expect any more from students than the skills necessary to pass state writing assessments. Or it may have something to do with the fact that we are failing to provide essential instructional elements that foster the complex thinking and learning required for excellence in writing, such as delivering focused instruction, modeling strategies, allowing students to select topics, providing adequate time for writing, and conferring with students to offer meaningful feedback. The NAEP, *Writing Next*, and *The Neglected "R"* reports cite both of these reasons, among others, for the disappointing performance of students.

We need to ensure students have enough time for writing.

Arthur Applebee, Judith Langer, Martin Nystrand, and Adam Gamoran (2003) report that we are not providing students with the time they need to become skilled writers, stating two-thirds of students spend less than an hour a week writing in or out of school. In *Writing Next*, Steven Graham and Delores Perin (2007) point out that the total time students spend writing is equal to only about 15 percent of the time they spend watching television. How, then, are students to become effective writers who can analyze and synthesize information? Spending more time teaching students how to write, giving them time to write for different purposes, and making time to provide targeted feedback are essential if students are to improve.

As part of its national writing agenda, *The Neglected "R"* report (National Commission on Writing, 2003) recommends that we "double the amount of time most students spend writing and require successful completion of a course in writing theory and practice as a condition of teacher licensing" (p. 3). These are certainly worthy goals: more time for students to write *and* for teachers to learn how to teach writing.

We need to apply technology to the teaching of writing.

"National technological infrastructure for education is as critical to the United States in the twenty-first century as highways were in the twentieth" (National Commission on Writing, 2003, p. 4). As I travel the country, visiting schools, I see evidence of a technological revolution. Electronic whiteboards, digital visual presenters, laptop computers, and LCD projectors are coming in the front door while chalkboards and overhead projectors are going out the back. The teachers are excited, but in the quiet of late afternoon, they often confide that they are not likely to receive the assistance they need to teach writing confidently with these devices. They don't feel prepared, so they approach technology cautiously.

Students, on the other hand, seek every opportunity to use technology, figuring it out as they go. In "Digital Natives, Digital Immigrants", Marc Prensky (2001) explains that because today's students are being raised on technology, they have developed cognitive thinking patterns different from ours, which is why they are less intimidated by new electronic devices. Interestingly, however, they don't see much of what they create with those devices, such as e-mails, text messages, and instant messages, as writing. "This disconnect matters because teens believe good writing is an essential skill for success and that more writing instruction at school would help them" (Lenhart, Arafeh, Smith, & Macgill, 2008). If middle school students believe that writing matters in the real world but don't view electronic communications as writing, we should broaden their definition. This generation's affinity for technology defines them as learners, and tapping into that is critical to teaching them to write.

We need to show teachers how to change practice.

In *Because Writing Matters*, members of the National Writing Project (2003) synthesized writing research and described its implications for teachers. A persistent theme throughout the document is the urgent need for high-quality training, citing that few preservice and practicing teachers of English and content areas receive more than a token amount of training in writing instruction.

And yet middle school teachers are expected to teach writing and use what students create as a means to assess what they know and can do. Writing may well be how we connect the dots in learning, but unless students have teachers who know how to nurture and support them, it is difficult to envision a future that is much different from the present.

We must administer fair and meaningful assessment.

To be effective writing teachers, we must understand what students can and can't do. To accomplish this, we need a highly reliable and accurate assessment tool. Enter the traits of writing. After being applied and refined for more than 20 years, the Trait Model is now the gold standard of classroom-based analytic writing assessment. (See Chapter 2 for background information on the model.)

But during this same period, teachers have also been barraged by large-scale state assessments that aim to pinpoint student achievement in math, reading, writing, and other key subject areas. As these assessments have rolled into our schools and *over* many teachers, they've stolen precious time for instruction. Teachers need better assessment tools—ones that will help them plan and execute instruction.

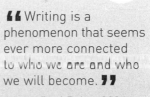

❝ Writing is a phenomenon that seems ever more connected to who we are and who we will become. **❞**

—Paul Prior, 2006

Principles for Creating Confident, Capable Middle School Writers

- **We must speak a common language based on the traits.**
  Respond to student writing according to individual traits, using the same language from day to day and year to year to develop a deep understanding of how writing works.

- **We must nurture process learning.**
  Value process over product in a classroom where writing is encouraged and celebrated every day.

- **We must use criteria to set the standard.**
  Use criteria, or clear indicators, to describe what we believe students must learn and to measure their progress.

The State Writing Assessment

Exciting conversations about writing instruction are happening in teachers' rooms across the country. But when the topic turns from classroom practice to large-scale, high-stakes assessments, the conversation often comes to a grinding halt. Everyone—students, teachers, administrators, parents, and community members—is impacted by them. Although their form varies from state to state, their purpose is the same: to determine how well students are meeting clearly defined and enumerated standards for writing. It's a huge national effort that costs untold millions of dollars each year. In 2001–2002, the state of California spent 221.3 million dollars on its assessment program (Legislative Analyst's Office, 2002, p. 1). The entire amount was not allocated for writing assessment, of course, but even a fraction of that cost, multiplied across 50 states, is a staggering amount of money to design, administer, and score writing assessments and report their results.

Who Is Served by the State Writing Assessment?

Researcher and author P. David Pearson explains, "Standardized tests probably do serve the needs of the general public and policy makers when they try to answer the question How are our schools doing?" (Brenner, Pearson, & Rief, 2007, p. 261). Taxpayers rightly demand to know their investment is paying off, that students are meeting and perhaps even exceeding the standards. Assessment provides accountability, plain and simple.

> **❝** There is a mismatch between what assessment could actually do (celebrate accomplishments) and what high-stakes assessment do (highlight failures). **❞**
>
> —Kylene Beers, Robert Probst, and Linda Rief, 2007

Now for the bad news: Since large-scale, high-stakes assessments have such a high public profile, they often become the de facto curriculum in many classrooms. "Teachers defer to the test designers as the experts, and embrace the test itself as the curriculum," notes researcher George Hillocks, Jr. (2002, p. 198). These teachers teach only those skills necessary to pass the test. They administer practice tests over and over, hoping this repetition will improve student scores. And it doesn't. In fact, students often do worse, according to Tommy Thomason and Carol York (2000), because they fall victim to testing fatigue.

We can't surrender the curriculum to test makers; it's far too important. So let me say right here and now, the test is not a curriculum, and neither are the traits. The traits are an assessment that should guide writing instruction; they serve teachers and students as they work together in the writing process classroom. Chris Gallagher and Amy Lee remind us, "When rubrics are used only to assign students numbers, they are counterproductive" (2008, p. 159). I would take their wise point a step further: When assessment becomes the end and not a means to enhance learning, we have lost our way.

When Assessments Are Scored Holistically

The state writing assessment is often scored holistically. That means trained scorers rank and sort student writing, using a single rubric or scoring guide, to provide a simple answer to complex questions such as "Are students meeting the standards?" and "Are groups of students improving overall?"

Holistic scoring is used for the following purposes:

- To gain insight about an entire group's performance: "Our eighth graders have improved overall." "The sixth grade outperformed the seventh."

- To show how many students have met or exceeded the standards at different grade levels: 12 percent of the eighth-grade class did not meet the writing standard; 59 percent met the standard; 29 percent exceeded the standard.

- To rank and sort individual performances: Jayson received the highest score, while Mita got the lowest.

- To place students into district and school level programs: talented and gifted, advanced placement, special education, and Title I

- To grade using percentages, points, or letters such as A, B, C, D, and F

Holistic scores are valid and useful, but broad. They do not provide specific diagnostic information to guide instruction.

The Advantage of Taking a More Analytic Approach

Analytic assessment is individualized, focused, and precise because it requires us to look at writing from multiple perspectives. Like scorers of holistic assessments, scorers of analytic assessments use a rubric or scoring guide. But they use those rubrics and scoring guides to determine multiple scores for a piece of writing, rather than just one. The Trait Model is a form of analytic assessment.

Analytic scoring is used for the following purposes:

- To provide details about individual students' writing performance and document progress over time

- To target strengths and weaknesses that inform instruction: "Frankie has learned to narrow his idea, but needs to add detail." "Le has mastered punctuation, but is struggling with spelling."

- To give the writer specific, focused feedback that will help him or her revise and edit. "What if you moved this part to the very beginning to create a stronger lead, Raheem? Try it and see if that organization choice improves the piece."

- To confer with students about their writing progress: "Lily, look at how much more you know now about word choice and how to use words well than you did at the beginning of the year!"
- To develop classroom lessons designed to teach and reinforce specific skills

Analytic assessment is process driven. Therefore, it is my preferred classroom assessment method, and the traits are the best analytic model I've found in 35 years of teaching and researching. (For a chart that helps you convert scores from a six-point scoring guide to percentages and, from there, to letter grades, see the file entitled "Grading Student Work" on the CD that accompanies this book.)

Holistic and analytic assessments serve different functions but can support one another. Think of it this way: No one wins on *American Idol* by skipping rehearsals and showing up for performance night. But by regularly practicing songs and embracing recommendations from professionals (analytic), each contestant stands a shot. Participants learn not only the fundamentals of singing, but also the skills that will make or break their performance. Writing works in the same way.

Dear Ruth,

A while ago, I began e-mailing you and sharing the writing success we have had in the sixth grade (which is split between two schools) since using your six trait materials to teach writing. To this point, the only proof I had to back up our accomplishments was the many pieces of writing my students produced. I am now proud to share our success on the state writing assessment (the MEAP in Michigan) with you, too.

Junior High #1 reported that 100 percent of last year's sixth-grade students are proficient in writing (up from 85 percent in 2006). Of those students, two were special needs. One student was considered a "reluctant writer" until he entered my classroom, and the other had one of the highest scores on the actual written (essay) part. Very cool!

Junior High #2 reported that 96 percent of last year's sixth-grade students are proficient in writing (up from 63 percent in 2006). The three students considered "not proficient" are special-needs kids. The year before, each received a score of 0 out of 6 on the writing (essay) portion. This year, each scored a 3. That is tremendous improvement!

In a district as large as ours, these writing scores will stand out and many other teams will want learn how we helped students improve so much. We will begin by saying how important reading your book is to the process.

All last year, our administrator supported us as we built our writing program, and you can imagine how excited he is to be able to show other administrators good old-fashioned data. We are very proud as well; we have never seen this much progress in writing in one year. Our challenge this year is a very large class, but we are finding that our program has a similar impact on them as well.

I hope that you are as excited as we are about this news. I couldn't wait to share with you the actual data that proves, conclusively, that the traits help students become great writers.

J. J. Koehn

sixth-grade teacher

Shelby Township, Michigan

What the State Writing Assessment Doesn't Measure

It's easy to get caught up in large-scale assessment, whether it's holistic or analytic—and the external demand to improve students' performance. But we must also consider the internal demand: our personal drive to help students learn. If we want middle school students to learn the critical skills and habits needed to write well, we have to move from the sidelines to the playing field, get dirty, take hits right along with them, and be there for every practice and game. As teachers, we must actively participate. We are their coaches.

I was reminded of that recently when I attended the talent show organized by my friend Bridey Monterossi, a music teacher at a school with more than 1,100 middle school students. She staged, scored, lighted, choreographed, and costumed the 20-act show that featured 75 students, diverse in every way—height, size, color, shape, experience, and skill.

Two days before the show, Bridey called in tears, convinced she'd never pull it together in time: kids left the dress rehearsal early or hadn't shown up at all, forgot lines, botched dance moves, couldn't find the right pitch, missed lighting and sound cues, and tried to sneak in much-too-revealing costumes. Even the principal backed out in the final hours. In short, the show was shaping up to be a disaster.

But when the curtain went up and each student stepped up to perform, it all came together. One group dedicated a song, "Big Girls Don't Cry," to a classmate who'd died earlier in the year. They showed a video of their friend singing the same song in the car, smiling radiantly, full of life. There was not a dry eye in the house. At that moment it didn't matter that the kids were a bit out of tune or that the sound system had failed.

A talented eighth-grade boy sang a ballad, strumming his guitar, while what sounded like the entire female population of the school screamed at the top of their lungs and rushed the stage. Cell phones lit the darkened auditorium as hundreds of girls took pictures and videos. It reminded me of the way I felt as a young teenager when the Beatles hit America. Sheer, unadulterated hero worship.

That day ended in triumph. But not all days in middle school end that way. Many are frustrating, complicated, maddening, and sad. It's that range of highs and lows that scares off many teachers. Emotions can rule the day like unwelcome guests. Teaching middle school is challenging, plain and simple. But then those magic moments crop up to remind us why we're there, like Bridey's talent show. I don't know anyone who became a teacher solely to administer the state writing assessment. Do you?

I believe middle school students have a deep and abiding hunger for writing, reading, and learning. They deserve the best content, instruction, and assessment we can serve up.

Five Truths About Middle School Students

Here are some of the "truths" I've discovered about middle school students over the past thirty years, which have helped me understand students better and respect them more:

1. They have a hard time remembering things.

They don't remember to put their names on their papers even though they did this automatically in elementary school. They don't remember where they put their papers, their backpacks, or that all-too-important permission slip. In fact, they remember hardly anything they consider mundane, no matter how desperately the adults in their lives wish they did. It doesn't mean they aren't learning.

2. They don't like to do ordinary, repetitive tasks.

They detest homework for the sake of homework, formula-driven prompts, black-line masters designed to teach them things they already know. (Who can blame them?) They like to be occupied with work that matters to them. They like being active. In fact, they crave it.

3. They must talk to learn.

Talking is as essential to middle school students as breathing. In silent classrooms, students are cut off from one another and become bored and frustrated. In classrooms where talking is valued, the energy level is palpable. Talking is how middle school students process their world and make sense of it.

4. They adore technology.

They "get it" in ways that we, as adults, never will. They will gladly show us what they know if given the opportunity to use computers, cell phones, iPods, interactive whiteboards, and on and on. If we find a way to make technology an integral part of our writing instruction, just imagine what our students might do.

5. They aren't high school students.

Their strengths and weaknesses are different from older kids'. Yes, they have passion and energy, but with these come moodiness and unbridled emotion. They should be taught for who they are now, what works for them now, what is meaningful now. This is the best preparation for what comes later. Likewise, the best middle school teachers aren't frustrated high school teachers, nor are they latter-day elementary teachers. We bring unique skills, passions, and characteristics to our work. The patience, flexibility, and humor required at every level, K to 12, are critical to success in middle school.

Final Thoughts

The grocery store cashier I described at the start of this chapter had it all wrong. I didn't deserve her pity because I taught middle school. I deserved respect and understanding, and so did my students. Middle school students can become amazing writers, as I'm sure you've seen in your practice and will see in this book. So, instead of taking pity, the cashier should have said to me, "Good for you! It's quite an adventure, I bet"—and thrown in a bottle of aspirin, on the house.

CHAPTER 2

The Writing Traits and the Writing Process:

What They Are and How They Came to Be

Although they may seem like late-twentieth-century creations, the writing traits—the qualities of good writing—and the writing process—the act of prewriting, drafting, sharing, revising, and editing—have been around since the invention of the pen. They are and have always been what writers think about as they compose. And good teachers have been showing students how to use them long before they became fashionable.

Just take a look at these pieces written by an eighth grader from South Pasadena, California, in 1964.

First draft:

"Today"

Today is a regular school day. I go to my clases which are mostly OK and then I go home. My favorite part of the day is sleeping because I love to sleep and could sleep all day and all night. My least favorit class is typing because Im not good at it and it takes me the whole class period to do the warm up exercise.

I love music and the Beatles are my favorite group. Especially Ringo. I love him so much. Shindig is my favorite tv show and I adore KRLA radio station.

When the weekends come I usually clean my room and listen to music, and have slumber parties with my friends. We do lots of fun things like staying up all night pretending to meet the Beatles and what that would be like. We talk about boys non stop, too. I like going to Confirmation class too. I'm learning a lot their.

A day in the life of this author is pretty normal, I guess. Its not that exciting, but it is MY LIFE!

After creating multiple drafts and conferring with her teacher, Miss Spellacy, here's where the girl landed.

Final draft:

"Today"

Today is a day filled with boys, music, Beatles, friends and school. The latter of which seems to occupy most of my time, spare or otherwise.

A typical day in the life of the author begins with the dreadful feeling that it's time to get up. I really can't understand where the night has gone to. One minute it's here, the next minute it's light. Sometimes I wish it were always night so I could sleep all the time.

Slowly, though, I make my way from my bed. Over my bed hang my pictures of the Beatles. They are arranged like the ones on the next page only with faces.

Then it's off to the breakfast table for a very quick meal while I read the comics. And then I'm off to school.

My hands are usually cold as I walk into my first period typing class and I sit down to do a warm-up exercise which usually takes me all period to do correctly. I don't consider typing one of my better subjects.

The bell for my second period class rings and I begin a frantic struggle to get to my second period English class. And so the day rambles on—brunch, Algebra, Study, Lunch, Social Studies, P.E., Spanish.

Much to my surprise, the day does end, and I'm on my way home to do my homework. Sound exciting?

This only happens on a ratio of 5:2 (did I say ratio? Algebra must be getting to me) though, and those two awaited days are upon us.

Saturday and Sunday are the highlights of my week, and if I can't sleep all the time, my second choice would be to have seven Saturdays and Sundays a week.

Saturday is usually spent sleeping and cleaning my room. Then it's off to a show or a baby-sitting job, and before I know it, it's Sunday. Sunday morning is spent in Church and in the afternoon I hurriedly prepare for my Confirmation class. It's very interesting and I enjoy it immensely, but even it doesn't last forever. Soon I'm on my way to make a dent on that homework I've been putting off all weekend.

And there you have it, "Today" in my life. I enjoy it a lot and plan to enjoy it no matter what I do or where I am.

Today is a day filled with boys, music, Beatles, friends, and school. The latter of which seems to occupy most of my time, spare or otherwise.

A typical day in the life of the author begins with the dreaded feeling that it's time to get up. I really can't understand where the night has gone to. One minute it's here, the next minute it's light. Sometimes I wish it were always night so I could sleep all the time.

Slowly, though, I make my way from my bed. Over my bed hang my pictures of the Beatles. They are arranged like the ones on the next page only with faces.

Then it's off to the breakfast table for a

What changed between the first and the final draft? Everything. This eighth grader did everything a skilled writer typically does. She:

- Developed and clarified the idea using original thinking and distinctive details
- Organized those details to create a logical flow
- Infused the piece with her individual perspective and insight to create voice

- Chose lively, original, and appropriate words to engage the reader and convince him or her that she knows what she's talking about

- Created sentence fluency by wording her sentences in a variety of ways— and by weaving them together seamlessly

- Followed standard conventions to enhance meaning and ease the reading experience

I try to remember the lessons Miss Spellacy taught me as I write today. Yes, this is my piece, from my autobiography—a yearlong, grueling project that resulted in a ten-chapter, handwritten, hand-stitched book. Miss Spellacy and I met many times over the course of the year as I struggled to meet her high standards. Draft by draft, chapter by chapter, my autobiography took shape. Miss Spellacy was the first teacher to show me how to write. She didn't just assign writing, she taught writing. Every day she presented new ways to discover what my classmates and I wanted to say and express it clearly. In 1964, no one knew about the writing traits and the writing process as we know them today, but they were alive and well. Lucky for me, Miss Spellacy knew that.

The Writing Traits

As I mentioned earlier, the Trait Model is a highly reliable and accurate form of assessment—and more. It is simple, logical, easy to understand, and, most important, effective as a tool for planning and carrying out writing instruction. Let's take a closer look at each trait:

Ideas: the piece's content—its central message and details that support that message.

Organization: the internal structure of the piece—the thread of logic, the pattern of meaning.

Voice: the tone and tenor of the piece—the personal stamp of the writer, which is achieved through a strong understanding of purpose and audience.

Word Choice: the vocabulary the writer uses to convey meaning and enlighten the reader.

Sentence Fluency: the way words and phrases flow through the piece. I call sentence fluency the auditory trait because we "read" for it with the ear as much as the eye.

Conventions: the mechanical correctness of the piece. Correct use of conventions (spelling, capitalization, punctuation, paragraphing, and grammar and usage) guides the reader through the text and makes it easy to follow.

Presentation: the physical appearance of the piece. A visually appealing text provides a welcome mat. It invites the reader in.

At the model's core are fundamental principles: conducting high-quality assessment that leads to focused instruction, establishing clear goals for teaching and learning, using a shared vocabulary to talk about writing, and weaving revision and editing together seamlessly and strategically. Embracing these principles is critical if we are to reform the way writing is taught in middle school (Graham & Perin, 2007). The traits allow us to break writing down so we can talk to our students about it, determine what is working and what isn't, and target the specific skills that students need.

This book was conceptualized and created for you, the middle school teacher. You'll find all-new customized scoring guides and teaching materials for each trait—exciting new resources that I developed based on feedback from middle school teachers and their students. They're teacher tested and student approved!

On the scoring guides, each trait is broken into four subsets, called "key qualities," which enable you to pinpoint how well students are mastering essential skills.

Ideas

Finding a Topic
The writer offers a clear, central theme or a simple, original story line that is memorable.

Focusing the Topic
The writer narrows the theme or story line to create a piece that is clear, tight, and manageable.

Developing the Topic
The writer provides enough critical evidence to support the theme and shows insight on the topic. Or he or she tells the story in a fresh way through an original, unpredictable plot.

Using Details
The writer offers credible, accurate details that create pictures in the reader's mind, from the beginning of the piece to the end. Those details provide the reader with evidence of the writer's knowledge about and/or experience with the topic.

Organization

Creating the Lead
The writer grabs the reader's attention from the start and leads him or her into the piece naturally. He or she entices the reader, providing a tantalizing glimpse of what is to come.

Using Sequence Words and Transition Words
The writer includes a variety of carefully selected sequence words (such as *later*, *then*, and *meanwhile*) and transition words (such as *however*, *also*, and *clearly*), which are placed wisely to guide the reader through the piece by showing how ideas progress, relate, and/or diverge.

Structuring the Body

The writer creates a piece that is easy to follow by fitting details together logically. He or she slows down to spotlight important points or events, and speeds up when he or she needs to move the reader along.

Ending With a Sense of Resolution

The writer sums up his or her thinking in a natural, thoughtful, and convincing way. He or she anticipates and answers any lingering questions the reader may have, providing a strong sense of closure.

Voice

Establishing a Tone

The writer cares about the topic, and it shows. The writing is expressive and compelling. The reader feels the writer's conviction, authority, and integrity.

Conveying the Purpose

The writer makes clear his or her reason for creating the piece. He or she offers a point of view that is appropriate for the mode (narrative, expository, or persuasive), which compels the reader to read on.

Creating a Connection to the Audience

The writer speaks in a way that makes the reader want to listen. He or she has considered what the reader needs to know and the best way to convey it by sharing his or her fascination, feelings, and opinions about the topic.

Taking Risks to Create Voice

The writer expresses ideas in new ways, which makes the piece interesting and original. The writing sounds like the writer because of his or her use of distinctive, just-right words and phrases.

Word Choice

Applying Strong Verbs

The writer uses many "action words," giving the piece punch and pizzazz. He or she has stretched to find lively verbs that add energy to the piece.

Selecting Striking Words and Phrases

The writer uses many finely honed words and phrases. His or her creative and effective use of literary techniques such as alliteration, similes, and metaphors makes the piece a pleasure to read.

Using Specific and Accurate Words

The writer uses words with precision. He or she selects words the reader needs to fully understand the message. The writer chooses nouns, adjectives, adverbs, and so forth that create clarity and bring the topic to life.

Choosing Words That Deepen Meaning

The writer uses words to capture the reader's imagination and enhance the piece's meaning. There is a deliberate attempt to choose the best word over the first word that comes to mind.

Sentence Fluency

Crafting Well-Built Sentences

The writer carefully and creatively constructs sentences for maximum impact. Transition words such as *but*, *and*, and *so* are used successfully to join sentences and sentence parts.

Varying Sentence Types

The writer uses various types of sentences (simple, compound, and/or complex) to enhance the central theme or story line. The piece is made up of an effective mix of long, complex sentences and short, simple ones.

Capturing Smooth and Rhythmic Flow

The writer thinks about how the sentences sound. He or she uses phrasing that is almost musical. If the piece were read aloud, it would be easy on the ear.

Breaking the "Rules" to Create Fluency

The writer diverges from standard English to create interest and impact. For example, he or she may use a sentence fragment, such as "All alone in the forest," or a single word, such as "Bam!" to accent a particular moment or action. He or she might begin with informal words such as *well*, *and*, or *but* to create a conversational tone, or he or she might break rules intentionally to make dialogue sound authentic.

Conventions

Checking Spelling

The writer spells sight words, high-frequency words, and less familiar words correctly. When he or she spells less familiar words incorrectly, those words are phonetically correct. Overall, the piece reveals control in spelling.

Punctuating Effectively and Paragraphing Accurately

The writer handles basic punctuation skillfully. He or she understands how to use periods, commas, question marks, and exclamation marks to enhance clarity and meaning. Paragraphs are indented in the right places. The piece is ready for a general audience.

Capitalizing Correctly

The writer uses capital letters consistently and accurately. A deep understanding of how to capitalize dialogue, abbreviations, proper names, and titles is evident.

Applying Grammar and Usage

The writer forms grammatically correct phrases and sentences. He or she shows care in applying the rules of standard English. The writer may break from those rules for stylistic reasons, but otherwise abides by them.

Presentation

Applying Handwriting Skills

The writer uses handwriting that is clear and legible. Whether he or she prints or uses cursive, letters are uniform and slant evenly throughout the piece. Spacing between the words is consistent.

Using Word Processing Effectively

The writer uses a font style and size that are easy to read and a good match for the piece's purpose. If he or she uses color, it enhances the piece's readability.

Making Good Use of White Space

The writer frames the text with appropriately sized margins. Artful spacing between letters, words, and lines makes reading a breeze. There are no cross-outs, smudges, or tears on the paper.

Refining Text Features

The writer effectively places text features such as headings, page numbers, titles, and bullets on the page and aligns them clearly with the text they support.

In addition to the new scoring guides mentioned on page 31, the book includes other trait-based resources for writing assessment and instruction, designed specifically for middle school:

- Scored and critiqued student papers for each trait
- Tips for understanding each trait, written by and for middle school students
- Four Think Abouts for each trait, based on key qualities—questions students need to ask themselves as they revise and edit their work
- Suggestions for using a student writing folders to ensure practice in each trait
- Trait-focused warm-ups, lessons, and activities, based on key qualities
- Recommendations for young adult books that you can use to model how professional writers apply the traits

- An accompanying CD with:
  - Student-friendly scoring guides aligned to the teacher's scoring guides that enable students to assess their own work in each trait
  - "Rules to Remember" pages for spelling, punctuation, capitalization, and grammar and usage
  - Tips on grading and guidelines for turning a rubric score into a grade
  - Scoring guides for assessing student work by mode (narrative, expository, and persuasive), with accompanying scored, critiqued benchmark papers and conference planners
  - Many of the reproducible forms from this book

Some History on the Writing Traits

The Trait Model is more than an approach to assessing and teaching writing. It's a vocabulary teachers use to describe their vision of what good prose looks like in its different forms. The model is rooted in writing research, writing pedagogy, and the combined wisdom of thousands of teachers. For those of us who have spent our careers thinking deeply about teaching writing, it's hard to remember a time when the traits were not a part of teachers' lexicon.

The model is based on the groundbreaking work of Paul Diederich and his colleagues (1961, 1974), who documented, categorized, and standardized readers' responses to a large sample of writing and created an analytic rating system emphasizing five factors: ideas, mechanics, organization, wording, and flavor (1974).

In 1985 teachers in Beaverton, Oregon, took that work and blended it with emerging ideas about performance assessment in all academic areas, including writing (Popham, 1995; Stiggins, 1994; Wiggins, 1998). Specifically, they organized recurring qualities of writing into six categories, or traits, and created a scoring guide that clearly articulated levels of performance for each. Then they used the scoring guide to assess student writing at many grade levels and refined it as necessary to improve its accuracy and reliability. In the process, the traits began taking hold and impacting writing classrooms across the country and the world.

The traits were further refined and expanded in the 1990s at the Northwest Regional Educational Laboratory (NWREL) in Portland, Oregon, where I was a researcher. My work focused on perfecting the scoring guide and developing trait-based classroom materials. The model was expanded when a study by Italian psychologist Remondino (Diederich, 1974) was rediscovered, which discussed the importance of "graphics," or the physical aspects of writing. (Diederich and his colleagues called this "handwriting, neatness.") So we folded "graphics" into the Trait Model as "presentation."

During these years, I scoured the research, read books on writing instruction, and haunted classrooms asking, "What happens when students write? What is easy for them? What is challenging? What evidence can we gather to prove important learning has occurred?"

Now, more than 20 years later, in my role as an independent writer and consultant, I continue to analyze the research, read books on writing instruction, and seek answers to important questions that affect classroom teachers and their students. I spend time with teachers across the country, gathering ideas and materials to improve student writing, and I pore over papers written by middle school students at all proficiency levels, sample lessons, and activities.

This work also inspired me to revise the scoring guides to meet the needs of middle school teachers. These guides allow us to do much more than assign a score to a paper. They allow us to do the following:

- Assess student writing across seven key dimensions, accurately and reliably
- Tell students what they're doing well in their writing and what needs attention, using precise, trait-specific language
- Plan and organize lessons not only by trait, but by the four key qualities that make up each trait

The thoughtful discussion of the needs of middle school writers and of the ways to use the traits successfully makes this book unique among professional resources. It will give you the support you need to teach students at a complex yet marvelous period in their lives.

Where's the Proof That the Trait Model Works?

Evidence that the model helps student writers succeed can be found in published research and in the students' work itself. In this section, I discuss both.

In Published Research

Over the past 20 years, qualitative and quantitative studies have been carried out to assist teachers, administrators, and policy makers in using analytic writing assessment to reform teaching—including studies on the Trait Model. In a three-year study that I helped conduct in the Kent School District, a large, urban district in Washington, the writing of students in grades 3, 6, 9, and 11 was assessed using the traits scoring guide. The following results show the increase of sixth graders who met the writing proficiency standards, which was typical of students in all four target grades:

- Ideas—from 49% to 78.1%
- Organization—from 43.3% to 64.1%
- Voice—from 41.4% to 73.1%
- Word Choice—from 44.7% to 75.5%

- Sentence Fluency—from 54.4% to 63%
- Conventions—from 57.2% to 68.2

(Arter, Spandel, Culham, & Pollard, 1994)

I was fortunate to participate in the initial research on the Trait Model, which was funded by the U.S. Department of Education and conducted by the Northwest Regional Educational Laboratory in 1992 to 1993. The results were conclusive: students who were taught according to the model improved as writers significantly more than students who weren't. The report, *Study Findings on the Integration of Writing Assessment and Instruction* (Siera, 2005), along with summaries of other studies and data from schools and districts in which the model is being implemented, is available at http://www.nwrel.org/assessment. Additionally, results from a recent federally funded six-year study, *Experimental Study on the Impact of the 6+1 Trait Writing Model on Student Achievement in Writing* (Coe, Hanita, Nave, Nishioka, & Smiley), are scheduled to be available 2011.

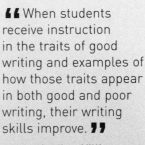

❝ When students receive instruction in the traits of good writing and examples of how those traits appear in both good and poor writing, their writing skills improve. **❞**

—Joellen Killion, 1999

In the Work of Students

Perhaps the most compelling evidence that the model works is in the writing that results from implementing it. There is nothing like seeing improvement with your own eyes and documenting it with a scoring guide to make you feel successful as a writing teacher. To prove it, take a look at this piece written by a seventh grader at the beginning of the year.

Harry Potter

The Harry Potter series by J.K. Rowling have been a big hit. Rowling has written seven great books; <u>Harry Potter and the Sorcerer's Stone</u>, <u>Harry Potter and the Chamber of Secrets</u>, <u>Harry Potter and the Prisoner of Azkaban</u>, <u>Harry Potter and the Goblet of Fire</u>, <u>Harry Potter an the Half-Blood Prince</u>, and <u>Harry Potter and the Deathly Hallows</u>.

As I said before, the Harry Potter books have been a BIG hit. Now, there are Harry Potter videogames, Harry Potter legos, Harry Potter calendars, pillows, posters, stuffed animals, action figures, computer animated software and more.

Also, as you probably know, Harry Potter movies are out, based on the best-selling Harry Potter books. Not all are out yet, but some are. The first movie, <u>Harry Potter and the Sorcerer's Stone</u> is approximately two hours and thirty-four minutes long, and has spectacular graphics.

I would strong advise peoples of all ages to read these fabulous books, watch the movies, and dig up anything else on the magical world of Harry Potter.

After seven months of learning about the traits and applying them to his writing, the same student wrote the following piece. Keep in mind, he wrote both pieces independently.

Bugs and Glitches

All computers have bugs and glitches but just one has them all. Microsoft. The very essence of all things that come from the evil pits of computer Hell! In my mind, when I see a commercial of Microsoft computers, my head starts to throb like a bucking bronco.

Just one Microsoft computer has the unwilling power to bend the human mind, with countless bugs, and an eternity of glitches. If you go on the internet, and go to any website (such as www.littlePinkPony.com one of the most kind and gentle sites on the net) it says you have committed an illegal operation, and that the program must immediately quit. Yeah, like visiting a site called little Pink Ponys is a crime.

Microsoft computers also wastes thousands of dollars in energy costs, because their computers don't go to sleep automatically! What kind of IDIOT would waste thousands of dollars in energy costs?! A mindless one, that's for sure. If the person that is reading this has a Microsoft computer, I suggest you get a brand new iMac. Anything is better than a pc.

You don't need a federally funded study to validate the positive impact the traits had on this student. His work speaks for itself. He has learned a great deal in a short time, showing progress in each trait.

Ideas: The first piece lacks substance. The writer simply lists details rather than using them to support his main point. He does not provide a compelling reason to read the Harry Potter books, as he proposes. In the second piece, however, he clearly states a point of view, offers good details and examples (though inflammatory, perhaps), and leaves the reader with a strong sense of his purpose for the writing.

Organization: The first piece is organized by paragraph, which makes perfect sense. But it contains little momentum because everything feels equally important. The beginning works a little better than the conclusion, but neither part is strong. The second piece, however, draws the reader in and ends with an action statement. The transitions between paragraphs are less predictable and work more effectively. The piece has momentum, even if you don't agree with the author's position.

Voice: The first piece has no voice. It's a series of lists, a halfhearted attempt at an assignment in which the writer is not invested. There is no energy. On the other hand, the voice in the second piece is over the top. It's great to see this passion and conviction from a seventh-grade writer. But, depending on his audience, he might want to tone down the voice a little.

Word Choice: The words in the first piece are clear, but lack sparkle. Repetition of the name *Harry Potter* is a problem. In the second piece, however, the writer selected the right words to convey his opinion. He uses phrases such as "very essence," "like a bucking bronco," and "eternity of glitches," which stand out. It might be worth having a short conversation with him to explain that some readers might be turned off by passages like "fiery pits of computer Hell," despite the fact that they paint a clear picture.

Sentence Fluency: The sentences in the first piece are grammatically correct, but lack flow. They just aren't well crafted or connected. In the second piece, however, the writer demonstrates control over the length of sentences, structure, and their relationship to one another. Sentences such as "Yeah, like visiting a site called little Pink Ponys is a crime" prove he's a risk taker.

Conventions: The writer struggles a bit with spelling, punctuation, and grammar, based on how he handles conventions in both papers. But the papers are readable. It wouldn't take much editing to create final, polished works.

Clear, measurable progress is every teacher's dream, and it doesn't happen by itself. This writer's teacher embraced the traits. In the seven months between the drafting of the first piece and the second, she conducted many lessons on revision and editing, based on the key qualities of the traits. She held conferences with students. She worked with them in small groups, focusing on very specific areas of need. It seems to have worked.

The Writing Process

Though the act of writing is highly individualized, most writers follow a predictable series of steps, or a process, when they compose. In its most generic form, that process looks like this:

> **ᴸᴸ** Good writing may be magical, but it's not magic. It's a process, a rational series of steps and decisions that all writers take. **ᴶᴶ**
>
> —Donald Murray, 1985

    Prewriting: The writer comes up with a topic for the work.

    Drafting: The writer commits his or her ideas to paper in rough form.

    Sharing: The writer gets feedback on the draft from the reader or listener.

    Revising: The writer reflects on the draft and makes choices that lead to a clearer, more engaging piece.

    Editing: The writer "cleans up" the piece, checking for correct capitalization, punctuation, spelling, paragraphing, grammar, and usage.

    Finishing/Publishing: The writer creates a final copy, and often takes it public.

It's a flexible, recursive process—not a lockstep and sequential one—with a long history.

Some History on the Writing Process

What follows is a summary of the qualitative and quantitative research on the writing process that has been documented over the past five decades.

The 1960s

In the early 1960s the National Council of Teachers of English commissioned a study by prominent researchers Richard Braddock, Richard Lloyd-Jones, and Lowell Schoer to document the methods teachers were using to teach writing in elementary and secondary schools and which, if any, were effective. The report, *Research in Written Composition*, (1963) stated that there was "only a rudimentary understanding of teaching writing" (p. 5) by classroom teachers at all levels. Pointing to a lack of consistent terminology and methodologies, the researchers concluded "the field as a whole is laced with dreams, prejudices, and makeshift operations" (p. 5). The report also denounced the teaching of isolated grammar skills, noting that, in addition to being ineffective, the time-honored practice thwarted teachers' attempts at showing students how to compose for real purposes. This new thinking set the stage for a more process-based approach to teaching writing—one that emphasized the creation of the product over the product itself.

The 1970s

The practical reality of shifting instruction from product to process became the focus of study during the 1970s. Researchers Janet Emig (1971) and Sondra Perl (1979) explored how writers write, and individually identified a process for writing that could be taught in composition classes. They concluded that composition is not a straightforward, linear process. They argued that writing should be a search for meaning, one that only becomes clear when the writer engages in a process over time. This research provided the foundation of what would come to be known as "the writing process" or five stages writers follow to compose: (1) prewriting, (2) drafting, (3) revision, (4) editing, and (5) finishing/publishing.

Arthur Applebee (1986) sums up the 1970s as a time that produced a "ground swell of support for 'process approaches' to learning to write" (p. 95). Teachers responded favorably to the research since traditional methods were not producing many inspired writers; students rarely wrote more than one draft, added or deleted details, or reorganized text. However, although teachers were excited, they did not immediately change their practices. The reason to an extent, Applebee argued, was the lack of professional materials and staff development opportunities available to them.

The 1980s

With landmark works such as Donald Graves's *Writing: Teachers and Children at Work* (1983), Donald Murray's *A Writer Teaches Writing* (1985), and Lucy Calkins's *The Art of Teaching Writing* (1986), the professional literature took a huge step toward showing teachers how to apply the writing process. Examples of effective instructional strategies filled these books, allowing teachers an inside view into some exceptional classrooms. The authors based their ideas on the notion that young writers need to think for themselves—and write for clear purposes, in a variety of modes and formats.

These authors advocated conferring with students and having them share with peers after drafting. Classroom teachers and educational researchers noticed improvement in writing when students received meaningful feedback on drafts and were taught how to apply revision and editing skills to strengthen their writing (Graves, 1983). In short, the work of authors, researchers, and teachers proved that the writing process is not a rigid series of steps; it's a menu of flexible, recursive actions writers take to make their message clear and memorable.

The 1990s

The 1990s brought a proliferation of new professional books that refined and extended ideas for teaching writing, such as Ralph Fletcher's *What a Writer Needs* (1992), Donald Graves's *A Fresh Look at Writing* (1994), and Lucy Calkins's new edition of *The Art of Teaching Writing* (1994). The writing workshop, first described in Donald Graves's *Writing: Teachers and Children at Work* (1983) and depicted so vividly in Nancie Atwell's *In the Middle* (1987), emerged as a favored structure for implementing a process approach to instruction. The workshop typically includes mini-lessons on writing craft; teacher modeling; student choice of topic, mode, and genre; extended time to draft, revise, and edit; and individual and small-group conferences. For better or worse, publishers jumped on the bandwagon and produced a plethora of curriculum materials inspired by the workshop model.

The 1990s was also the decade of educational standards, which were recommended and, in some instances, demanded at the national and state levels. Those standards grew out of English/language arts scope and sequence guidelines that varied across districts and states. Realizing the value of having common standards for teaching and learning, the International Reading Association and the National Council of Teachers of English took the bold and controversial step of creating a joint document, *Standards for the English Language Arts* (1996), which contains national standards that embrace the writing process: "Students employ a wide range of strategies as they write and use different writing process elements appropriately to communicate with different audiences for a variety of purposes" (p. 25).

Today

With this interest in writing, it's not surprising that assessments of all sizes and shapes emerged to measure how well students were meeting the standards. As such, the 2000s will undoubtedly be remembered as the testing decade. Some of those assessments provided an authentic glimpse of students' capabilities in writing by allowing ample time for writing and choice of topics. But most provided little more than the dull rumble of collective data.

As I mentioned earlier in the chapter, the traits of writing emerged as an accurate and reliable assessment model used by individual teachers and whole states, such as Arizona, Washington, Kansas, and Oregon, to name a few. Furthermore, other states, such as Texas, New York, South Carolina, and Illinois, adapted the model to meet their needs. Today, the traits are present in one form or another in most state writing assessments, in the National Assessment of Educational Progress, and in the writing component of the SAT and ACT.

My colleagues and I also found that when the traits and their key qualities are taught, not just assessed, student writing dramatically improves. We've developed a deep understanding of what good writing looks like. And, for the first time, we can explain to middle school students how to make their writing strong. When we talk about the key qualities of the ideas, organization, voice, word choice, and sentence fluency traits, students finally understand what revision is and why it is hard. In fact, they glom onto those key qualities like a writing life preserver and use them to revise. And when we teach the conventions trait, which is made up of spelling, capitalization, punctuation, paragraphing, and grammar and usage, students become editors who know just what to do to make their writing readable. Teaching students how to revise and edit is finally in our grasp.

My discovery parallels what research tells us: Direct instruction in revision and editing strategies, supported by guided practice, is essential to helping students apply the writing process with success (Applebee, 1986; Atwell, 1987; Calkins, 1986; Cramer, 2001; DeFoe, 2000; Pritchard & Honeycutt, 2006). And "although most researchers agree that the strategies and mental processes involved in the writing process are recursive and interlocked, many have discovered that studying one component at a time makes an enormously complex task more manageable" (Pritchard & Honeycutt, p. 281). Simply put, those components are the traits: ideas, organization, voice, word choice, sentence fluency, conventions, and presentation, and how they are exhibited in the revision and editing stages of the writing process.

Final Thoughts

It's taken two decades for me to understand how the writing traits and the writing process originated and are interrelated. And now I use that understanding in my work to offer an assessment-driven system for teaching writing—one that is manageable, flexible, student centered, and results oriented. In this next chapter, I introduce you to that system.

CHAPTER 3

Embedding the Traits Into the Process

The writing process and the traits support one another well. Think of the traits not only as an assessment tool, but also as an instructional tool for helping students learn to revise and edit—in essence, learn to apply the writing process. The traits don't stand alone in the writer's world; they melt into the process like dawn into day. When we use the language of the traits to better understand the stages of the writing process, it becomes a cornerstone for teaching writing effectively. To see what I mean, take a look at how the steps in the writing process align with the traits:

Prewriting: The writer comes up with a topic for the work.	→	**Predominant traits:** ideas, organization, voice
Drafting: The writer commits his or her ideas to paper in rough form.	→	**Predominant traits:** word choice and sentence fluency
Sharing: The writer gets feedback on the draft from the reader or listener.	→	**Predominant traits:** ideas, organization, voice, word choice, sentence fluency
Revising: The writer reflects on the draft and makes choices that lead to a clearer, more engaging piece.	→	**Predominant traits:** ideas, organization, voice, word choice, and sentence fluency
Editing: The writer "cleans up" the piece, checking for correct spelling, capitalization, punctuation, paragraphing, and grammar and usage.	→	**Predominant trait:** conventions
Finishing/Publishing: The writer creates a final copy, and takes it public.	→	**Predominant trait:** presentation

Building a System of Teaching

To help students become better writers, they need to understand the steps in the writing process, particularly the difference between revision and editing, and they need instruction on the key qualities of the traits along with opportunities to apply them in their own work. There are prepackaged, ready-to-go writing materials galore out there, but before you spend your money, remember that "stuff" doesn't improve writing. *Writing* improves writing. Decades of research and classroom observation prove it.

However, teaching students to write by writing takes so much time. You need a system—one built on best practices but manageable, and that gets the results you want. A system that serves all students, those who excel at writing and those who don't—one that blends process with traits, so students learn how to think and talk about what they produce, and revise and edit it accordingly.

In this chapter, I present a system that is flexible enough to work in any middle school classroom and simple enough to sustain throughout the year. I share what I've learned about what to teach (and what not to) and how to get organized.

What You Should *Not* Do in Your Teaching

Let's begin with things to avoid. For efficiency's sake, it might be tempting to assign specific traits to each grade level—perhaps ideas and content in grade six, voice and word choice in grade 7, sentence fluency and conventions in grade eight. Don't. Imagine a conference with a sixth-grade student in which you say, "Gosh, Ronita, I'd love to discuss your excellent choice of verbs, but that will have to wait until next year." Ridiculous, right? Students need all the traits all the time. If you separate the traits across years, even months, they lose their power because students don't have all the information they need in order to write well.

That said, you'll probably want to focus on one trait at a time at the beginning of the year to familiarize students with it and build their skills in applying them—but, please, never for more than a couple of weeks per trait. To linger too long on any one trait sends a message that the traits you're not teaching don't matter as much, and that's just not true. Serve students the full-deal meal—all seven traits.

How Students Learn to Write	How Students Do Not Learn to Write
• By watching the teacher model his or her own writing	• By being taught "how to trait"
• By practicing in context	• By filling out work sheets and responding to isolated drills
• By writing every day	• By writing infrequently
• By writing to figure out what they know or want to know	• By only completing assignments
• By using technology	• By only using paper and pencil
• By working with others, talking and sharing	• By working alone, silently
• By focusing on process	• By focusing exclusively on product
• By writing for real purposes and audiences, on topics that matter to them	• By writing for purposes and audiences that are unclear, on topics they don't care about

What You Should Do in Your Teaching

For students to write well, you must teach specific skills that experienced writers use as they draft, revise, and edit. We make this process more transparent for students when we show them how to use the key qualities of the traits to guide their thinking as they write. Remember, we're teaching students to write, not "to trait." There is a huge difference. A system for putting all the writing pieces together is represented in this chart:

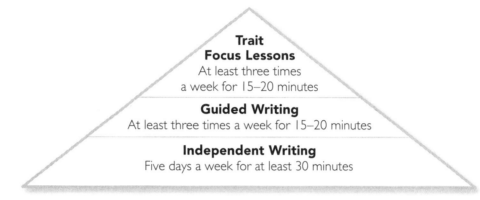

Trait Focus Lessons
At least three times a week for 15–20 minutes

Guided Writing
At least three times a week for 15–20 minutes

Independent Writing
Five days a week for at least 30 minutes

Trait Focus Lessons

A focus lesson is a short, teacher-led demonstration of a specific writing skill. The difference between a focus lesson and a traditional mini-lesson is that in a focus lesson the teacher zeroes in on a key quality of a trait, whereas in a mini-lesson she teaches any skill for any subject. (See pages 31–34 for a complete list of key qualities.)

Focus lessons are not a new idea, but organizing instruction systematically around them, trait by trait, just might be. The best way to choose topics for focus lessons is by assessing student writing to figure out its strengths and weaknesses, using the scoring guides that appear throughout this book. For guidelines on how to do that, see pages 50–51.

Once you have assessed student work, choose an appropriate lesson, based on the greatest area of need. Since each of the seven traits has four key qualities, you'll need at least 28 lessons to cover all the bases. To get you started, I've provided sample lessons in the chapters that follow. However, don't forget to scour your own resources for lessons, revising them as necessary to align with the traits and their key qualities. It's true what they say: everything old can be new again.

Guided Writing

Imagine presenting a focus lesson on a particular writing-related skill, such as using sequence and transition words effectively (key quality #2 for organization). Students are attentive. They listen as you explain what sequence and transition words are and how to use them.

They follow along as you use them in a draft of your own work and join you in a lively discussion about what they notice. Then, to seal the deal, you hand them a work sheet designed to reinforce the skill. Most students complete it successfully. The lesson ends. The next time your students write, however, they don't apply that skill. What happened? Your lesson went so well. Or did it? If students can't use the skill in their own writing, why waste valuable instructional time teaching it?

Consider using guided writing in addition to or even instead of assigning work sheets. Judith Langer and Arthur Applebee (2003), building on the work of Jerome Bruner and others, use the metaphor of "instructional scaffolding" to describe this practice, in which students are presented with a task they can't do independently but could with the support of a skilled teacher. The goal is to wean the student off the teacher so he or she can carry out the task independently. Allowing students to try out new skills on drafts of their writing is essential to understanding and internalizing how writing works. Students need to practice skills, under your guidance, if you expect them to apply those skills to longer, more complex, self-generated projects.

I know what you're thinking. This sounds good in theory, but if every time you present a new skill you must also plan time for helping individual students practice and master it on their own, you'll go nuts. To preserve your sanity, I propose having students keep writing

A Routine for Guided Writing

In order for guided writing to be successful, students need to use their writing folders often. To ensure that happens, follow these steps:

1. Plan a focus lesson for a small group or the whole class, based on a key quality of one of the traits. Use your assessment results of student work to determine which key quality to teach. Have students take out the anonymous piece of student writing from their folders and project the same piece for all to see. (See page 48 for details.)

2. In front of the group, model how to revise or edit for the key quality. Make your changes right on the piece, using colored pens and explaining what you are doing and why. Do not rewrite the piece. Instead, do what real writers do: cross out, circle, insert, draw arrows, use editing symbols, write in the margins, and so forth. Encourage students to revise or edit their copies of the same piece right along with you.

3. Tell students to choose a partner, select a draft from their writing folders, and use their student-friendly scoring guide to assess the piece for the key quality addressed in your focus lesson. Have partners check scores for accuracy and discuss how to revise or edit the piece.

4. Provide time for students to revise or edit their drafts on their own or with their partners. Walk around the room, offering ideas to students who need assistance and praising students who are successfully applying the skill, noting specifically what they are doing well.

5. Ask students to read their revised or edited piece aloud to their partner. When both students have finished, ask them to reassess their pieces, using the student-friendly scoring guide. Have students discuss parts that improved and parts that need further work.

6. Have students return their work to their writing folders and store the folders away safely, so they are readily available the next time you plan a focus lesson with guided writing practice. Feel free to change pieces in their folders as students tire of them.

folders that contain their own drafts, selected by you. This method is simple, draws upon available resources, and allows students to practice new skills in the context of their own work.

Implementing Guided Writing With a Writing Folder

A writing folder is the ideal tool to help students gain new skills. In it, they store rough drafts to use for practicing revision and editing skills as they are taught. Begin by giving each student a plain folder, which they can personalize if you wish. Help students gather the following items for the folder:

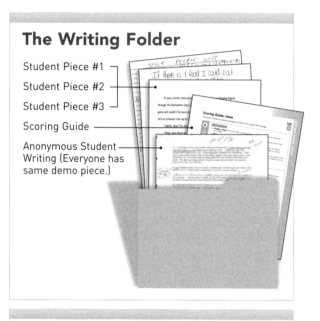

The Writing Folder

Student Piece #1

Student Piece #2

Student Piece #3

Scoring Guide

Anonymous Student Writing (Everyone has same demo piece.)

Tips for Managing the Writing Folder

- Store the folders in a central area of your room or, if you work in different locations throughout the day, on a cart. Keep them within your view, not in lockers, not in backpacks, not anyplace other than where they belong.

- In your records, indicate when students successfully apply a focus-lesson skill, but don't grade the drafts on which they applied it. Remember, this is practice.

- Retire a piece when you or the student decides it's finished or the student grows tired of it. Choose another piece to replace it in the folder.

- **The student-friendly scoring guides** (located on the accompanying CD) These guides are organized around the same key qualities for each trait as the teacher versions. They enable students to assess their draft before and after guided writing practice to determine their progress.

- **Two to four pieces of students' own work in draft form** The papers should be rough. After all, if there's no room for improvement, how will students use them to practice the new skills you teach in focus lessons and guided writing? They should also be short, less than a page. Quickwrites, literature responses, short-answer essays, and journal entries are excellent choices.

- **One piece of anonymous student writing in draft form** Use this piece, which you can copy from this book or find on your own, to model revising and editing strategies that you teach in the focus lessons and guided writing. By listening to you think aloud and watching you work, students learn to apply strategies in their own drafts. Vary the piece over time. After it's been worked on several times, ask students to make a final copy and turn it in. Then give them a new practice piece for your next set of lessons.

Traits of Writing: The Complete Guide for Middle School

Independent Writing

I've found that students need to write independently for at least 30 minutes a day, five days a week to maximize their learning. During that time, they should be working on one or two extended pieces of writing each grading period that require them to use all their newly acquired and established trait-focused skills and apply all steps in the writing process: prewrite, draft, share, revise, edit, and finish/publish.

Ideas for these pieces can come from your curriculum or from the students themselves. You might ask them to write a persuasive essay on the most influential U.S. president of the twentieth century, a review of *The Absolutely True Diary of a Part-Time Indian* by Sherman Alexie, or an explanation of what happens to an unfortunate victim of a Venus flytrap. Or you may ask students to try their hand at a fiction or nonfiction genre that you're covering in a reading unit. Of course, what's most important is that the students like their topics and feel compelled to write about them.

During independent writing, circulate around the room, stopping to talk to students who need support. But don't feel obliged to spend the same amount of time with each one. Instead, carry out one of the following types of conferences, based on what you observe.

The Quick Stop *(for students who are working well and don't have questions, 1 minute)*

Even students who are engaged in writing appreciate being told they're on track. Stop by the writer's desk and ask him to tell you how it's going. If he tells you "Fine!" and keeps working, acknowledge his progress by saying something like, "You seem to be on a roll. I won't stop you. But, if you have any problems or have a part you'd be willing to read me in little while, let me know. Come and find me if I don't get back as quickly as I'd like."

Tips for Using Trait-Specific Language in Conferences

- Name the trait you're addressing. Let your comments teach students about the trait along with helping to make their pieces stronger. Use language from the scoring guide.

- Avoid superficial responses, such as "Nice job" and "Good work." Instead, use specific words and phrases from the scoring guide, such as "The sound of your sentences in the third paragraph is poetic. Thank you for working on the *sentence fluency* to make reading a pleasure." Or "You have several *ideas* working here. So, let's zero in on the most important one to explain in more detail so your writing has a clear focus."

- Avoid using the word *but* in your comment, and try using *and* instead. *And* reinforces the process and doesn't negate what you've already said. For example, you could say, "The way you begin your piece really draws me in, and now, to take the organization even further, let's think of a way to conclude that wraps it up and gives the reader something important to think about."

In Chapters 4–10, I offer examples of trait-specific language in handy sections entitled "Conference Comments."

The Stop and Chat *(for students who have a quick question or straightforward problem, 2–3 minutes)*

If you notice a student slowing down or looking concerned, or who has her hand in the air and wants your attention, stop by and ask how you can help. This student may need the assignment clarified or may have a specific question you can help answer, such as "How else can I end this without saying, 'Thank you for reading my paper.'?" Talk with this student until she's sure she can move on. If you wish, leave a sticky note with some of the ideas from your conversation. You might encourage the student to pair up with a classmate to try one of those ideas.

The Stop and Stay *(for students who need a lot of help, 4–5 minutes)*

Sometimes writing doesn't go well. If you have a student who is totally lost about how to proceed, pull up a chair and plan to stay for a while. Ask what is stopping him, and listen carefully. You may need to write what the student says, so he has something to work with after you leave. Or brainstorm ideas using a resource: "Let's find five things polar bears need to survive and write them here." Or use technology such as Microsoft Word or PowerPoint to get the writer going.

Assessing Writing Using the Trait Scoring Guides

Practice makes perfect. So in each of the chapters that follow, you'll find examples of scored sample papers to study before assessing your own students' papers. When you're ready to score your students' papers, follow these steps:

1. Collect the student papers you want to assess for a particular trait.

2. Copy the scoring guide for the trait you're covering, since you'll want to write on it, highlight key descriptors, and make notes. You'll find the guides on the accompanying CD and on the following pages.
   - Ideas, page 65
   - Organization, page 101
   - Voice, page 147
   - Word Choice, page 185
   - Sentence Fluency, page 225
   - Conventions, page 267
   - Presentation, page 309

3. Read the scoring guide's descriptors for each of the three performance levels.
   - High—6 (Exceptional) and 5 (Strong)
   - Middle—4 (Refining) and 3 (Developing)
   - Low—2 (Emerging) and 1 (Rudimentary)

4. Read one of the student papers carefully. As tempting as it might be, avoid skimming and scanning. Even the most experienced reader is surprised now and again.

5. Assess the paper for the trait, assigning a score of 1 to 6 and a level of "low," "middle," or "high." Begin by asking yourself if the paper is strong or weak in the trait. If you feel it is strong, focus on the descriptors at the high level, 5 and 6, and match them to the paper. Assign a score of 5 if the paper captures each key quality or a score of 6 if it exceeds each key quality. If you feel the paper is weak in the trait, focus on the descriptors at the low level, 2 and 1, match them to the paper, and assign a score. If you feel the paper is somewhere in the middle, assign a 3 or 4, depending on how closely it matches the descriptors for those scores.

As you become comfortable with trait-based assessment and instruction and your students produce a critical mass of work, feel free to score papers for more than one trait at a time. Similarly, when your students write extended pieces—important pieces that they've revised and edited—score them according to all the traits, even if you haven't covered particular traits in depth, to determine how those pieces are working as a whole. Remember, we teach writing, not traiting.

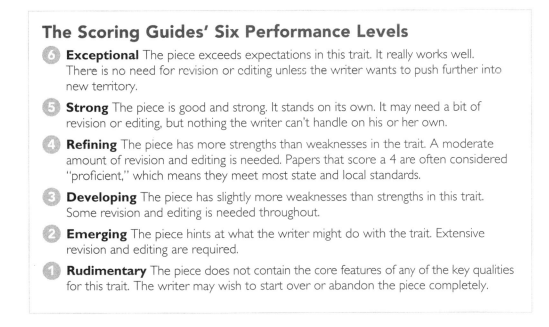

The Scoring Guides' Six Performance Levels

6 Exceptional The piece exceeds expectations in this trait. It really works well. There is no need for revision or editing unless the writer wants to push further into new territory.

5 Strong The piece is good and strong. It stands on its own. It may need a bit of revision or editing, but nothing the writer can't handle on his or her own.

4 Refining The piece has more strengths than weaknesses in the trait. A moderate amount of revision and editing is needed. Papers that score a 4 are often considered "proficient," which means they meet most state and local standards.

3 Developing The piece has slightly more weaknesses than strengths in this trait. Some revision and editing is needed throughout.

2 Emerging The piece hints at what the writer might do with the trait. Extensive revision and editing are required.

1 Rudimentary The piece does not contain the core features of any of the key qualities for this trait. The writer may wish to start over or abandon the piece completely.

Understanding the Modes and Formats of Writing

Do you want to stick your fingers in your ears when your students ask:

"What was the assignment again?"

"Why do we have to do this?"

"Will we be graded?"

"Is this what you want?"

"How long does it have to be?"

All of the above.

Taking time to teach students the *whys* and *whats* of writing right along with the *hows* can nip questions like these in the bud. Don't make students guess. Whether you're asking them to write something as teacher-directed as a one-page summary, a short story, or a 200-word editorial, or as student-directed as a journal entry or an extended research project, explain your reasons for the assignment and encourage questions. I've always found that spending time explaining, listening, and clarifying up front is time well spent because afterward students are much more likely to buy into the assignment. It also saves me from endlessly repeating the same information.

As I explained in Chapter 2, the traits of writing help us break down writing into manageable pieces so, over time, students see how writing works. However, the traits don't help us address the *whys* (modes) or the *whats* (formats) of writing. So in this section, I discuss the different modes of writing and explore the basic question "Why am I writing?" From there, I discuss the many formats of writing as I examine the question, "What am I writing?" Once you have a firm understanding of modes and formats, you'll be better equipped to teach students the *hows*—or the traits—of writing, within the system described on pages 44–50.

The Modes of Writing

There are three basic modes of writing: narrative, expository, and persuasive. According to George Hillocks, Jr. (2002), these modes help the writer establish a purpose for the writing and make that purpose clear to the reader. Many educators consider "descriptive" to be a mode, and it makes sense. However, writers rarely write only to describe, preferring to use description to enhance writing in one of the three core modes. In light of that, I prefer to focus on the narrative, expository, and persuasive modes and recommend using descriptive in service of them.

Narrative writing's purpose: to tell a story

The narrative writer typically:

- Offers a clear, well-developed story line
- Includes characters that grow and change over time

- Conveys time and setting effectively
- Presents a conflict and resolution
- Surprises, challenges, and/or entertains the reader

Expository writing's purpose: to inform or explain

The expository writer typically:

- Informs the reader about the topic
- Transcends the obvious by explaining something interesting or curious about the topic
- Focuses on making the topic clear for the reader
- Anticipates and answers the reader's questions
- Includes details that add information, support key ideas, and help the reader make personal connections

Persuasive writing's purpose: to construct an argument

The persuasive writer typically:

- States a position clearly and sticks with it
- Offers good, sound reasoning
- Provides solid facts, opinions, and examples
- Reveals weaknesses in other positions
- Uses voice to add credibility and show confidence

By zeroing in on the purpose of the writing, the writer establishes why he or she is writing the piece and, in the process, is likely to narrow his or her topic. For example, if a student chooses to write about cell phones, he or she might zero in on the purpose, select a mode, and narrow the topic along one of these lines:

Narrowed topics for a narrative piece

- Tell about the time he lost his cell phone in a pile of lunchroom garbage.
- Tell about his parents' reaction the moment the first big phone bill arrived.
- Tell about the time he accidentally dropped his cell phone in the toilet.

Narrowed topics for an expository piece

- Explain how to use a cell phone.
- Explain a new model's many cool features.
- Explain the benefits of text messaging and ways to get good at it.

Narrowed topics for a persuasive piece

- Persuade his parents to give him a cell phone.
- Persuade the phone company to remove unfair charges from the bill.
- Persuade the principal to allow students to bring cell phones to class.

According to authors Chris W. Gallagher and Amy Lee (2008), "We are dealing with purposes for writing: it provides information, tells a story, or makes an argument. We know that most good writing does more than one of these things at a time" (p. 15). In other words, the best writing usually contains elements of all three modes. A persuasive essay, for example, might contain stories, descriptions, and facts to make its case. A strong narrative includes facts and descriptions as the plot unfolds. If the writer blends elements of modes while clearly maintaining his or her purpose, it's a sign of maturity. Learning how to blend modes is a writing milestone to celebrate.

The traits of writing cut across all three modes. Regardless of his or her purpose for writing—telling a story, informing and explaining, or constructing an argument—the writer must come up with an original idea, organize his or her thoughts logically, find a voice that's right for the audience, pick the best words possible and use them to create sentences that flow, and, of course, check conventions for accuracy and present the work neatly and legibly. The mode is the umbrella under which all seven traits fit snugly.

As a rule of thumb, don't just ask students what they want to write. Ask them to explain why they are writing it, too. Their answers may surprise you. A student may want to create an essay that's as satisfying to read as a good short story. Or a memoir that takes into account meaningful world events. Or an editorial for the local paper that contains a poem to hammer home her argument. When you help students clarify their purposes for writing right from the start, you energize them. You encourage them to do the hard thinking that writing demands. (For further discussion about modes, mode-specific scoring guides, and examples of scored narrative, expository, and persuasive papers by middle school students, see this book's accompanying CD.)

The Formats of Writing

Once the writer determines why he or she is writing a particular piece, the next step is to figure out the form it will take. Visualize going into a bookstore. You wouldn't ask the clerk for an expository book. You'd ask for the category or genre of the book you want: novel, memoir, cookbook, self-help, romance, and so forth.

When you locate the right section (books on travel, for instance) and start browsing, you notice that individual titles are not all organized in the same way. A guidebook on Belize might be organized by types of food, local points of interest, currency, places to stay, and so on. Yet another book in the same section might be made up of stunning captioned photographs that capture everyday life in Belize. You might come across a book of journal entries documenting the author's traveling experiences in Belize and the surrounding area. In other words, individual titles on the same topic come in different formats.

There are so many formats and so little time. If a list were assembled of all the formats writers use, they'd fall into two categories: those that are typically taught and assigned in school, such as essays, short stories, and letters, and those that aren't, such as

A Menu of Formats to Teach Students

advertisements	editorials	package copy
advice columns/letters	e-mail	personalized license plates
affidavits	encyclopedia entries	PowerPoint presentations
anecdotes/stories	greeting cards or texts	prophecies and predictions
announcements	historical accounts	proposals
applications	indexes	public notices
biographical sketches	instructions	requests
blurbs: book covers/TV listings	Internet blogs, wikis, pages	résumés
board game instructions	interviews (real/imaginary)	reviews
brochures	introductions	science notes/observations
bumper stickers	job specifications	screenplays
captions	journal entries	skits
children's books	lab reports	slogans
comics/comic books	last wills and testaments	songs
commentaries	letters	story beginnings
consumer guides or reports	lists	storyboards
contest entries	math problems and solutions	summaries
data analyses	memos	survival manuals
debate outlines/notes	menus	tables of contents
definitions	monologues	telephone dialogues
dialogues	mottoes	test questions
dictionary entries	news stories—paper/radio/TV	wanted posters
directions	newspaper columns	word puzzles and games

e-mails, advertisements, and applications. We typically teach the first group for a reason: they're the formats that students are required to know for state writing assessments. But by teaching only those formats, we're doing our students a disservice, inhibiting them from understanding the full range of ways writers convey their ideas. To become skilled writers, students need to be taught the many, many forms writing can take and be given chances to practice them, using all they know about traits, process, and modes.

Keep in mind, however, that format should not drive the writer's message. Topic and purpose should drive it—and format should be chosen based on how the topic and purpose will be conveyed most effectively. Once the writer establishes what he wants to write about and to whom he wants to write, he's in a good position to choose a format that will work for readers. For example, if the writer wants to tell a story, there are a variety of formats to consider, such as a short story, a play, or a personal journal entry.

The essay is a commonly assigned and maligned format. But there's nothing inherently evil about the essay. Students must, in fact, develop skills necessary to craft well-written essays; it's a format they will use often throughout their school careers. The essay gets into serious trouble, however, when a rigid format hijacks the content. There is no worse offender in this regard than the five-paragraph essay. Putting structure before content doesn't work. In a five-paragraph essay, writers know, before any thinking begins, they will have an introduction, three main points, and a conclusion that looks a lot like the introduction. Cramming this artificial structure down the throats of young writers is a surefire way to turn them off of writing. According to Hillocks (Ezarik, 2004), "the most frequently taught 'basic essay structure' is the five-paragraph theme. The problem is that it does not represent any real essay I have ever seen, and it is not basic in any way. Everything about it indicates that it short-circuits thinking. In fact, I think it is taught so that students do not have to think." (p. 66).

When composing an essay, the writer should create as many paragraphs as necessary to say thoroughly what he or she needs to say, as clearly and convincingly as possible. A wise teacher once told me that there is a big difference between the five-paragraph essay and an essay that has five paragraphs. So right she was.

Opening the door to different formats gives students choices and motivates them to write. And, in my experience, it allows us to inject a lot of fun and creativity into the curriculum without sacrificing content. Nancie Atwell puts it well: "When teachers admit the many possible forms that school reports might take, then they also admit the strong possibility that writers will enjoy writing as well as learn from it" (1990, p. 163).

Final Thoughts

I thought Miss Spellacy was a mean ogre. I kicked and screamed my whole way through her eighth-grade autobiography project, asking, "Who does she think I am, a writer or something? Kids don't write books." Now I get it. Kids *do* write books and anything else they put their minds to.

You can be the Miss Spellacy for your students. Support them when they feel overwhelmed, recharge them when they lose energy, and praise them when they demonstrate effort and show progress. They may not appreciate the great gift you give them today. They are teenagers, after all. But writing well is necessary for success in life, whatever path they choose. So encourage them to stick with it, be patient, demand a lot, keep your eye on the prize, and never lose sight of the fact that systematic, student-centered instruction in traits, modes, and formats, combined with a solid understanding of the writing process, is at the very heart of a successful writing program.

In Part Two, I provide a close-up view of the revision traits: ideas, organization, voice, word choice, and sentence fluency. These are critical qualities of writing that must be assessed carefully and taught creatively if your students are to become skilled writers. Read on to find out how.

PART TWO
The Revision Traits

Revision literally means "to see again." To make their writing as logical, clear, and cohesive as possible, writers need to do just that: draft and then see what is working and what isn't. From there, they rework the text, based on what they feel it needs to meet their purpose for writing and satisfy their audience. Often, however, as most teachers know, students struggle with revision or skip it altogether. Students are not sure how to choose an idea and convey it clearly, organize the piece, use a voice that is appropriate for the audience, select "just-right" words or phrases, and/or come up with well-built sentences that flow. Our task as their teachers is to show them how.

Revision: ideas, organization, voice, word choice, and sentence fluency

Editing: conventions (spelling, capitalization, punctuation, paragraphing, and grammar and usage) and presentation

This is exactly why the traits are so powerful. They enable us to show students how to break down their writing into manageable parts and focus their attention on building the skills that make their writing strong. In this part, I focus on the revision traits—ideas, organization, voice, word choice, and sentence fluency—showing you how to use their key qualities as a basis for assessment and instruction. (In Part Three, I focus on the editing traits: conventions and presentation.)

Using the language of the traits from year to year and applying their key qualities are important to making revision doable for your students.

To introduce or reintroduce students to revision, demonstrate where the traits fit within the writing process and how each trait is aligned to either revision or editing.

1. Review the writing process with students as outlined on page 44 and show them how the traits work within it.

2. Give each student a copy of the student-friendly scoring guides found on the CD to refer to throughout the year, as they apply the traits.

3. Make a chart like the one above and hang it prominently to remind students that the first five traits align with revision and the last two with editing.

When discussing writing with students, use the terms *revision* and *editing* accurately to reinforce the difference between them. You should see an immediate change—for the better—in how students approach the writing process.

CHAPTER 4

Ideas:

To Snorkel or to Scuba Dive?

While walking down the hallway of a middle school in Beaufort, South Carolina, last year, I overheard part of a sixth-grade writing lesson. I glanced into the classroom and was struck by the body language of the students; they were leaning forward, totally enthralled by what the teacher, Mr. Sheppard, was saying. I caught Mr. Sheppard's attention and silently mouthed, "May I stay and watch?" He smiled, nodded, and continued.

In one hand, he held a diving mask and snorkel. In the other, he had another mask, but this one was connected to an oxygen tank leaning against his chair. "I've been teaching middle school writing a long time," he said. "What I've noticed every year is that many kids present their ideas in a very general way. For example, you might write, 'It was huge.' 'I was scared.' 'Times were bad.' And although I get the drift of what you are saying, I've read it a million times before. You expect me, the reader, to fill in the details. But that's the writer's job, not the reader's. You need to include specific details that help me see, really see, the idea."

The students' attention began to fade. I found myself wondering, just as they probably did, what this had to do with the props in Mr. Sheppard's hands. But he continued, "Think about it like this. When you snorkel, you put your mask on your face, you put the air hose in your mouth, and you swim along the water's surface, looking down in fascination at what lies beneath. Maybe there's a coral reef, a shipwreck, or plants with schools of colorful fish swimming around them. It's fun to see what's there. I enjoy snorkeling.

"But when you scuba dive, you swim right down into those schools of fish and feel them brush up against you. You touch the plants, examine the coral, and explore the shipwreck, taking note of the odd bits of this and that on the ocean floor. You swim out of the light and into the dark. Scuba diving is harder and requires more skill than snorkeling. And there are greater risks. But, ultimately, it's a more satisfying experience, wouldn't you agree?"

Of course the students did, and so did I. In fact, I found that I was no longer standing in the doorway; I was inside the classroom, watching and listening intently as the lesson unfolded.

"Now," said Mr. Sheppard, "what I want you to do is pick a draft from your writing folder. Then, read the draft aloud to a partner. Together, find three snorkel details—details that could go deeper. Circle them. Then rewrite each one in the margin or on another piece of paper to create a scuba piece. I'm going to give you about ten minutes to try this. We'll share the results at the end."

What a moment. Mr. Sheppard's use of snorkel and scuba gear was brilliant, because it made the old adage, "Show, don't tell," crystal clear and memorable. And, he used the writing folder to put this new understanding into action. I stayed long enough to watch students choose a draft, find a partner, and begin revising for this key quality of the ideas trait: using details.

Later that day, I spoke with Mr. Sheppard. He told me that during small-group share, one student admitted that he was neither snorkeling nor scuba diving when he wrote his draft. He was sitting on the beach. I had to laugh because, honestly, as writers, aren't we all stuck on the beach sometimes?

The Ideas Trait: A Definition

The ideas trait is about how writers plunge into the water to experience the unknown and use what they discover to make meaning for the reader. It is the piece's content—its central message and the details that support that message. The piece shows strength in the ideas trait when its topic is narrow and clear and its details are specific, interesting, and accurate. It is focused and well developed and contains original thinking because the writer knows what he or she wants to say and anticipates the reader's every question. To accomplish this, the writer must apply the key qualities of this trait, with skill and confidence:

* Finding a Topic

* Focusing the Topic

* Developing the Topic

* Using Details

> **❝**Your idea gives the reader the chance to fly with you. **❞**
> —Cassidy, grade 7

Why Students Struggle With Ideas

I think of the ideas trait as the "never-ending trait" because no matter how old you are, no matter how much writing you do, no matter how much you improve over time, finding ideas and writing about them clearly and compellingly is a challenge. Small wonder, then, that middle school writers find the ideas trait difficult to master. Here are some reasons.

They Stray From the Topic

As students think about what they want to say, they sometimes wander off the assigned topic to a related one—or go in a completely different direction. An assignment to write a page or two about the censorship of *Fahrenheit 451*, for instance, may prompt a student to think about a time she encountered censorship and how she felt about it, which might lead to writing a piece about a school rule she thinks is unfair—a far cry from the *Fahrenheit 451* assignment. You might be tempted to score this piece low in the ideas trait. But remember, we assess for the quality of the idea, not for having the "right" idea. It's quite possible that the student developed a strong piece although it was not on the topic you expected.

Students stray from the topic for many reasons: they aren't interested; they don't have much to say; they aren't clear about the purpose. If you take time to sort out why the student's writing diverged from the assignment, you can help her get back on track. Maybe she needs to do more research, change modes, or use a different format to become more engaged with the topic. Or maybe she isn't aware that what she's writing isn't what you assigned. We can redirect students who write off topic without condemning them: "Tonya, this is a very interesting piece you are developing on censorship in Afghanistan. However, I still need your book review on *Fahrenheit 451*. Keep working on the Afghanistan piece during writing workshop. I'll be happy to help you with it then."

They Don't Know How to Pick Topics

Students who have been fed a steady diet of teacher-generated prompts often flounder when asked to choose a topic of their own. Finding their own topic means thinking, and many students would rather the teacher do the thinking for them.

Our students will never get better at finding topics unless we provide them with ample opportunities to try. So strike a balance between providing students with topics and asking them to find topics on their own. Finding their own topics will be harder for them, of course. But, in time, they'll discover that it's far more satisfying—and therefore more motivating—to revise and edit a piece of writing based on their own idea than someone else's.

If your classroom is filled with long-faced students asking, "What should I write about?" it's time to teach them how to look within themselves to discover their own ideas for writing. We want to shift their thinking away from "writing right" to writing well.

They Don't Understand the Benefits of Prewriting

If students don't use prewriting to think through audience and purpose, gather information, and carefully plan details—if they just start writing once they've come up with a topic—their piece will surely wind up too general. Their lack of effort will show on the first draft. Yet getting students to slow down and think through possibilities before composing can be a hard sell. Many students just want to fulfill the requirement and move on. So, we have to show students the benefit of narrowing their topic before they begin to write. For one thing, it makes their writing more interesting. For another, it makes it more focused:

General Topic: The Internet

Focused Topic: How have current events been influenced by the existence of the Internet?

General Topic: *American Born Chinese* by Gene Luen Yang (2006)

Focused Topic: What questions do you have for Gene Luen Yang, author of *American Born Chinese*, that relate to any of the big ideas or themes presented in the graphic novel?

Focused topics lead to writing with a clear purpose. A general topic just sits there, waiting to be turned into something. Students who struggle to make topics work would do well to slow down during prewriting and think through their options until they find one they can get excited about. Then, they can gather the information needed to make their idea clear. Their writing will be stronger as a result.

Assessing Student Work for Ideas

The following six sixth-grade papers represent a wide range of skills in the ideas trait. Review the scoring guide on page 65, read each paper carefully, assess the paper for the ideas trait by following the steps on pages 50–51 under "Assessing Writing Using the Trait Scoring Guides," and then read my assessment to see if we agree. Use your own students' writing for further practice.

The papers were all written in the narrative mode, in response to the prompt "Tell about a time you will always remember." That said, you shouldn't need to know the prompt to score the papers. If you find yourself wondering what the topic was intended to be, that's an indication that the piece is not strong in the ideas trait. If the writer has done his or job well in the ideas trait, the topic will be crystal clear.

I chose papers written at the same grade level, in the same mode, and to the same prompt so that you can focus on the issue at hand, ideas, without other factors serving as distractions. But keep in mind, it's critical that students learn to develop ideas regardless of the grade they're in, the mode they choose, or the prompt they're given. Clear, well-supported ideas should be found in all writing, all the time. Even though I focus on ideas, I've scored the papers in all the traits (except presentation, since the papers are typeset) in case you need additional samples to practice scoring or use in your instruction.

Scoring Guide: Ideas

The piece's content—its central message and details that support that message.

6

HIGH

EXCEPTIONAL

A. Finding a Topic: The writer offers a clear, central theme or a simple, original story line that is memorable.

B. Focusing the Topic: The writer narrows the theme or story line to create a piece that is clear, tight, and manageable.

C. Developing the Topic: The writer provides enough critical evidence to support the theme and shows insight on the topic. Or he or she tells the story in a fresh way through an original, unpredictable plot.

D. Using Details: The writer offers credible, accurate details that create pictures in the reader's mind, from the beginning of the piece to the end. Those details provide the reader with evidence of the writer's knowledge about and/or experience with the topic.

5

STRONG

4

MIDDLE

REFINING

A. Finding a Topic: The writer offers a recognizable but broad theme or story line. He or she stays on topic, but in a predictable way.

B. Focusing the Topic: The writer needs to crystallize his or her topic around the central theme or story line. He or she does not focus on a specific aspect of the topic.

C. Developing the Topic: The writer draws on personal knowledge and experience, but does not offer a unique perspective. He or she does not probe deeply, but instead gives the reader only a glimpse at aspects of the topic.

D. Using Details: The writer offers details, but they do not always hit the mark because they are inaccurate or irrelevant. He or she does not create a picture in the reader's mind because key questions about the central theme or story line have not been addressed.

3

DEVELOPING

2

LOW

EMERGING

A. Finding a Topic: The writer has not settled on a topic and, therefore, may offer only a series of unfocused, repetitious, and/or random thoughts.

B. Focusing the Topic: The writer has not narrowed his or her topic in a meaningful way. It's hard to tell what the writer thinks is important since he or she devotes equal importance to each piece of information.

C. Developing the Topic: The writer has created a piece that is so short, the reader cannot fully understand or appreciate what he or she wants to say. He or she may have simply restated an assigned topic or responded to a prompt, without devoting much thought or effort to it.

D. Using Details: The writer has clearly devoted little attention to details. The writing contains limited or completely inaccurate information. After reading the piece, the reader is left with many unanswered questions.

1

RUDIMENTARY

Having My Own Room

I have my own room no brother to sleep with. He takes up all the room and I could not sleep at all. So I told my mom and dad they called to get a new bed and he had his own room and I had my own room. The next morning My brother got out of his bed, he felt relaxced. He got some eggs and toast ate all of it

When he went back to sleep and had a lot of deams. Every time he gets up my mom and dad have to give work. My parents and my brother are playing butzz, I don't get to have fun. After the day was done I have to go to bed. Then I asked my dad to see if my brother cody would move to Tennessee and dad said yes and moved my brother there. I said good by to My brother when we left Tennessee and I was sad.

Time to Assess for Ideas

Writing that lacks focus can be a big problem in the ideas trait. This piece is an example of exactly that. It begins with a general nod to the topic and then digresses. What eggs and toast have to do with getting one's own room is a mystery, as is what's going on in the whole second paragraph. In general, the piece rambles and completely lacks focus.

Ideas	
Score	**1: Rudimentary**
Range	**Low**

Other Traits	
Organization	1
Voice	2
Word Choice	2
Sentence Fluency	1
Conventions	1

A Finding a Topic

The writer has not settled on a topic and, therefore, may offer only a series of unfocused, repetitious, and/or random thoughts.

There is a lot going on in this piece and it's confusing. The writer would do well to pick one of these potential ideas—his room or his brother who moved to Tennessee—and develop it.

B Focusing the Topic

The writer has not narrowed his or her topic in a meaningful way. It's hard to tell what the writer thinks is important since he or she devotes equal importance to each piece of information.

This is dead on. The brother's breakfast, the writer's dreams, going to work, and playing games are details that have been given the same importance to bigger ideas such as getting his own room or witnessing his brother move away.

C Developing the Topic

The writer has created a piece that is so short, the reader cannot fully understand or appreciate what he or she wants to say. He or she may have simply restated an assigned topic or responded to a prompt, without devoting much thought or effort to it.

This is a short, undeveloped piece. The writer starts to explain why getting his own room matters, but quickly loses focus and provides details that roam all over the place.

D Using Details

The writer has clearly devoted little attention to details. The writing contains limited or completely inaccurate information. After reading the piece, the reader is left with many unanswered questions.

Is this piece about getting a room of your own or losing your brother? Details such as "He takes up all the room and I could not sleep at all" are good but they are few and far between and don't connect clearly to an obvious main idea.

The Baseball Game

When I was 3 years old my dad took my brother and I to a baseball game. The Royals were playing the Oakland A's. We got there early to watch them warm up. Finally the game started, The first pitch of the game the A's leadoff hitter hit a homerun. During the game the Royals only got 5 hits In the end the Royals lost 10-1. I left the game happy and full of the food I bought with the money I kept begging for. from then on I was an A's fan.

Time to Assess for Ideas

This little piece has big potential. But for now it's mainly a list of routine events and facts. As it stands, the reader can't help but ask, "So what?" because the writer hasn't found anything meaningful to write about apart from the obvious. It's more than a random, disconnected collection of thoughts, however, because it covers the writer's experience of going to the baseball game. But it's very general and lacks focus.

Ideas	
Score	**2: Emerging**
Range	**Low**

Other Traits	
Organization	3
Voice	1
Word Choice	2
Sentence Fluency	2
Conventions	2

A Finding a Topic

The writer has not settled on a topic and, therefore, may offer only a series of unfocused, repetitive, and/or random thoughts.

> *It's easy to see the general idea the writer is going for here. But the writer does not provide a focused story of his day or explain why he's telling the story in the first place. One line, "I left the game happy and full of the food I bought with the money I kept begging for," is intriguing and worth developing in the next draft.*

B Focusing the Topic

The writer has not narrowed his or her topic in a meaningful way. It's hard to tell what the writer thinks is important since he or she devotes equal importance to each piece of information.

> *This is an all-too-common "bed-to-bed" narrative, in which the writer covers a whole day in a single breath and devotes equal importance to each detail. It's difficult to discern what makes this event special enough to be the topic of the paper.*

C Developing the Topic

The writer has created a piece that is so short, the reader cannot fully understand or appreciate what he or she wants to say. He or she may have simply restated an assigned topic or responded to a prompt, without devoting much thought or effort to it.

> *This piece is very short. The writer outlines high points of the game, but he doesn't develop them with a sense of purpose or provide a unique perspective.*

D Using Details

The writer has clearly devoted little attention to details. The writing contains limited or completely inaccurate information. After reading the piece, the reader is left with many unanswered questions.

> *Broad strokes: Baseball. The A's. The Royals. The warm-up. The home run. The score. Then one nice moment where we get something truly interesting—begging for food and getting it.*

Winning First Place!

This story is about winning first place at a cheerleading competition. But before we get to winning lets go back to the morning of competition.

This morning my mom came into my room and woke me up saying "get up it is time to get ready for competition." I got out of bed and went to take a shower. Then I went downstairs to get my hair done. I was trying to eat my breakfast while my mom was tugging and pulling on my head. After, my mom made sure that all the cheerleaders were there and then we left.

Once we go to B. High School, we went to go warm-up. Everything was going pretty good until a girl came in late and she didn't even have her hair in a ponytail! So while she got her hair done the rest of the squad warmed up their stunts. One stunt fell and we all got worried. That stunt group tried it again and got it. Next, we went out on the floor to practice our formations.

Now as we get ready to go out and show what we have worked on for 3 long months. The group in front of us is going off the floor. We spirit onto the floor, as we wait for the music to start, knots are forming in all of our stomachs. But this was it, one shot to show them what we've got. As the music starts up we smile and do the routine that we learned. We finished and spirited off the floor.

Time to Assess for Ideas

This piece starts out like the last paper on the baseball game because the writer doesn't reveal why the topic matters to her in any real detail. However, there are a few moments where we get a glimpse at what she's thinking and feeling. As a reader, I found myself hungry for more of those moments. Events like these can be turning points in the lives of young teens, but this writer doesn't open up much to let us understand why cheerleading tryouts mattered so much to her. Dear Writer: Open the door to insightful details and let me in!

Ideas	
Score	**3: Developing**
Range	**Middle**

Other Traits	
Organization	4
Voice	3
Word Choice	3
Sentence Fluency	4
Conventions	5

A Finding a Topic

The writer offers a recognizable, but broad theme or story line. He or she stays on topic, but in a predictable way.

The topic is recognizable, for sure, but very broad and unfocused for most of the paper. There's nothing new in here for the reader.

B Focusing the Topic

The writer needs to crystallize his or her topic around the central theme or story line. He or she does not focus on a specific aspect of the topic.

There is no "main idea," "big issue," or "lesson learned." The writer relays facts, and that's about it.

C Developing the Topic

The writer draws on personal knowledge and experience, but does not offer a unique perspective. He or she does not probe deeply, but instead gives the reader only a glimpse at aspects of the topic.

We understand what happened and that it mattered to this writer, but not why it mattered. Her urgency and anticipation are clear. Her reasons for feeling them aren't.

D Using Details

The writer offers details, but they do not always hit the mark because they are inaccurate or irrelevant. He or she does not create a picture in the reader's mind because key questions about the central theme or story line have not been addressed.

A significant detail doesn't appear until the third paragraph: "She didn't even have her hair in a ponytail." With precious few exceptions the details in this piece address commonly understood information about the topic.

Thing to Remember

The thing that I will want to remember is all the fun I had with my family at my grandmas house. I want to remember the fun I would have when I was with my cousins over at my grandmas house. We would go there for every holiday except Holloween. On Thanksgiving we would go out side just the kids and play games like tag or roming around but the thing we did the most was hide and go seek. We would play if rain, snow, blistering heat, whatever. Hide and go seek was a way to get away from parents and have fun. My grandma's land scape of her house was so big that it could be used for a football feild. It was all down hill even her house was. My grandma lived ther for so long our parents wer little they went there to. Every one brought there food they have made and brought it over and had a dinning table full of food. The food our family brought was always good. We would have a fiest with diserts and hams. and drinks, mash potatos. We would stay inside if it was to cold. Inside we would eaither talk or we play dodge ball up in my grandmas room with pillows and stuffed animals. My grandmas hous was everyones favorit place to be. The women talked and perpared the food to eat, werering wher we were. The men sit and talk about work and what was new in their life. My grandma always sitting there quite and inocently. She is no longer with us but I will always remember her and her beautiful home.

Time to Assess for Ideas

I really like this piece; it's exactly what I'd like to see go in the writing folder so the student can work on it further until it becomes tight, focused original writing. However, in its present form, I was left yearning for the details that would allow me to experience this family's warm relationships. They are definitely on the right track, though. I'd urge the writer to rethink those details in favor of more sensory ones—all the wonderful things he saw, heard, tasted, smelled, and felt at his grandmother's house during holidays. Don't let the spelling and other conventional errors distract you from seeing a good idea in the making.

Ideas	
Score	**4: Refining**
Range	**Middle**

Other Traits	
Organization	5
Voice	5
Word Choice	4
Sentence Fluency	3
Conventions	3

A Finding a Topic

The writer offers a recognizable, but broad theme or story line. He or she stays on topic, but in a predictable way.

The idea is not as polished as it could be, but it's heading in a good direction. The writer has pretty much provided a list of events. He focuses on what happened at Grandma's place. Now he needs to tell us what it was like.

B Focusing the Topic

The writer needs to crystallize his or her topic around the central theme or story line. He or she does not focus on a specific aspect of the topic.

The writer understands that being at his grandmother's was special and is worth writing about, but dances around the big idea.

C Developing the Topic

The writer draws on personal knowledge and experience, but does not offer a unique perspective. He or she does not probe deeply, but instead gives the reader only a glimpse at aspects of the topic.

Just when the writer provides specific examples of what makes his experiences memorable, he throws in broad ones. It's uneven, making for a rocky read.

D Using Details

The writer offers details, but they do not always hit the mark because they are inaccurate or irrelevant. He or she does not create a picture in the reader's mind because key questions about the central theme or story line have not been addressed.

The details that pepper this piece are relevant, but lean toward common. Fine-tuning them by focusing on the senses will move the piece up the ideas scale.

The Top Thrill Dragster

We were traveling to Ohio for our family vacation. My dad, mom, brother, and I were going there for a week, specifically to go to Cedar Point. Cedar Point is an amusement park that has sixteen roller coasters, and a bunch of rides. The best ride that is there is called The Top Thrill Dragster.

The Top Thrill Dragster is an astounding four hundred and twenty feet high. It is a roller coaster that is so tall, if you stair at the very top for a few seconds you'd sprain your neck. It is a roller coaster that shoots you off from a stop, sending you on a wild ride that jerks you from zero to one hundred and twenty miles per hour, in four seconds.

The lines for the ride were horrendous. Waiting for three hours was nothing. As we waiting, not so patiently, you could hear zoooom, and awww off in the distance! While I stood in line I timed how long the ride was. It took only twenty seconds to go straight up four hundred and twenty feet and straight down four hundred and twenty feet. A perfect right angle.

As the ride starts, it shoots you off and it takes your picture. Flash. On your way back down when the ride is almost over, it takes your picture again. Flash. Then you get to look at it in the photo booth. We bought a picture, and it was hilarious. I keep it tucked into my binder as a reminder of this awesome day.

The weather that week was perfect. Sunny with a light breeze. We rode the Top Thrill Dragster twice that week because the lines were so long. When the week was over I told my dad that I would like to come back again, sometime. I loved our trip to Cedar Point and the Top Thrill Dragster.

Time to Assess for Ideas

In this piece the writer is clear about what she wants to show the reader, and the details that develop the piece focus on that main idea, especially the specific and sensory ones in the body of the text. It's almost as though, in the middle, the writer pulls out binoculars and focuses them, but neglects to use those same settings at the beginning and end. Some work on the introduction and conclusion would easily bring this piece up one more step in the ideas trait.

Ideas	
Score	**5: Strong**
Range	**High**

Other Traits	
Organization	4
Voice	4
Word Choice	4
Sentence Fluency	4
Conventions	4

A Finding a Topic

The writer offers a clear, central theme or a simple, original story line that is memorable.

No problem here. The story line is both simple and original. The writer captures thrill of the ride in the middle by weaving together sensory details effectively.

B Focusing the Topic

The writer narrows the theme or story line to create a piece that is clear, tight, and manageable.

Thank goodness this writer focused on just one ride. So often, middle school writers try to cover the entire vacation, and it just doesn't work.

C Developing the Topic

The writer provides enough critical evidence to support the theme and shows insight on the topic. Or he or she tells the story in a fresh way through an original, unpredictable plot.

The writer provides enough evidence to make it clear that the ride was exciting and memorable. It goes beyond "Because I said so."

D Using Details

The writer offers credible, accurate details that create pictures in the reader's mind, from the beginning of the piece to the end. Those details provide the reader with evidence of his or her knowledge about and/or experience with the topic.

There are many great details: "shoots you off from a stop," "zoom and awww," horrendous lines, hilarious pictures. These work well. Details like these are needed in the introduction and conclusion as well.

An Event I'll Always Remember

The hands on the clock were frozen. 11:35p.m. I'd been standing in line for three hours with Ryan, my sixteen-year-old brother. Mom paid him to take me to Barnes & Noble to get the last book in the Harry Potter series, can you believe it? He didn't want to come because he was afraid of what all his friends would say, but twenty bucks speaks louder so here we were. And besides, he'd do anything to drive now that has his license, even hang out with me.

The books were stacked and ready for we greedy readers, but no one was allowed to touch them until the stroke of midnight. 25 minutes to go. I didn't think I'd make it. My feet hurt so bad. Standing in line like that with hundreds of other wizards and muggles was exhausting. There were little kids running around everywhere. Why? They didn't care about Harry Potter like I did, I could tell. They were just there for something to do. It was really annoying.

To pass the time, I'd been through two mocha frappachinos and looked at every book in the fantasy section. There were some there I liked, like *Dragonslayer*, but none of them made my heart race like Harry Potter. It was so exciting – the last book. Would Harry die? Would Dumbledore return from the dead? Would He-Who-Cannot-Be-Named show himself? I could not wait another minute to find out. As soon as I got my hands on the book I was going to start reading and not quit until I turned the last page.

I check and rechecked my wristband. We were in the gold group, the third to get books. All evening I'd been eyeing the stacks, trying to estimate how many books there were and how many people would get theirs first. Darn. I should have paid more attention in math class when we were doing estimating, I guess. But, it looked like I'd get mine. I wasn't positive. I heaved a huge sigh of relief, however, when it got even closer to midnight and the store manager rolled out one more palate of books. Great. I thought. Now I'm for sure going to get my own copy TONIGHT.

The clock creeped closer and closer to midnight and the crowd got more and more restless. All those kids dressed like Harry or Hagrid were looking pretty tired. There were even some grown ups with tattoos and makeup to get them in the spirit. I thought they looked dumb, but at least they were there.

Finally. Midnight. The first group raced up to get their books. I wished I had a blue wristband. I wished my mom had let me come earlier, but I had to be a little more patient. Then, the green group. The book stacks were dwindling. There must have been 200 people in the groups ahead of me. I kept eyeing the stacks and the line. Surely I'd get mine soon. Finally, the gold group was called and I pushed my way up to the front and grabbed a book. My brother, who had wandered off all evening and left me alone (thank goodness) paid for it, and pushed me toward the door. "Come on, Matt. Let's go. Hurry up." You didn't have to tell me twice. I could hardly wait to crack the cover.

I started reading, "The scar had not pained Harry for nineteen years. All was well." All was well, indeed. My wait was over. But just then, my brother reached over and grabbed the book out of my hands. "You can wait. I'm gonna read it first," he said with a sneer.

"Like heck," I told him. And grabbed it back. It might have been the only time he let me win. And then my muggle brother drove me home.

Time to Assess for Ideas

You don't have to be a J. K. Rowling fan to appreciate what this writer had to go through to get a copy of *Harry Potter and the Deathly Hallows* on the night it was released. Insightful details on a focused topic, woven together with a wizard's touch, make this a standout piece. I had a similar experience standing in line until 2 a.m. in Lee's Summit, Missouri, that same night—and relived that experience upon reading this well-told story.

Ideas	
Score	**6: Exceptional**
Range	**High**

Other Traits	
Organization	6
Voice	6
Word Choice	5
Sentence Fluency	6
Conventions	6

A Finding a Topic

The writer offers a clear, central theme or a simple, original story line that is memorable.

The piece is simple, straightforward, and clear. Though hundreds of thousands of people stood in line at bookstores that night, only this writer could tell this story. Bravo!

B Focusing the Topic

The writer narrows the theme or story line to create a piece that is clear, tight, and manageable.

One night. One event. One perspective. The piece is focused on what matters—getting inside this experience and telling the story well.

C Developing the Topic

The writer provides enough critical evidence to support the theme and shows insight on the topic. Or he or she tells the story in a fresh way through an original, unpredictable plot.

There's no doubt this writer went through a lot to get his copy of Harry Potter and the Deathly Hallows. *The piece is unique. It works because the writer goes beyond the story line and reveals himself and his perspective so clearly.*

D Using Details

The writer offers credible, accurate details that create pictures in the reader's mind, from the beginning of the piece to the end. Those details provide the reader with evidence of his or her knowledge about and/or experience with the topic.

Details such as frozen clock hands, a brother who has to be bribed to take him to the bookstore, mocha "frappachinos," eyeing the stacks, the colored wristbands, and so many others work well to bring this piece to life.

Conference Comments

If the piece scores high in ideas, 5 or 6, say something like:

> "I felt like I was right there with you, waiting impatiently for my own Harry Potter book. Your <u>idea</u> was clear and stayed focused. Outstanding work."

> "The details you wrote helped me picture this <u>idea</u>, allowing me to experience this memorable night right along with you. Thanks for taking me inside this story."

If the piece scores in the middle, a 3 or 4, say something like:

> "Choosing an event like this is a good start at selecting an <u>idea</u> worth writing about. Did you have a favorite moment? Are there some that don't matter as much? Revising to make the special moments stand out will make your <u>idea</u> clear."

> "What is a specific moment that stands out about cheerleading tryouts? Why don't you start your piece there to get into the <u>idea</u> right away?"

If the piece scores low, a 1 or 2, say something like:

> "I think you have something to build on with this moment about the food and how you nagged to get it all during the game. I'd certainly like to read more about that <u>idea</u>."

> "You've written a list of events about the baseball game, and now I'm curious what they mean to you. Make a quick list of three <u>ideas</u> about why this baseball game was special. Then pick one and try writing about that single <u>idea</u>. See where it takes you."

Teaching Writing With the Ideas Trait

Writing must make sense, and that's what the ideas trait is all about—choosing a topic, narrowing it down, and supporting it with enough details to make the message clear and engaging. To help you help students do that, I've organized the remainder of this chapter into sections that correspond to the ideas trait's four key qualities:

* Finding a Topic

* Focusing the Topic

* Developing the Topic

* Using Details

> **ff** I think working with ideas is like music. I love how Mozart's pieces have notes that weave in and out and around each other to create perfect harmonies. I think that all great composers were probably good writers, too. **JJ**
>
> —Makita, grade 8

Within each section, I provide four types of teaching resources:

A Think About: A list of four critical questions that keep students focused on important aspects of the key quality. Think Abouts provide a self-check for students to use as they draft and revise their work. Give students a copy of the Think About and review it with them before conducting the accompanying focus lesson. (The Think Abouts are peppered throughout the pages that follow and on the CD that accompanies this book.)

A Warm-Up: A quick, teacher-led activity that provides practice in the key quality. Warm-ups take about ten minutes to complete.

A Focus Lesson: A teacher-led demonstration of how skilled writers apply the key quality to their work and how students might apply it to their own, with an extended practice component. Focus lessons can take a whole class period or longer.

Two Activities: Creative, classroom-tested ideas that allow students to try out skills and strategies that you share in warm-ups and focus lessons. Activities can take five minutes or 50, depending on your students' needs and interest levels, and can be carried out by students independently or in small groups.

Although there are a total of 20 Think Abouts, warm-ups, focus lessons, and activities for the ideas trait in the pages that follow, you'll want more—good teachers always do. Check professional resources, search children's books for exemplary passages, and look in your files for material to create your own warm-ups, focus lessons, and activities.

Key Quality: Finding a Topic

Many students think that if they haven't discovered a spaceship in their backyard or ridden an alpaca in Uruguay, they have nothing interesting to say. But many good topics for writing stem from normal, everyday events. How students bring their own, original spin to those events is what makes their writing special. Use the following Think About to expand students' notions about selecting a topic.

Reproducible on CD

THINK ABOUT:

- Have I chosen a topic that I really like?
- Do I have something new to say about this topic?
- Am I writing about what I know and care about?
- Have I gathered enough information about it so that I'm ready to write?

WARM-UP   Finding a Topic

Distribute copies of the Think About. Ask students to clear their minds and come up with a cool invention they could use at school—something that would make life easier, less stressful, and/or more fun. Some ideas:

- A homework machine
- An automatic essay writer
- A bully-proof force field
- A remote control for your teacher
- The ultimate hall pass that transports you somewhere fun
- A cleaning machine for backpacks and lockers
- A flavor and texture enhancer for cafeteria food

Once they come up with their topic, have them spend five minutes (and only five minutes) writing about their inventions in detail and, if they like, illustrating them. When they're finished, share the following example with students and have them share theirs.

> Here he comes. That kid who scares the daylights out of everyone. He kicks, he hits, and he spits, and is just disgusting to be around. I know he must be lonely and need friends, but it's hard to be his friend when he acts so mean all the time. Oh no. He's coming right over my direction. I better activate my new, Bully-Proof Force Field. Here it goes; I hope it works. BZZZZZZ. I can feel the energy all around me now. And here he goes, trying to kick me, but his leg hits the invisible force field and he is thrown backwards. As he stumbles to get back on his feet, he throws a punch that is also repelled. Now he's shaking his head and leaving. Good thing. According to the directions, the Bully-Proof Force Field only works for one minute.

FOCUS LESSON   Finding a Topic

Finding topics in readily available resources, such as newspapers and magazines, is a useful skill for students. Those resources provide valuable fodder for fiction and nonfiction writing. In this lesson, students search *USA Today* for topics and then write articles in the more student-friendly style of *Upfront*, a teen newspaper from the *New York Times* and available online. In the process, they learn not only about finding a topic, but also a thing or two about voice. You can substitute any newspaper or magazine you wish, as long as you end up with two publications that have significantly different writing styles.

Materials:

- multiple copies of *USA Today* and *Upfront* (or newspapers of your choice)
- chart paper and markers
- paper, pens, pencils

What to Do:

1. Arrange students into small groups. Give each group a copy of *USA Today* and assign them a section: National and International News, Money, Sports, Life, and so forth.
2. Ask members of each group to scan their section for an interesting article to read in depth.
3. Once they've chosen an article, have one group member read it aloud. Then have all members discuss the article, determine its topic, and write the topic on a sheet of paper so it can be shared. Remind groups to zero in on the topic, not just the headline.
4. Ask groups to read several short articles from the front page of each section and record the topics on the same sheet of paper.
5. Bring the class together and have a member of each group share their topics. On chart paper, organize those topics by section. Here's an example:

USA Today

Section A National and International News	Section B Money	Section C Sports	Section D Life
The devastation from a category 4 hurricane	The effect of an economic slowdown on spendable income	The perfect draft choice for a pro football team	Why more people watch dramas than comedies on TV
The type of jobs on the increase in the US	Teenagers buy phones with IM capabilities	Why players always wear white in tennis	The best new movie coming out this week
Why young voters turned out for the first time	More money spent on pet treats than bread	Baseball team chooses unlikely mascot	The real story behind reality TV show success

6. Hand out a copy of *Upfront* to each group, have a member read an article aloud and determine the topic, and record the topic on the chart in the section it might belong in if it appeared in *USA Today*.

7. Using the chart as a guide, ask groups to put two topics together to create a whole new topic such as "Teens set record number of IMs after new baseball team mascot is made public."

8. Ask group members to write a short news article in the style of either *USA Today* or *Upfront* on their new topic.

9. Share articles as a class.

Lesson Extension

Ask individual students or small groups to write an article for a forthcoming issue of *USA Today*. Tell them to record the topic and its section on a separate sheet of paper. Then exchange papers, read each other's articles, and write down the paper's topic and the section in which they think it should be featured. Match what the writer had in mind to what the reader thought. Discuss the importance of having clear, focused topics.

ACTIVITIES Finding a Topic

Talking About Books

Ask pairs of students to write at least six e-mails (send and reply at least three times each) discussing a book they've both read, its main idea, and parts they enjoyed. Tell them to come up with a title for the e-mail based on the book's main topic. For example, if students wrote about *The Catcher in the Rye*, the e-mail messages might be entitled: "Holden Caulfield Examines His Life in This Timeless Bildungsroman." (Look it up; it was new to me, too!) Ask students to end their e-mail correspondence with a recommendation for a different book that has the same main topic as *The Catcher in the Rye*.

Writer's Notebooks

Often, the best topics are the ones students come up with themselves. As you work with students, encourage them to jot down in a notebook possible ideas for use in writing later—ideas that occur to them during science, social studies, health, fine arts, or English, or in everyday life. Let students select a notebook that makes them feel comfortable. Keep your own notebook and model how you jot down ideas for writing, words and phrases you like, intriguing information and observations, and questions to ponder. This is sure to silence the lament. "I don't know what to write about."

Key Quality: Focusing the Topic

Once writers select a topic, they determine a focus—a specific aspect of the broader subject. As they do that, they must consider the most important information to include and the best way to convey it. Use the following Think About to expand students' notions about focusing the topic.

THINK ABOUT:

- Have I zeroed in on one small part of a bigger idea?
- Can I sum up my idea in a simple sentence?
- Have I chosen the information that captures my idea best?
- Have I thought deeply about what the reader will need to know?

Reproducible on CD

WARM-UP   Focusing the Topic

Distribute copies of the Think About. Write the following paragraph on a chart or project it on the overhead. Read the paragraph and have students revise it on a separate sheet of paper, using the Think About questions to narrow the topic to one aspect of the main idea and add details to develop it.

> Turn your lights off in your home when you don't need them. Recycle your garbage. Go paperless. Hair products can be environmentally harmful. Be less wasteful. Grocery bags can be recycled. Take public transportation or carpool to save gas. Shopping. Don't leave the water running when you brush your teeth.

When they're finished, share the following example with students and have them share theirs.

> In today's world, it just makes sense to be less wasteful. We should recycle our garbage so we have fewer landfills. One simple way is to bring grocery bags to the store so you don't need a new one for every purchase. We can conserve energy by taking public transportation, carpooling, riding bikes, or walking more often. Our need for water can be reduced by simple acts such as not letting the tap run while brushing your teeth. And we can choose environmentally friendly products for our hair and for cleaning. Here's one more good idea to be less wasteful: go paperless. Why not use word processing instead of paper, even on a piece like this!

FOCUS LESSON Focusing the Topic

Learning to go from a general topic to a specific one is a skill students can and should learn. This lesson is easy because it doesn't require any preparation or create any papers to grade. And it's fun because it feels more like a game than a lesson. I call it "Narrow It" and play it whenever I have a few unexpected extra minutes.

Materials:

- electronic projection system or traditional overhead projector

What to Do:

1. Think of a broad topic such as animals, sports, weather, food, geography, books, or school. Remind students of the Think About so they have some sense of how writers focus on broad topics.
2. Divide the class into two groups.
3. Write the topic on the board and ask the first group to "narrow it"—to think about the topic and come up with a small issue related to it.
4. Ask someone from the first group to call out his or her answer and write it underneath the main topic. For example, if the broad topic is "food," students might call out "pizza."
5. Think aloud for students to show how you check to make sure that "pizza" is a subcategory of "food." Say, "Hmmm . . . Yes, pizza is a type of food, so that works."
6. Turn to the other group and ask its members to "narrow it." They should come up with a small issue related to "pizza." Again, provide time for students to think, ask for a response, and write it on the board. Students might say, "pepperoni." Think aloud to show students how you connect "pepperoni" to pizza.
7. If students give you a different type of food, such as "hamburgers," rather than a small issue related to pizza, write it on the board next to "pizza" to show them that both hamburgers and pizza are types of food, but "hamburgers" does not narrow the topic of pizza. Then ask students to choose one or the other and continue.
8. Return to the first group and say "narrow it again." Continue writing responses down until students have nothing else to contribute. In the end, your chart might look like the example on page 85.
9. When you have a focused topic, ask students to respond to this question: "If you had all the information you needed, which would be easier to write about, 'Food' or whether pizza is better hot or cold?" Students will likely respond that the focused topic would be easier.

10. Tell students that when they're confronted with a general topic in any class or on a state assessment, they should play the "Narrow It" game in their minds to arrive at an interesting and manageable topic.

Lesson Extension

If students want to write pieces based on the focused topic from the lesson, tell them to jot the topic down in their writer's notebooks and revisit it later during independent writing.

ACTIVITIES Focusing the Topic

From General to Specific

Give students a prompt they might encounter in school or on the state assessment, such as, "Discuss something you've learned about playing a sport or other activity." In small groups, have them transform the prompt into a dozen good, focused topics for writing, like these:

> The bus ride to soccer camp
>
> Losing out for starting position as the goalie
>
> The sound of my father's voice cheering me on from the stands
>
> The feel of ice underfoot on early morning Saturday games in October
>
> How I keep my too-big pants up during the game
>
> The difference between playing on grass or artificial turf
>
> The reasons I chose to play soccer instead of football
>
> How I can tell my coach is about to erupt
>
> The best halftime soccer snacks
>
> A move I learned that's made a difference
>
> How to head butt
>
> Why I would/wouldn't play again

Discuss with students which of their new topics are still "on topic" and which are too far removed and, therefore, might be deemed "off topic" by standardized test givers. Remind them to choose only "on-topic" ideas when taking tests—but to run with any topic in most other situations.

The Best and the Worst

Have your students brainstorm a list of real-world jobs that require a great deal of writing: a writer for a late-night talk show, a fund-raiser for a charity, a developer of video games, an author of children's books, and so on. Write the jobs on a chart. Divide the class into small groups and assign one of the jobs to each group. Ask group members to prepare a panel presentation explaining the best and worst parts of the job and present it to the class, using some sort of visual aid that illustrates key points, such as a chart or diagram. Hang their creations in a prominent place for everyone to read and think about. This activity teaches students that writing is a big part of most professions—a lesson they will come to learn on their own soon enough.

Key Quality: Developing the Topic

If they're writing nonfiction, writers develop their topic by focusing on the information readers need to understand it. If they're writing fiction, they do it by focusing on the details that move the plot forward. In both cases, the goal is to create a rich, solid, well-conceived piece of writing. Use the following Think About to expand students' notions about developing the topic.

Reproducible on CD

THINK ABOUT:

- Am I sure my information is right?
- Are my details chock-full of interesting information?
- Have I used details that show new thinking about this idea?
- Will my reader believe what I say about this topic?

WARM-UP Developing the Topic

Distribute copies of the Think About and have students develop the following piece with interesting, accurate information.

> Country music is America's music. It's what everyone likes. There should be a lot more country music on the radio.

When they're finished, share the following example with students and have them share theirs.

> Once known as country-western, country music is a favorite music genre in America today. It began as folk music that originated from the southern rural states, but widened its appeal from coast to coast after World War II. It's a unique style of music that is American, through and through. Some people find the topics of country music songs to be silly, but I think they express what Americans really value: family, home, hard work, love, religion, and how to survive hard times. Country musicians are my favorites, whether it's an old timer like Hank Williams or the new star Kenny Chesney. I wish there were more radio stations that played only country music; I'd listen to them day and night.

FOCUS LESSON Developing the Topic

Middle school students often jump to conclusions based on emotion, so this writing activity is designed to slow them down, allow them to gather information about a topic, and think it through before reaching a final conclusion. It helps you to have an energized, well-informed discussion with students prior to writing, which will stimulate their thinking and send a strong message about the importance of such work when it comes to developing topics.

Materials:

- a list of thought-provoking "I believe" statements:

> I believe that…
>
> Words can hurt.
>
> People learn from their mistakes.
>
> What goes around comes around.
>
> You can only depend on yourself.
>
> Money can't buy happiness.

- paper, pens, pencils

What to Do:

1. Label two corners of your classroom "Agree" and two corners "Disagree."
2. Tell students you are going to read a statement and that they should each go to one of the corners, based on whether they agree or disagree with that statement. Ask students to limit the number in each corner to eight.
3. Choose a statement from the list above and read it aloud.
4. Allow time for students to think about the statement (really think about it) and go to the corner of their choice.
5. Once the students have found their places, ask each group member to declare one reason why he or she agrees or disagrees with the statement. After hearing all the reasons, tell students to write down the one they agree with most.
6. Ask students to return to their seats, announce a second statement of your choice, and repeat steps 3–5. Follow the same procedure for the remaining statements.
7. When students have responded to all the statements, ask them to pick the one they feel most strongly about, find a couple of classmates who share the same opinion, and get into groups.
8. Have groups talk about their reasons for feeling strongly about the statement, write them down, and give a class presentation that begins with the statement, followed by all the reasons they agree or disagree with it. Use PowerPoint or Keynote for the presentations if available.

9. When everyone has finished presenting, allow the whole class to discuss the different points of view. Then ask students to talk specifically about the usefulness of gathering information from different sources to make their opinion more powerful, whether they're speaking or writing.

Lesson Extension

Ask students to prepare to debate one of the topics from the list above or from a list you generate together. But this time, if they agree with the statement, they must argue for the other side, using information they gather from classmates and print and online resources.

ACTIVITIES   Developing the Topic

Top-Ten List

Ask students to write a top-ten list of things every adult should know about middle school students. Encourage them to develop each point in a fun, truthful, and interesting way. Here are examples of two developed points:

1. We don't like to be told what to do. But if you don't tell us, we won't do it! And even when you do tell us, many times we won't do it unless you get mean about it. We're kinda flakey.

2. Remembering to put our names on our papers is harder than being blindfolded and sending a text message with our thumbs.

It's All About the Middle

On a sheet of paper, write the beginning, middle, and ending of a story, leaving room in between for students to write what happens. Here's an example:

Beginning: It was a dark and stormy night.

Middle: Where was she? We realized that we had to go outside and find Drizzle, our black Lab.

Ending: When we finally got home, we locked the door, turned on all the lights, and sat up the rest of the night, afraid to sleep.

Distribute copies to the class and ask students to fill in details that logically lead up to the last sentence.

Key Quality: Using Details

The writer uses details—fine points related to the topic—to give the reader the information he or she needs to understand and appreciate the writing. Details need to be vivid, credible, and accurate in order for that to happen. Use the following Think About to expand students' notions about using details.

THINK ABOUT:

- Did I create a picture in the reader's mind?
- Did I use details that draw upon the five senses? (sight, touch, taste, smell, hearing)
- Do my details stay on the main topic?
- Did I stretch for details beyond the obvious?

WARM-UP   Using Details

Distribute copies of the Think About and have students revise the following piece, using details to make the idea crystal clear.

> Parents should be cautious when choosing a babysitter. They should pick someone who is responsible and careful. The person should know first aid.

When they're finished, share the following example with students and have them share theirs.

> Ask kids what qualities they want in a babysitter, and they will probably tell you he or she should be fun and like to play. Although these are desirable traits in a good babysitter, the most important qualities are responsibility and safety. Here are some things parents should look for to be sure they choose a responsible and safe babysitter:
>
> - Communicates clearly by phone or e-mail her availability and any restrictions she has such as number of children, length of time she will stay, her hourly rate, and so on
> - Confirms the date and time
> - Arrives on time, happy and ready to engage with the children
> - Provides references
> - Dresses appropriately for play
> - Brings ideas for entertaining the children other than watching TV or a movie
> - Prepares healthy meals and snacks
> - Knows basic first aid and CPR
>
> If parents choose a babysitter with these qualifications, chances are, they've found someone who really enjoys the job. Kids will get what they want, and so will their parents.

FOCUS LESSON Using Details

Most middle school students understand the value of using details in their writing. However, it's not uncommon for them to use general details rather than the focused, specific ones that readers need to understand and fully appreciate what they're trying to say. In other words, students find snorkeling easy, but not scuba diving. In addition, once they get the hang of scuba diving, some students never come up for air; too many details can clutter the writing. Stephen King puts it this way: "Thin description leaves the reader feeling bewildered and nearsighted. Over-description buries him or her in details and images. The trick is to find a happy medium" (2000, p. 171). In this lesson, students focus on the details in a mentor text by popular author Gary Paulsen. Then they write high-quality details for their own piece, inspired by that text.

Materials:

- a copy of *How Angel Peterson Got His Name and Other Outrageous Tales About Extreme Sports* by Gary Paulsen
- paper, pens, pencils

What to Do:

1. Review the key qualities of the ideas trait with students. (See page 31 for a list.)

2. Tell them you are going to read a passage from Gary Paulsen's *How Angel Peterson Got His Name and Other Outrageous Tales About Extreme Sports* Ask them to listen carefully for details.

   > "Emil's real problem, or what would prove to be a problem, was that he was what folks called 'tight with a nickel.'"

3. Ask students what Paulsen tells the reader about Emil. What does it mean to be "tight with a nickel"? (cheap, thrifty, miserly, penny-pinching, stingy, and so on) Are their other details that bring this character to life? (no) Is this a showing or telling passage? (telling) Is it snorkeling or scuba diving? (snorkeling)

4. Read the rest of the passage to students, asking them to pay close attention to the details.

   > He was so tight that once I saw him buy a candy bar, eat half of it and then sell the remaining half to another boy in school for the full five cents the original candy bar cost. Six times in one day. This doesn't say much about the six boys who bought the half-bars, or about Emil's ethics, but it shows how far he would go to stretch a nickel. Actually, I was one of the boys who bought half a candy bar but in my defense it was late in the afternoon in history class, which was taught by the football coach, who related every aspect of history to football ("Caesar would have made a good quarterback.... Cleopatra would have made a good quarterback, if she had

been a man…. Napoleon would have made a good quarterback…. Robert E. Lee would have made a good quarterback….") and who had the most monotonous voice on the planet. When Emil offered me the half candy bar, I would have given him a dollar if he'd asked for it, I was that bored. (pp. 36–37)

5. Ask students what the reader learns about Emil in this passage that he or she doesn't from the first one. Discuss how Paulsen's details add clarity and richness to his writing, which, to a large degree, is what makes it so interesting.

6. Ask students to write a paragraph about a person who shares Emil's characteristics. If they don't know anyone like Emil, have them make up a person. As students are writing, write a paragraph of your own. When you and the students have finished, share your pieces and discuss them.

   Note how using details based on experience and knowledge makes writing more interesting, creates images in the reader's mind, focuses the topic, and adds voice.

Lesson Extension

Ask students to find a descriptive passage in a favorite book. Then group them in pairs, and have them read their passages to one another. Allow time for them to discuss how the details help to carve out a character, establish a setting, add important information, create a plot twist, and so on.

ACTIVITIES   Using Details

The Art of Details

From the art teacher or another source, borrow three art prints that contain many details, such as Raphael's "The School of Athens," Frank Dillon's "The Stray," or Bill Bell's "The Poker Club." Show one print to students for 15 seconds and ask them to write down what they see. Then show the second, and do the same, followed by the third. Ask students to tell you what they wrote for each print. Then, show the prints to students for two minutes each and ask them to add more details to their lists. Discuss the details they added the second time and the value of spending time finding them. Ask student to compare how art and writing are similar.

Getting Into the Details

Give students a general statement, such as "I love Friday," and ask them to work with a partner to brainstorm at least ten details that explain why Friday is their favorite school day. Have pairs share those details with the whole class and make one long list. Now ask students to select their favorite details, at least five but no more than ten, and choose the one they consider the most important. From there, have pairs write a paragraph describing all the great things about Friday, emphasizing one detail they feel is most important.

When they're finished, ask students to put their paragraphs on their desks and invite their classmates to walk about and read them. Later, discuss the techniques students used to focus the reader's attention on one detail more than others.

Mentor Texts for Middle School: Ideas

Here are some recently published books I use as mentor texts for teaching students about ideas. I hope that you and your students enjoy exploring them for shining examples of ideas in action.

Genius Squad by Catherine Jinks (Harcourt, 2008)

What is good? What is bad? These are two questions that Cadell Piggott must answer in this fast-paced and lively technology thriller, the sequel to 2007's highly acclaimed *Evil Genius*. Piggott and his nemesis/supposed father, Prosper English, are two of the richest, most textured characters I've discovered living between the covers of a book in a long time.

Notes From the Midnight Driver by Jordan Sonnenblick (Scholastic, 2006)

16-year-old Alex Gregory makes a huge, uncharacteristic mistake when he takes the family car out one night—drunk. He's caught, sentenced to community service, and, in the process, meets a cast of quirky characters with important lessons.

Suite Scarlett by Maureen Johnson (Scholastic, 2008)

On Scarlett Martin's fifteenth birthday, she's put in charge of the Empire Room, a suite at Manhattan's dilapidated Hopewell Hotel, owned by her zany yet loving family. Her job is to keep the room clean and care for its guests. When an eccentric visitor arrives to spend the entire summer, Scarlett's life is turned upside down as she confronts feelings about her sister, her brother, and herself.

Final Thoughts

Ideas may well be the never-ending trait since writers are always working on them. The time you spend teaching students where ideas come from and how to develop them effectively is critical to their success as writers. Finding a topic, focusing it, developing it, and using precise details to support it is where the writing begins. Once the writer has done that, he or she must structure all that good thinking. The next trait—organization—will offer the help we need.

CHAPTER 5

Organization:
Beyond the Formula

Take a look at the example of a sixth grader's writing on the next page. She has fresh ideas, enthusiastic voice, strong words, fluent sentences, and a solid command of conventions. But something's missing. Can you spot it?

Being a Superhero

If I could be any superhero for a day, it would most definitely be Superman. I mean, who is the most prominent figure when you think of superheros? Is it Spiderman, with his redundant "spidey" powers? Is it Robin with his gregarious personality? No, you think Superman, airborne high in the sky, saving people and ridding the world of evil one megalomanic at a time. Hence, that is why I chose him, the icon superhero legend.

If I was Superman, the first thing I would do is fly. I would fly as fast as I could, no matter how percarious the situation. I would soar with the birds, and fly to the top of Mount Everest. I would fly indiscretely and unnoticed above the clouds.

The next thing I would do if I was Superman is save people in distress. If there was gangsters attacking someone, I would save that person. If a drug store was being held up, I would save the store. If there was about to be a car crash, I would stop the cars with my super strength.

Finally, if I was Superman, I would vanquish all evil, annihilating one immoral person at a time with my virile powers. First, I would incarcerate Lex Luther for being sordid. Second, I would fly to a major automobile manufacturing company (which will remain nameless) and disable their pollution-making equipment. Finally, I would reverse the evil of global warming with a wide variety of powers.

As you can see, if you could be any superhero for a day, you too would want to be Superman. I just know it. Whats not to like about someone who can fly, save innocent people, and vanquish evil?

What's missing is a creative approach to organization. The structure is forced. The transitions from one paragraph to the next are predictable. The opening and ending are uninspired. Sadly, this writer has been sold a bill of organizational goods that just doesn't work. The five-paragraph essay is living inside her—and, although it may take surgery to remove it, I'd advise her to ditch the formula for a more natural and logical organization that supports her good ideas.

I've found that many teachers gravitate toward teaching formulas because they worry their students' work will be hopelessly disorganized without them. However, we can teach students how to organize their work without putting them in a straitjacket. Ernest Hemingway compared prose to architecture. It's an apt comparison because, without question, every structure needs a sturdy foundation: steel beams and concrete footings. But the purpose of the building dictates its design and determines whether it become a house, a church, a gas station, or a school. There are countless ways to design a building, just as there are countless ways to organize a piece of writing.

Another argument teachers make for teaching formulas is that state assessments and colleges demand them. But in fact, many state assessments and colleges don't. Texas is a prime example. To help students practice for the TAKS (Texas Assessment of Knowledge and Skills), the state provides model papers that receive the highest scores in organization, and there's not a formulaic one in the mix (Texas Education Agency [TEA], 2007). And as for the myth about what colleges want, Les Perelman, professor and director of the

Writing Across the Curriculum Program at the Massachusetts Institute of Technology, explains, "Most college instructors work to 'deprogram' students from the infamous 'five paragraph essay'" (Jaschik, 2007, p. 2), concluding, "the [five-paragraph] essay is a completely artificial and unnatural piece of writing" (p. 2). So much for those excuses.

What I've said here may make you uncomfortable. After all, teaching to a formula may be how you were taught to teach writing—or maybe, as a young person, you were taught to write that way yourself. Or you may see formulaic writing as the best way to help your students pass the state assessment. But make no mistake about it—formulas don't work. We have to accept that fact. Don't just take my word for it; take this excerpt from the policy brief by the Alliance for Excellent Education, *Making Writing Instruction a Priority in America's Middle and High Schools*.

> A rigidly formulaic approach to teaching writing has been the norm in America's schools for well over a century (Conners, 1997). To the extent that teachers do assign essays, they tend to insist that students use a specific organizational structure (most often the well-known "five paragraph essay") and write in a constrained impersonal style (often referred to as "academic," even though, in truth, no such universal style exists among the various academic disciplines).
>
> Advocates of the five-paragraph essay argue that such formulas can provide useful guidance for beginning writers, offering them a crutch upon which to rely until they are ready to try other styles and formats. However, there exists no evidence to support this theory, and most experts in writing instruction now argue that this approach does more harm than good, giving students the false impression that good writing involves nothing more than following a set of rules.
>
> Rather, the expert consensus holds that the best writing instruction teaches students to become comfortable with a wide variety of styles and formats, so they can communicate effectively with many different kinds of readers in many different contexts, adapting their writing to the particular situation and audience at hand. (2007, p. 4)

When I was younger, I liked to do paint-by-numbers. It was oddly pleasing to match the numbers to the bright colors, filling in small bits of the whole until the piece was complete. And when I'd stand back from my masterpiece, I fancied it to be a horse, a guitar, or a bowl of fruit. But when I moved closer, the effect faded and what I saw were the lines that separated each color. Was I painting? Sure. Was it art? No. Writing is the same. Students who draft a five-paragraph essay are writing. But is it effective? Usually not. When students get inside the writing process, when they think deeply about why they're writing and for whom they're writing, they reach their potential as writers who can use organization to make clear what they want to say.

The Organization Trait: A Definition

Organization is the internal structure of the piece—the thread of meaning, the pattern of logic. Typical structures include point-by-point analysis, chronological play of events, deductive logic, cause and effect, comparison and contrast, problem and solution, and order of importance and complexity. The structure the writer chooses depends on his or her purpose for writing and the intended audience.

Writing that is well organized unfolds logically from beginning to end. It starts with an introduction that creates a sense of anticipation for the reader. Events and information are presented in the right doses and at the right moments so the reader never loses sight of the main idea. Transitions from one point to the next are strong. Well-organized writing closes with a sense of resolution; the writer ties up loose ends and answers important questions, while leaving the reader with a thing or two to ponder. To accomplish all this, the writer must skillfully and confidently apply the organization trait's key qualities:

* Creating the Lead

* Using Sequence Words and Transition Words

* Structuring the Body

* Ending With a Sense of Resolution

> **"** Organization is like a big puzzle. It doesn't really matter where you start, but all the pieces have to fit together. **"**
>
> —Ali, grade 6

Why Students Struggle With Organization

Organization may well be the hardest trait to master. It's ironic, because it's one of the easiest to describe in the scoring guide: a well-organized piece contains a strong lead, a smoothly paced body that is punctuated with carefully chosen sequence and transition words, and a thoughtful ending. But writing a well-organized piece is a challenge for students at all grade levels, including middle school. Here are some key reasons why.

Their Introductions and Conclusions Are Uninspired

"Hi, my name is Ruth and I'm going to tell you about sedimentary rocks," is not a stellar introduction to a research paper. And "Thank you for reading my paper" doesn't work as a conclusion, either. On the other hand, when students write dull introductions and conclusions like these, at least they acknowledge the need for them. That's a start.

The introduction should work like a fishing fly, gently hovering over the surface of the idea until the reader spots it and bites. The conclusion should be the reader's catch and release. The writer hooks the reader, reels him in with the strength of the idea, gently removes the hook from his mouth, and sets him free. This is a difficult concept for many students to master because each day—whether fishing or writing—is different. Decisions about how to catch and release must be adjusted according to how the fish are biting.

But take heart, students can learn to write graceful introductions and conclusions. Just like fishing, it just takes practice and patience. The more ways students find to introduce their writing and wrap it up, the easier it becomes.

Their Pacing Is Too Fast or Too Slow

Sometimes when I read student writing, I come to the end of a page, turn it over expecting to find more, and find nothing. The student just stopped. At other times, I discover that the student doesn't truly get into the idea until the third page, leaving me to wonder whether the first two pages are even necessary.

When students write too much or too little, it's a pacing issue. They are not sure when to slow down to present details that make a point crystal clear, and when to speed up to move into critical new territory. This typically happens because they haven't read enough well-written texts to develop an awareness of pacing or been given the chance to apply that awareness to their own work. Students need to write the way we, as adults, drive—they need to know when it's important to focus on getting the reader to where she needs to go, and when it makes sense to take a detour to give the reader a better view of the landscape.

Their Transitions Are Too Common

First, *second*, *third*, *finally*, and *in conclusion*: transitions like these are much too common in middle school writing. Students lean on them like a crutch. But just as Amahl from *Amahl and the Night Visitors* found a way to walk without the crutch, students can find a way to write without relying too heavily on tired transitions. At first, Amahl was shaky. But he kept at it, gaining confidence with each step, until, to everyone's surprise, he could not only walk, but also run and, eventually, dance.

Middle school writers need to dance. They need to discard the transition words and phrases that were force-fed to them in earlier grades and replace them with logical turns of phrase to get readers from one point to the next. And they don't need a miracle to make that happen. They just need good models and plenty of practice.

Assessing Student Work for Organization

The following eighth-grade papers represent a wide range of skills in the organization trait. Review the scoring guide on page 101, read each paper carefully, assess the paper for the organization trait by following the steps on pages 50–51, under "Assessing Writing Using the Trait Scoring Guides," and then read my assessment to see if we agree. Use your own students' writing for further practice.

The papers were all written in the persuasive mode, in response to the prompt "Do you think it's better to be an only child or to have siblings?" The papers should provide a convincing argument for the writer's position on the topic and should employ a variety of approaches including pro and con, list of reasons, and stories and anecdotes, among others. There are many methods by which to achieve the ultimate purpose of the writing: to persuade.

I chose papers written at the same grade level, in the same mode, and to the same prompt so that you can focus on the issue at hand, organization, without other factors serving as a distraction. But keep in mind, it's critical for students to develop skills in organization regardless of the grade they're in, the mode they choose, and the prompt they're given. Good organization should be applied to all writing, all the time. Even though I focus on organization, I've scored the papers in all the traits (except presentation, since the papers are typeset) in case you need additional samples to practice scoring or use in your instruction.

Scoring Guide: Organization

The internal structure of the piece—the thread of logic, the pattern of meaning.

Reproducible on CD

6

HIGH

EXCEPTIONAL

A. **Creating the Lead:** The writer grabs the reader's attention from the start and leads him or her into the piece naturally. He or she entices the reader, providing a tantalizing glimpse of what is to come.

B. **Using Sequence Words and Transition Words:** The writer includes a variety of carefully selected sequence words (such as *later*, *then*, and *meanwhile*) and transition words (such as *however*, *also*, and *clearly*), which are placed wisely to guide the reader through the piece by showing how ideas progress, relate, and/or diverge.

C. **Structuring the Body:** The writer creates a piece that is easy to follow by fitting details together logically. He or she slows down to spotlight important points or events, and speeds up when he or she needs to move the reader along.

D. **Ending With a Sense of Resolution:** The writer sums up his or her thinking in a natural, thoughtful, and convincing way. He or she anticipates and answers any lingering questions the reader may have, providing a strong sense of closure.

5

STRONG

4

MIDDLE

REFINING

A. **Creating the Lead:** The writer presents an introduction, although it may not be original or thought-provoking. Instead, it may be a simple restatement of the topic and, therefore, does not create a sense of anticipation about what is to come.

B. **Using Sequence Words and Transition Words:** The writer uses sequence words to show the logical order of details, but they feel obvious or canned. The use of transition words is spotty and rarely creates coherence.

C. **Structuring the Body:** The writer sequences events and important points logically, for the most part. However, the reader may wish to move a few things around to create a more sensible flow. He or she may also feel the urge to speed up or slow down for more satisfying pacing.

D. **Ending With a Sense of Resolution:** The writer ends the piece on a familiar note: "Thank you for reading…," "Now you know all about…," or "They lived happily ever after." He or she needs to tie up loose ends to leave the reader with a sense of satisfaction or closure.

3

DEVELOPING

2

LOW

EMERGING

A. **Creating the Lead:** The writer does not give the reader any clue about what is to come. The opening point feels as if it was chosen randomly.

B. **Using Sequence Words and Transition Words:** The writer does not provide sequence and/or transition words between sections, or provides words that are so confusing the reader is unable to sort one section from another.

C. **Structuring the Body:** The writer does not show clearly what comes first, next, and last, making it difficult to understand how sections fit together. The writer slows down when he or she should speed up, and speeds up when he or she should slow down.

D. **Ending With a Sense of Resolution:** The writer ends the piece with no conclusion at all—or nothing more than "The End" or something equally bland. There is no sense of resolution, no sense of completion.

1

RUDIMENTARY

Only Child

I think being an only child woult be boring even if I had a sister it would be a lot more fun then being by my self. But being alone woult be fun but not as fun as having a brother or sister. Its also better to have 2 brothers or sisters. I woult rather have 2 or 3 brothers so I can more then 1 person by my side ant most activities more then 1 person.

Time to Assess for Organization

Organization can make ideas stand out. But if the ideas are underdeveloped, it's virtually impossible for a writer to show strength in organization, as proven by this piece, which begins clearly, and then rambles aimlessly. This writer only hints at what he thinks about the topic, so it's hard for him to organize the writing in a meaningful way. And it's hard for me to know how to advise him about organization until he thinks through his idea more completely.

Organization	
Score **1: Rudimentary**	
Range	**Low**

Other Traits	
Ideas	1
Voice	1
Word Choice	2
Sentence Fluency	1
Conventions	1

A Creating the Lead

The writer does not give the reader any clue about what is to come. The opening point feels as if it was chosen randomly.

> *The writer jumps in, restating and responding to the question. There is no real attempt to draw the reader into the piece and engage him or her.*

B Using Sequence Words and Transition Words

The writer does not provide sequence and/or transition words between sections, or provides words that are so confusing the reader is unable to sort one section from another.

> *"But," "I would rather," and "Also" link one sentence to the next. The piece is so short, however, that these simple connections are ineffective and even downright unnecessary. It seems as if the writer is using them for the sake of showing he is able to use them, rather than using them to organize the piece well. That said, of all key qualities of the organization trait, he is most successful at this one.*

C Structuring the Body

The writer does not show clearly what comes first, next, and last, making it difficult to understand how sections fit together. The writer slows down when he or she should speed up, and speeds up when he or she should slow down.

> *It's hard to determine whether the writer can speed up or slow down at key points because the piece is so short. He does not provide enough evidence to show control over pacing.*

D Ending With a Sense of Resolution

The writer ends the piece with no conclusion at all—or nothing more than "The End" or something equally bland. There is no sense of resolution, no sense of completion.

> *A scant 25 words separate the first line from the last line. The conclusion reiterates the writer's position, but does not sum it up in a meaningful way.*

Being an Only Child

I could get more presents. I wouldn't half to fight with them. I wouldn't have to share with them.

The first reason I would like to be an only child is more presents. I would get nicer and more expensive things. I would get more birthday presents. I really want a Juicy bag this year but my mom say NO WAY. I hope she will get me one anyway. All my friends have them. Their the best bags ever.

Another reason is I wouldn't half to fight with them. I could have my own clothes. I could get on the computer with out fighting. And I could eat all the snacks and drink the soda by myself. I dont think it's fair I have to share the good stuff with my brother. He's a pain and doesn't share with me. My sister is a little nicer though. Thank you for reading my story about being an only child.

Time to Assess for Organization

The writer begins by supplying one reason she'd like to be an only child getting more presents—but goes on to supply other reasons that are not ordered in any particular way. There is no introduction to speak of, and the conclusion is a groaner. The writer shows a glimmer of organizational know-how, but fails to apply it with any consistency or control.

Organization	
Score	**2: Emerging**
Range	**Low**

Other Traits	
Ideas	3
Voice	3
Word Choice	2
Sentence Fluency	2
Conventions	3

A Creating the Lead

The writer does not give the reader any clue about what is to come. The opening point feels as if it was chosen randomly.

There is no true lead. The piece just starts. The reader is left wondering what the piece is about and what comes next.

B Using Sequence Words and Transition Words

The writer does not provide sequence and/or transition words between sections, or provides words that are so confusing the reader is unable to sort one section from another.

"The first reason" and "Another reason" are the only attempts the writer makes to link ideas together. Since most of the piece's body is a list, the reader is left wondering what points are most important, how one detail connects to another, and how it all adds up.

C Structuring the Body

The writer does not show clearly what comes first, next, and last, making it difficult to understand how sections fit together. The writer slows down when he or she should speed up and speeds up when he or she should slow down.

The second paragraph works better than the first because the writer slows down long enough to explain her thinking about getting presents. But in the opening paragraph and the closing paragraph, she scampers from point to point.

D Ending With a Sense of Resolution

The writer ends the piece with no conclusion at all—or nothing more than "The End" or something equally bland. There is no sense of resolution, no sense of completion.

Disappointing. "Thank you for reading my paper about being an only child," is not an effective conclusion. I want this writer's thinking to add up to something important. I expect something more than an expression of gratitude.

Being an Only Child

Do you want to be an only? I don't. I would rather keep my siblings. I have three reasons why I would keep my siblings. My three reasons are that they take care of me, they are kind, and they are helpful.

The first reason I would is because they are kind. They are kind by watching me when my moms gone. They love me. They are just someone there. I could always play or hang out with them.

Another reason is because they take care of me. They feed me when no one's home. They let me spend the night when ever I want. They drive me anywhere I need.

Finally the reason is that they are helpful. They help me clean the house if we need something. They help me on homework. The most important thing is they are there for me.

Now you know why I want to keep my siblings. Yeah, sure they can be annoying but I will keep them.

Time to Assess for Organization

Here is a classic example of a writer who has shoehorned his ideas into a formula. The introduction is all too typical—a question followed by three points he plans to address. Yawn. The middle proves that the writer is aware of how to link points, but only in the most obvious way. And the piece ends predictably. This is the five-paragraph essay at its worst because it limits the writer's ability to strengthen skills in other traits.

Organization	
Score	**3: Developing**
Range	**Middle**

Other Traits	
Ideas	2
Voice	2
Word Choice	2
Sentence Fluency	2
Conventions	4

A Creating the Lead

The writer presents an introduction, although it may not be original or thought-provoking. Instead, it may be a simple restatement of the topic and, therefore, does not create a sense of anticipation about what is to come.

> *Double trouble on this introduction: a forced question followed by a list of what will be covered in the rest of the paper. Credit must be given for having an introduction, but that introduction needs an extreme makeover.*

B Using Sequence Words and Transition Words

The writer uses sequence words to show the logical order of details, but they feel obvious or canned. The use of transition words is spotty and rarely creates coherence.

> *How many times have you read papers that contain "The first reason," "Another reason," and "Finally" at the start of each paragraph? Too many, I suspect. Again, I must give credit to the writer for knowing it's important to lead the reader from one point to the next, but he could handle it far more artfully and far less predictably.*

C Structuring the Body

The writer sequences events and important points logically, for the most part. However, the reader may wish to move a few things around to create a more sensible flow. He or she may also feel the urge to speed up or slow down for more satisfying pacing.

> *Because they take care of you and because they are kind and helpful are good reasons to appreciate having siblings. But the writer has not focused on one reason more than another. As a result, there is no momentum and no high point.*

D Ending With a Sense of Resolution

The writer ends the piece on a familiar note: "Thank you for reading," "Now you know all about…," or "They lived happily ever after." He or she needs to tie up loose ends to leave the reader with a sense of satisfaction or closure.

> *"Now you know…" is an all-too familiar conclusion-starter. But it's followed by a statement that reveals the writer's true feelings about his brothers and sisters. So the piece ends on a high note—but the writer has to break out of the formula.*

Brothers and Sisters Are the Best

I would rather have brothers and sisters because they will always love you even though you drive them crazy. Brothers and sisters make everyday interesting, and can bring a smile to your face.

Brothers and sisters help you with problems you have. If you have siblings you will learn how to socialize at an earlier age. If you were an only child and you didn't have any siblings you probably wouldn't learn how to socialize as quickly. When you have a problem with your homework and you have an older sibling who took that subject you could ask them for help, because it is fresher in their minds. Brothers and sisters can help you feel better when you feel down. If you were an only child you would probably be bored by yourself because you wouldn't have anyone to talk to.

When you have siblings, you are able to experience more things, such as being able to give advice to others. You will have someone to talk to when you have an argument with your parents. Brothers and sisters will stick with you through thick and thin. You can always talk to them when you feel sad, because someone you cared about died. You never know your day is going to be like when you have siblings. If my parents hadn't adopted my older brother and sister, I probably wouldn't have experienced having siblings. I don't always get along with my brother and sister. But you would still feel a little bit of love for them.

In my opinion siblings are people you should cherish. Even though they don't always like you. You should always love them and respect them. They are one of life's many gifts. If you didn't have siblings your life probably wouldn't be the same today. You probably wouldn't have someone who understands what your going through because they went through the same.

Time to Assess for Organization

There's a lot to be said for this piece's organization. The writer uses organizational techniques effectively. The introduction is present, though not compelling, and the body rambles in places. But the writer has, for the most part, corralled the ideas logically, distributes them logically, and ends with big-picture thinking.

Organization	
Score	**4: Refining**
Range	**Middle**

Other Traits	
Ideas	4
Voice	4
Word Choice	4
Sentence Fluency	4
Conventions	5

A Creating the Lead

The writer presents an introduction, although it may not be original or thought-provoking. Instead, it may be a simple restatement of the topic and, therefore, does not create a sense of anticipation about what is to come.

This introduction simply states the topic. But acknowledging that brothers and sisters can bring a smile to your face brings a smile to my face. It's a nice touch that suggests what's to come. The introduction needs revision, but not a complete overhaul by any means.

B Using Sequence Words and Transition Words

The writer uses sequence words to show the logical order of details, but they feel obvious or canned. The use of transition words is spotty and rarely creates coherence.

How one idea links to the next is sketchy. The writer would be well advised to make those connections clearer to the reader. For example, what is the link between learning to socialize and helping with homework? And giving advice and sticking with you through thick and thin? In a nutshell, the piece lacks sequence and transition words.

C Structuring the Body

The writer sequences events and important points logically, for the most part. However, the reader may wish to move a few things around to create a more sensible flow. He or she may also feel the urge to speed up or slow down for more satisfying pacing.

The introduction and conclusion are in better focus than the body because the writer tries to say too much in the middle two paragraphs. As a reader, I'm with her one moment and lost the next. She'd be wise to cluster key points into separate paragraphs.

D Ending With a Sense of Resolution

The writer ends the piece on a familiar note: "Thank you for reading," "Now you know all about…," or "They lived happily ever after." He or she needs to tie up loose ends to leave the reader with a sense of satisfaction or closure.

The writer tries to provide the reader with something to think about at the end, which is admirable. However, her conclusion is awkwardly constructed. As with the introduction, all the pieces are there. It's just a matter of retooling them a bit.

Never Boring!

Picture this: total chaos. Can you? I would pick that any day over boredom. I'm just not the kind of person who likes the same thing day in and day out. Which is probably why I think having brothers and sisters is a lot better than being an only child. At my house you never know what's going to happen next. My brother can surprise you at any minute. He leaves my mom shaking her head at what he says and does. My sisters get in big fights and yell and scream so loud the neighbors probably wonder if they should call for help. Even our dog, Julip, runs for cover when they get into it.

Despite all of the fighting, we have lots of fun. Along with that, we work together on projects and share games and music. I download songs for my iPod and give them to my brother. No sense in him buying the same song. He does the same for me, though I'm not really crazy about his music. Like I said, he's unpredicatable which shows up in his taste in music, too.

Sometimes I wonder what it would be like to be an only child. Seriously. Who wouldn't want their stuff left alone and to be the total focus of their mom's life? I wouldn't mind having more time, just her and me. And, I admit, it annoys me when I see my siblings have been using my art materials or when I have to go hunting for toothpaste.

It seems like that's how it is in life. You get some things you want, but you have to trade them for things you don't. My brother and sisters get on my nerves but I can't imagine one day without them. They are what keeps things interesting. I like the chaos more than quiet. Give me a crazy brother and sisters any day over boredom.

Time to Assess for Organization

This piece flows. Although the beginning may be a bit forced, it gets my attention. The ideas are grouped logically in the middle. The ending is smart because it zeroes in on a big, culminating issue: Life is a series of compromises. I'm particularly impressed by how the writer introduces an idea in the first paragraph—the brother's unpredictable nature—and revisits it in more detail in the second. The writer's thinking about siblings—both the good and bad—is the thread that runs through this piece from beginning to end, and one of the reasons the piece's organization works well.

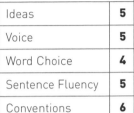

Organization	
Score	**5: Strong**
Range	**High**

Other Traits	
Ideas	5
Voice	5
Word Choice	4
Sentence Fluency	5
Conventions	6

A Creating the Lead

The writer grabs the reader's attention from the start and leads him or her into the piece naturally. He or she entices the reader, providing a tantalizing glimpse of what is to come.

I give the writer credit for trying to get our attention right from the start, even though the construction is a bit contrived. A stronger place to begin might be "At my house, you never know what's going to happen next." Of course, that would mean reworking the conclusion as well.

B Using Sequence Words and Transition Words

The writer includes a variety of carefully selected sequence words (such as *later*, *then*, and *meanwhile*) and transition words (such as *however*, *also*, and *clearly*), which are placed wisely to guide the reader through the piece by showing how ideas progress, relate, and/or diverge.

"Even our dog," "Despite all of the fighting," and "Sometimes I wonder" are phrases that knit the piece together, without smacking the reader between the eyes. The piece flows largely because sequence and transition words were carefully chosen and positioned.

C Structuring the Body

The writer creates a piece that is easy to follow by fitting details together logically. He or she slows down to spotlight important points or events, and speeds up when he or she needs to move the reader along.

This piece hums along. It lacks a real high point, but it proceeds smoothly.

D Ending With a Sense of Resolution

The writer sums up his or her thinking in a natural, thoughtful, and convincing way. He or she anticipates and answers any lingering questions the reader may have, providing a strong sense of closure.

The writer has the right idea for the conclusion, but the execution needs a bit of work. I appreciate the ways she attempts to echo the introduction in the conclusion, but it could be more artfully executed. Using the exact words "chaos" and "boredom" is the easy out. She could revise the introduction and the conclusion to be more graceful so they complement one another.

Missing Shanna-Banana

"You make me sick! You get on my nerves! I can't wait for you to go to college!" These were words I often said to my sister before she went away to college. I couldn't wait to be the only child at home. No more taking turns watching T.V., playing on the computer or talking on the phone. No more rummaging through her closet for my new sweater, just to discover a big-old stain right on the front. All of this sounded good but in reality, since she left, life has been pretty boring. I thought it would be nice being an only child for a change, but it isn't. It's lonely!

When Shanna was here, I took her for granted. Friday night was always game night. I know, kinda cheesy, but it was fun to get Boardwalk and Park Place when all she had were the utilities. Now I have no one to play board games with. It's boring staying up late watching movies by yourself. I miss not having another teenager in the house to talk to, fuss at, and act silly with. I will never admit it to my sister, but she made life more interesting.

I've lived life as a sibling and now as an only child. Each has its advantages, but right now, being an only child is not much fun. In fact, it is downright awful. Since Shanna left, when my parents are going to be gone for a while, I have to have a babysitter. I hate babysitters! They're mean, they're lazy and they ask to many questions! I never had to have a babysitter when my sister was here. She just left me alone most of the time. I didn't appreciate that until now.

On the other hand, my parents are a little quicker with the cash. They give me more spending money so I can go to the movies with my friends or go shopping. Before, they would have to split it between my sister and me, and I always got less since I was younger. They also let me stay up later. I like that. And, I can have more sleepovers now that it's just me.

The biggest change is how lonely I feel without my sister. She was always there – even when I didn't want her to be. She made me laugh, and she understood me. She used to call me "Doodlehead" which I hated. I'd call her "Shanna Banana" which she hated just as much. It's funny how you miss the little things most of all.

I wish she'd come back more often. My parents only have me to worry about and sometimes they pay way too much attention to what I wear, eat, how long I talk on the phone and if my homework is done. It's not as great as I thought it would be to be an only child. When "Shanna Banana" was here, they used to nag her about being messy and getting good grades for college. It took some of the pressure off. Now I get it double. I wish my family had stayed the same. I wish I had been smart enough to appreciate what I had when I had it, even if it meant being a "Doodlehead."

Time to Assess for Organization

An introduction that grabs your attention; multiple, well-argued points that build to a high point; and a conclusion that reveals a deep understanding of family roles make this an especially well-organized piece. It's an example of how a good writer engages the reader using a structure that supports the idea, rather than smothering it.

Organization	
Score	**6: Exceptional**
Range	**High**

Other Traits	
Ideas	6
Voice	6
Word Choice	5
Sentence Fluency	6
Conventions	6

A Creating the Lead

The writer grabs the reader's attention from the start and leads him or her into the piece naturally. He or she entices the reader, providing a tantalizing glimpse of what is to come.

The use of dialogue is a good choice for this piece. It's personal. Using her own experience to draw the reader in is an effective technique.

B Using Sequence Words and Transition Words

The writer includes a variety of carefully selected sequence words (such as *later*, *then*, and *meanwhile*) and transition words (such as *however*, *also*, and *clearly*), which are placed wisely to guide the reader through the piece by showing how ideas progress, relate, and/or diverge.

Used sparingly but with precision, transition words link ideas throughout. Within paragraphs, the writer proceeds logically, without leaving the reader wondering where she is heading or how one idea relates to another.

C Structuring the Body

The writer creates a piece that is easy to follow by fitting details together logically. He or she slows down to spotlight important points or events, and speeds up when he or she needs to move the reader along.

The writer slows down at key points to give the reader a clear picture of what she is talking about. She then speeds to the next point. The high point—where she reveals the pet names she and her sister call one another—is poignant. Indeed, the little things are what we miss the most. Then the writer ends the piece. Nice pacing.

D Ending With a Sense of Resolution

The writer sums up his or her thinking in a natural, thoughtful, and convincing way. He or she anticipates and answers any lingering questions the reader may have, providing a strong sense of closure.

This is a wonderfully complicated ending. It wraps up the loose ends with style and insight. I love how the writer uses "Doodlehead" and "Shanna Banana" while musing about the piece's universal theme.

Conference Comments

If the piece scores high in organization, 5 or 6, say something like:

> "Your thinking about being both a sibling and an only child is well structured and controlled from beginning to end. In other words, it's well paced—and that pacing is a big reason your <u>organization</u> works so well."

> "Your use of transition words is effective. Now, let's fine-tune the introduction and conclusion to make the <u>organization</u> really stand out."

If the piece scores in the middle, a 3 or 4, say something like:

> "You've included some terrific details in the body of your piece. Now let's <u>organize</u> them so they flow logically, one to the next, by using appropriate transitions and sequence words."

> "First, let's generate a list of key points and match them with details that support your main idea. Then, let's <u>organize</u> them, beginning with an introduction that grabs the reader and sets the stage for what's to come."

If the piece scores low, a 1 or 2, say something like:

> "The <u>organization</u> of your piece will be stronger if you think about what the reader needs to know in the beginning, middle, and end. Let's start by coming up with a great idea for an introduction."

> "You started with reasons it's boring to be an only child, so keep going down that road to keep your ideas <u>organized</u>. Can you think of other reasons to add to this paragraph?"

Teaching Writing With the Organization Trait

> **❝** There's a lot more to this organization business than a beginning, middle, and end. It's actually very complicated. **❞**
>
> —Devon, grade 6

All the great ideas in the world won't add up to a strong piece of writing if they aren't organized logically. In fact, ideas and organization go hand in hand: without organization the ideas are impossible to follow; without ideas there is nothing to organize. Writers must first arrive at a main idea and come up with supporting details. Then they have to consider various formats to find the one that fits the idea best, and apply it. It's no easy job. So don't get discouraged if your students seem to need help with organization every time they write. To make teaching organization more manageable, I've organized the remainder of this chapter into sections that correspond to its key qualities:

* Creating the Lead
* Using Sequence Words and Transition Words
* Structuring the Body
* Ending With a Sense of Resolution

Within each section, you'll find a warm-up exercise, a focus lesson, and two activities, as well as a Think About to help students focus on important questions to ask themselves as they organize their writing. (The key qualities and Think Abouts are also included on the CD that accompanies this book.)

Key Quality: Creating the Lead

Writers get one chance to make a good first impression. When their lead, or introduction, is strong, the reader becomes intrigued and wants to read on. He or she is hooked upon the writer's first cast. Use the following Think About to expand students' notions about creating the lead.

THINK ABOUT:
* Did I give the reader something interesting to think about right from the start?
* Will the reader want to keep reading?
* Have I tried to get the reader's attention?
* Did I let the reader know what is coming?

WARM-UP   Creating the Lead

Distribute copies of the Think About and encourage students to write a new lead for the following piece that hooks the reader and informs him about what's to come.

> Animals are important in our world. My favorite animal is the gecko because I saw one in Hawaii last year on our vacation. But, this paper isn't about geckos, it's about saving the polar bear.

Once students have written a new lead, ask them to share it with a partner and compare revision techniques. Have them discuss problems with the original piece's lead, and the solutions writers have for fiction and nonfiction. When they've finished, share the following example and ask them to figure out the lead technique(s) used:

> "They cling precariously to the top of what is left of the ice floe, their fragile grip the perfect symbol of the tragedy of global warming" (Mouland, p. 1). The image of the magnificent polar bears, struggling to survive as the earth warms and their natural habitat thaws, has gained national and international attention. But could it be too late to save them? Scientists are conflicted on the cause of global warming and therefore, the solutions are not clear either. While they argue, form study committees, and play politics, every day more polar bears drown. Every day. It's time to take action.

FOCUS LESSON   Creating the Lead

A strong introduction can have an impact on the reader, right from the get-go. Whether they're writing fiction or nonfiction, writers need to put themselves in the reader's shoes and think about what will get her attention so she will read on. This lesson provides an opportunity for students to practice composing catchy leads and try them out to see if they are successful.

Materials:
- Writing Formats/Topics reproducible (page 118 and CD)
- Types of Leads reproducible (page 119 and CD)
- sets of cards featuring the different types of leads, one per card (Create enough sets for half the students in your class.)
- paper, pens, pencils

What to Do:
1. Distribute the Writing Formats/Topics and Types of Leads reproducibles to student pairs. Have them select one writing format/topic and one type of lead and list their two choices at the top of a sheet of paper.
2. Ask students to write a lead that will grab the reader's attention, based on their two choices.
3. When they've finished, distribute a set of cards to each pair.

4. Ask a member of each pair to read his or her lead aloud. After he or she has read, ask the other students to identify the lead type by holding up a card for all to see. Continue the process until all leads have been read aloud and identified.

5. Vote on the most effective leads and discuss them. What made them so effective? Note the similarities and differences between leads for fiction and nonfiction.

6. If time allows, ask students to pick a new writing format/topic and type of lead, and write another lead.

Lesson Extension

Write a weak lead in front of the whole class, such as "I'm going to tell you about a time I got really scared." Then ask students to consult their cards and pick a lead that would be more effective. Reach consensus on the best choice. Come up with a lead of that type and write it on chart paper or the whiteboard, thinking aloud as you go so students get a glimpse into your process. Compare the two leads and discuss why one is better than the other. Then, ask students to come up with their own formats/topics and write leads for them.

> " I used to have trouble thinking of a good beginning, but my teacher said to start in the middle. I tried that and it works. I go back and write the lead later. "
>
> —Julianne, grade 6

Writing Formats/Topics

A campaign commercial for a political candidate

A classified ad for a used car

An encyclopedia entry about the Venus flytrap

A "help wanted" notice

A short story about a mysterious murder

A blog entry about a favorite book

The opening lines of a trailer for a new movie

An advertising headline for a restaurant

A biography about a famous historical figure

Types of Leads

Analogy or comparison – compares or contrasts two different things

Anecdote or case history – provides a real-life scenario or nonfiction story

Direct address – addresses reader using second person "you"

Fact – contains an interesting bit of information about the topic

Metaphor – a figure of speech to show how two unlike things are similar in one important way; states something *is* something else

Description – explains the setting, characters, or factual events

One word/phrase – starts with a specific image or sound such as "Zing!"

Controversial statement – takes a stand on the topic

Statistic – reveals a detail about the topic, based on quantitative data

Summary – crystallizes what will be addressed

From *A Writer's Guide to Nonfiction* by Elizabeth Lyon (2003), adapted for middle school.

ACTIVITIES   Creating the Lead

The Good, the Bad, and the Ugly

Give students 15 minutes to look through books, newspapers, magazines, and other print materials for the best lead and the worst lead they can find. Read each student's two choices aloud, and have the class score them from 1 to 10, (1 = low, 10 = high). Discuss the scores and create a list on the board of dos and don'ts for writing leads. Reread the top three scorers for both categories, and vote to select winners. Post the best and worst leads for students to refer to as they write. Ask students to add more "good, bad, and ugly" examples as they find them while reading.

Fade In

Screenplays often have good leads and, therefore, make good examples for students to follow. Download a strong opening of a screenplay from a movie or TV show of your choice. (I've had good luck at http://www.oscars.org/awards/nicholl/scriptsample.pdf.) Share the opening with students and talk about what makes it effective. Then give them the cue "Fade in" and ask them to write the opening lines of a new movie or TV show, following the format of your example. When they've finished, invite students to share their leads with the class. Discuss which ones would most likely draw in people their own age, older people, and younger people.

Key Quality: Using Sequence Words and Transition Words

There's a lot more to good organization than getting started. Writers also need to use sequence and transitions words to show how their ideas connect and interrelate. This is critical to making their writing easy to follow and understand. Use the following Think About to expand students' notions about using sequence and transition words.

Reproducible on CD

THINK ABOUT:

- Have I used sequence words such as *later*, *then*, and *meanwhile*?
- Did I use a variety of transition words such as *however*, *because*, *also*, and *for instance*?
- Have I shown how the ideas connect from sentence to sentence?
- Does my organization make sense from paragraph to paragraph?

A Partial List of Sequence Words and Transition Words

To continue a line of thinking:	To signal the wrap-up:
also	indeed
clearly	in the final analysis
furthermore	in conclusion
because	therefore
besides	all in all
since	
as well as	**To restate a point within a paragraph:**
it is easy to see that	in other words
	that is to say
To change a line of thinking:	in short
however	
on the other hand	**To show sequence or time:**
but	after
yet	as soon as
nevertheless	at first
	at last
To begin a paragraph or line of thinking:	before
certainly	earlier
granted	in the first place
no doubt	in the meantime
obviously	later
of course	meanwhile
true	next
unquestionably	soon
in general	then

WARM-UP   Using Sequence Words and Transition Words

Distribute copies of the Think About and the following piece of writing. Have students circle the transition words.

> It was then that we realized making a deep enough hole for this huge tree was going to be a challenge. "Thanks." At long last, when the work was done, we stood back, admiring our handiwork. Not so surprisingly, we didn't feel like doing any of the chores my mom left for us when she went to work. After we paid for it, we carried it home. Luckily, there was a nursery only a few blocks from my house. Unfortunately it took a long time and wore us out. We ate lunch then we left to pick out the perfect tree. It was summer break, and my friends and I were looking for something to do. "Mom's

gonna love this," I told them. Even though the rock-hard dirt made our work nearly impossible we dug a good-sized hole for the blue spruce. The tree was heavier and bigger than we expected. After a while, we decided to plant a tree in the backyard that would give us shade on hot, late summer days.

Ask students to work with a partner and revise the piece on a separate sheet of paper, using the Think About questions to help them put all the information in a more sensible order. They may wish to organize the text into two paragraphs. When students have finished, have them share what they wrote. You can also share the model that follows. Remind students there is no "right way" to organize a piece of writing. What's most important is that the piece be logical and make sense.

It was summer break, and my friends and I were looking for something to do. *Not so surprisingly,* we didn't feel like doing any of the chores my mom left for us when she went to work. *After a while,* we decided to plant a tree in the backyard that would give us shade on hot, late summer days. *Luckily,* there was a nursery only a few blocks from my house. We ate lunch, *then* we left to pick out the perfect tree. *After* we paid for it, we carried it home. The tree was heavier and bigger than we expected.

It was then that we realized making a deep enough hole for this huge tree was going to be a challenge. *Even though* the rock-hard dirt made our work nearly impossible we dug a good-sized hole for the blue spruce. *Unfortunately,* it took a long time and wore us out. *At long last,* when the work was done, we stood back, admiring our handiwork. "Mom's gonna love this," I told them. "Thanks."

FOCUS LESSON   Using Sequence Words and Transition Words

Using sequence and transition words skillfully—connecting ideas so the reader sails through the text—comes with practice. Examining mentor texts by favorite authors can also help. In this lesson, students put the jumbled paragraphs from a piece by Gary Paulsen into the correct order. Then they do the same with sentences from a paragraph by Cullen Murphy. These finely organized passages don't rely on the most common sequence and transition words. Rather, they contain more subtle turns of phrase to guide readers from one point to the next, so students will have to read carefully and then use what they learn to revise a piece of their own.

Materials:
- electronic projection system or traditional overhead projector
- paper, pens, pencils
- one set of jumbled cut-apart paragraphs from Gary Paulsen's *Winterdance: The Fine Madness of Running the Iditarod* (page 124 and CD) (Create enough sets for half the students in your class.)

- one set of jumbled cut-apart sentences from Cullen Murphy's "Lulu, Queen of the Camels" (page 125 and CD). (Create enough sets for half the students in your class.)
- copies of the original, intact pieces to project (page 125 and CD)

What to Do:

1. Review the importance of using sequence and transition words to organize writing. Remind students that strong organization leads the reader through the ideas smoothly and logically.
2. Give student pairs a set of jumbled cut-apart paragraphs from Gary Paulsen's *Winterdance.* Tell them to reorder the paragraphs so the piece makes sense from beginning to end. Encourage them to look for sequence and transition words and other elements Paulsen uses to show how ideas relate one to the next.
3. Once they've settled on an order, tell students to number the paragraphs from 1 to 8.
4. Display the original passage and compare it with the students' versions. Discuss any differences. Encourage students to call out specific sequence and transition words and phrases and other cues they used to determine the logical order of the passage.
5. Give pairs a set of jumbled cut-apart sentences from the paragraph from Cullen Murphy's "Lulu, Queen of the Camels." Provide time for students to place the sentences in the correct order. When they've finished, tell them to number the sentences from 1 to 10.
6. Ask for a volunteer from each pair to read his or her newly organized paragraph aloud. Compare that version to the paragraphs of other pairs of students.
7. Display the original passage. Compare each pair's version of it. Discuss differences and similarities and the difficulty students may have had putting this paragraph in order because it lacks traditional sequence and transitions words. Remind students that sophisticated writing doesn't always rely on the crutch words, preferring instead to use logical turns of phrases to guide the reader through the text.
8. List the ways students ordered the sentences to make a coherent paragraph. Encourage students to share the clues within the text (transitional words and phrases, logical sequencing, pronoun-antecedent agreement, and so on) that helped them decide a sensible order for the sentences.
9. Discuss how ordering paragraphs within a passage was different from and similar to ordering sentences within a paragraph.
10. Ask students to look at a draft of their own writing, noting places to add sequence and/or transition words or other order clues to strengthen the organization.

From *Winterdance: The Fine Madness of Running the Iditarod*

By Gary Paulsen

I do not hold the record for the person coming to disaster soonest in the Iditarod. There have been some mushers who have never left the chutes. Their dogs dove into the spectators or turned back on the team and tried to go out of the chutes backwards. But I rank close.

There is a newspaper photo somewhere showing me leaving the chutes, that shows Wilson with his tongue out the idea of his mouth and a wild look in his eye as he snakes the team out and away from the starting line with a great bound. (It also shows me apparently smiling; for the record the smile is not humor but the first stages of rictus caused by something close to terminal fright.)

We made almost two blocks. The distance before the first turn. Wilson ran true down the track left by the previous thirty-one teams. Until the turn. At the end of the block there was a hard turn to the right to head down a side street, then out of town on back trails and alleys and into the trees along the highway away from Anchorage.

I remember watching the turn coming at alarming speed. All the dogs were running wide open and I thought that the only way to make it was to lean well to the right, my weight far out to the side to keep the sled from tumbling and rolling.

I prepared, leaned out and into the turn and would have been fine except that Wilson did not take the turn. He kept going straight, blew on through the crowd and headed off into Anchorage on his own tour of discovery.

I could not stop them. The sled brakes and snowhook merely scraped and bounced off the asphalt as we passed, tearing it off the car (why in God's name are they all made of plastic?), and for a space of either six blocks or six miles—at our speed, time and distance became irrelevant—I just hung on and prayed, screaming "WWHOA!" every time I caught my breath. Since I had never used the command on the team before it had no effect whatsoever and so I got a Wilson-guided tour of Anchorage.

I heard later that at the banquet some people had been speaking of me and I was unofficially voted the least likely person to get out of Anchorage. Bets were made on how soon I would crash and burn. Two blocks, three. Some said one. It was very nearly true.

We went through people's yards, ripped down fences, knocked over garbage cans. At one point, I found myself going through a carport and across a backyard with fifteen dogs and a fully loaded Iditarod sled. A woman standing over the kitchen sink looked out with wide eyes as we passed through her yard and I snapped a wave at her before clawing the handlebar again to hang on while we tore down her picket fence when Wilson tried to thread through a hole not much bigger than a housecat. And there is a cocker spaniel who will never come into his backyard again. He heard us coming and turned to bark just as the entire team ran over him; I flipped one of the runners up to just miss his back and we were gone, leaving him standing facing the wrong way barking at whatever it was that had hit him. (1994, pp. 144–145.)

From "Lulu, Queen of the Camels"
By Cullen Murphy

Geckos darted about.

In the stockades the females have been separated from the males.

Early one morning Lulu Skidmore pulled off the highway and on to this road.

The sandy embankment on both sides was strewn with the yellow fruit known as desert apples.

The desert in Dubai is as much a time as it is a place: it begins the moment resistance to it relents.

Down the road a little ways was a compound of low-slung ocher buildings.

Twenty-five miles southeast of Dubai, at Nakhlee, on the highway to Hatta, a gatepost sign you could easily miss marks an unpaved road to the right.

The desert runs unbroken from Dubai City to the Hajar Moutains.

The males have been separated from one another.

Camels stood in wire stockades everywhere: black camels from Saudi Arabia, tan camels from the Emirates, white camels from Sudan.

From "Lulu, Queen of the Camels"
By Cullen Murphy

The desert in Dubai is as much a time as it is a place: it begins the moment resistance to it relents. The desert runs unbroken from Dubai City to the Hajar Moutains. Twenty-five miles southeast of Dubai, at Nakhlee, on the highway to Hatta, a gatepost sign you could easily miss marks an unpaved road to the right. Early one morning Lulu Skidmore pulled off the highway and on to this road. The sandy embankment on both sides was strewn with the yellow fruit known as desert apples. Geckos darted about. Down the road a little ways was a compound of low-slung ocher buildings. Camels stood in wire stockades everywhere: black camels from Saudi Arabia, tan camels from the Emirates, white camels from Sudan. In the stockades the females have been separated from the males. The males have been separated from one another. (2000, p. 140)

ACTIVITIES Using Sequence Words and Transition Words

Tell It Like It Is

Write each sequence and transition word from page 121 on an index card and shuffle the deck. Ask one student to start a story by coming up with and reciting an opening line. Then, ask him or her to select a classmate to go next. Have the chosen classmate draw a card and, using the word or phrase on the card, add the next sentence to the story. Continue until either all students have had a chance to build the story, the story reaches a natural conclusion, or all the cards are drawn. Discourage students from getting too caught up in the story itself and instead have them focus on the use of sequence and transition words. Expect the stories to be wacky as students help one another figure out how to use sequence and transition words. Try this activity for nonfiction pieces as well.

Sequence Word Scavenger Hunt

Put students into teams of three or four and challenge them to gather over the course of the following week as many examples of sequence and transition words as they can find in signs, brochures, billboards, menus, and other functional print materials outside of school. Teams should record the words and phrases and their sources. At the end of the week, give teams time to compile their lists. Ask each team to report its final number and give examples of the words it found. Announce the winning team, crown its members "Sequence Kings and Transition Queens for the Day," and, as a prize, let them free-read or freewrite for the remainder of the class period. Discuss with the other students where the winning team found the most examples of sequence and transition words and whether any of those sources surprise them. Kings and Queens can join in, if they wish.

Key Quality: Structuring the Body

When writers develop the body of a piece of writing, they expand on an idea touched on in the introduction, using details to support that idea. So it's important for the body to be structured well so that details unfold logically, clearly, and smoothly. Writers must also have command of pacing. They must be able to highlight important points by lingering on them and move quickly through less important ones so the reader doesn't get bogged down. Use the following Think About to expand students' notions about structuring the body of their writing.

THINK ABOUT:

- Have I shown the reader where to slow down and where to speed up?
- Do all the details fit where they are placed?
- Will the reader find it easy to follow my ideas?
- Does the organization help the main idea stand out?

WARM-UP Structuring the Body

Distribute copies of the Think About and the following paragraph. Have students revise the paragraph by putting details in a more sensible order and using pacing to highlight the most important ones.

> John Wilkes Booth was born on May 10, 1838. He was a stage actor. Booth threatened to kill Lincoln several times. He shot and killed Abraham Lincoln on April 14, 1865. He died several days later.

When students are finished, share the following example with them or write one of your own.

> John Wilkes Booth is famous *and* infamous for the assassination of Abraham Lincoln at the Ford Theatre in Washington, D.C., April 14, 1865. Booth shot and killed Lincoln while the president and his wife were enjoying the play *Our American Cousin*, thus making it the first presidential assassination in U.S. History. What is not as well known, however, is that Lincoln's assassination was part of a larger conspiracy to not only kill President Lincoln, but Vice President Andrew Johnson, Secretary of State William H. Seward, and General Ulysses S. Grant as well. Booth and accomplices Lewis Powell, David Herold, and George Atzerodt intended to throw the government into a state of panic and therefore allow the Confederate government time to reorganize and continue fighting the Civil War that was going badly for the South. Lincoln was killed, but attempts on the lives of the others were thwarted. Booth was chased down and shot a few days later, marking the end of one of the most tragic chapters in American history.

FOCUS LESSON   Structuring the Body

Knowing what is and isn't important to include in a piece of writing is challenging for many middle school writers. It's easy for them to get caught up in the details without focusing on a main idea and, in the process, lose sight of their purpose for writing. One way to help them is to model how to revise a piece with obvious organizational flaws. In the lesson that follows, students discover what happens when writing contains too many unimportant details, and its pacing is out of control.

Materials:

- a first draft that needs work in organization (page 130 and CD) and a revision (page 131 and CD)
- electronic projection system or traditional overhead projector
- paper, pens, pencils
- draft pieces from students' writing folders

What to Do:

1. Discuss the importance of using details in writing. Remind students that coming up with details is part of the ideas trait, but structuring them within a piece of writing is part of the organization trait.

2. Make sure students are familiar with the concept of pacing—the way ideas flow in a piece of writing. Compare what writers do to create pacing to what runners do to win a race: they speed up and slow down as needed, always keeping an eye on the finish line. The finish line for writers is a solid piece of writing with a structure that supports the ideas.

3. Share the first draft on page 130, a story from my life, with your students, or write one of your own.

4. Ask students to give you feedback on the piece's organization. Of course, it needs a better lead and ending, so acknowledge that if a student mentions it. Also, record their ideas for structuring the body more effectively. Here is some feedback middle school students have given me after sharing this piece with them:

   - "It skips around. I got lost."

   - "Once you start with one idea, don't drift away. It needs to make sense why you are changing to something else. Your writing could use some transitions."

   - "Rides, food, driving—you are all over the place. Maybe you could link two of these ideas together, but not all three."

   - "Trying to follow this story is like reading a road map in the pitch black." (Ouch!)

   - "Your beginning just starts in the middle of nowhere and your ending leaves me flat. Both should be more interesting."

5. Share the revision on page 131—or take your students' good advice, revise your own piece after class, and share it with the class the next day.

6. Ask the students to note the changes between the first draft and the second, centering your discussion on the piece's body. List their observations on the board or projector. Here are some comments students have offered me in the past:

   - "You tied everything together."
   - "I wasn't sure how you'd write a piece on chili cheese fries but it's really a comparison between the food at Disneyland and the food you grew up with. I see that now."
   - "Grouping the details in paragraphs two and three really made a difference."
   - "I like how you brought in details about your own life when you were younger. Nice transition."
   - "What does 'E ticket ride' mean? I'm not sure I get your ending."

   (More about this in the next section, Ending With a Sense of Resolution.)

7. Invite students to revise a draft in their writing folders, focusing on structuring the body so details fit together and creating pacing that leads to a high point.

Lesson Extension

Give students a copy of your revised piece and ask them to write the topic of each paragraph next to it in the margin. Then, ask them to circle its high point, the place where the main idea is made clear. Discuss. Ask them to underline each detail that helps them build an understanding of the main idea. Finally, ask them to put a box around the sequence and transition words that keep the piece flowing. Discuss.

Disneyland

At Disneyland there were a lot of people who wanted to ride on the same rides as we did, so we had to wait in line for a long time. That part wasn't so great, but except for that, Disneyland was a lot of fun. My favorite ride was Splash Mountain, but I liked the food there, too. There was popcorn and chili cheese fries. My son, Sam, really liked the hamburgers there because they were barbecued and had a lot of good stuff on them, but I liked the chili cheese fries the best. Sometimes we make them at home now because they were so good. Anyway, Sam and I had a great time at Disneyland. He liked the ride with the bumper cars. He wanted to drive since the day he was born. He stood in line on his 16th birthday to get his license the minute the DMV opened up. He got to practice driving at Disneyland. It was fun.

Disneyland

My mouth still waters at the thought of those delicious chili cheese fries. The potatoes so hot they almost burn the top of your mouth; the cheese, melted to just the right temperature, gently oozing down the side of the dish; the aroma of chili pungent with the Texas Prairie spices. I couldn't believe it; I was finally at Disneyland, and my senses were going wild.

Most people remember a thrilling ride, or the crowds of people milling around the acres and acres of land designed to help visitors forget their everyday lives for a few precious hours. Not me. I remember the food—rich, delicious, and everywhere. Pleasures for the palate, just another dimension of this magical kingdom designed to fulfill every wish and dream.

You see, when I was growing up, we ate plain food. Good, healthy, wholesome food (at least by 1960s standards), but plain. Meatloaf, tuna on toast, chicken and dumplings, fruit in Jell-O molds, and at least a weekly dose of liver. That's why now that I found myself at Disneyland, surrounded by rides, shops, and sights designed to create a lifetime of memories, what amazed me most were the chili cheese fries. Gloriously hot, gooey, savory, chili cheese fries. Ahhh . . . they were definitely an E-ticket ride.

ACTIVITIES Structuring the Body

What Matters?

Sometimes it's hard to discern what is truly important in students' writing because they devote equal weight to every event or fact they present, rather than focusing on a single event or fact and offering details to support it. Give students lists of details from a story about getting a new puppy and an essay about what makes the fall season special, such as the ones below, and ask them to tell you which details should be developed, which should be reordered, and which should be left out entirely.

Fiction: "Getting Gus"	Nonfiction: "Fall Feelings"
I woke up.	Fall is a season of contrasts.
I put on my green shirt.	The leaves fall off the trees.
I found a pair of matching socks.	It's colder at night than in the summer.
I ate cereal for breakfast.	Replace your batteries at the end of daylight saving time.
I wanted a dog to keep me company.	They are red, gold, and orangey-rust.
I took him home.	New TV shows start in the fall.
I brushed my teeth.	Raking the leaves is not much fun.
I got a new puppy from my best friend.	I love putting warmer blankets on my bed and snuggling under them at night.
I named him Gus.	Leaves can be used for compost.
I went to school.	Trimming dead flower blossoms makes plants stronger and healthier in the spring.
I went home.	Animals gather food for the long winter ahead.
Gus and I went to bed.	Leaves can be bagged and left for recycling.

And With a Musical Touch

Ask students to make a list of the different types of music, such as rock, country, and alternative, using print and electronic resources. Share the lists with the class. Ask each student to select one type of music and partner with a classmate who selected a different type. Give each student five minutes to brainstorm what makes his or her chosen type of music special: it makes you want to dance, it's easy to sing to, it puts you to sleep, it makes you feel good, and so on. At the end of five minutes, ask partners to share their lists and talk about the item that stands out as the most important or interesting. Ask students to write a short piece about their choice of music and share the results.

Key Quality: Ending With a Sense of Resolution

A great beginning draws readers in, and a great ending leaves them satisfied. There are no "right" or "wrong" endings. There are only endings that are more or less satisfying. And finding ones that work is not easy. That's why students cap off their pieces so often with "That's all I have to say about…," "Thank you for reading my paper," "Then I woke up and it was only a dream," and the time-honored "The end." These are endings, no doubt, but they don't satisfy. A good ending ties up loose ends and brings the reader to a new level of thinking, while softly echoing the piece's overarching theme. No wonder writing endings is so difficult—that's a lot for a middle school writer to handle. Use the following Think About to expand students' notions about what makes a good ending to fiction and nonfiction.

Reproducible on CD

THINK ABOUT:

- Have I wrapped up all the loose ends?
- Have I ended at the best place?
- Do I have an ending that makes my writing feel finished?
- Did I leave the reader with something to think about?

WARM-UP   Ending With a Sense of Resolution

Distribute copies of the Think About and the following persuasive piece on why a school district should provide a laptop for every student. Have them revise the ending in a way that leaves their reader wanting to take action.

> These are the three reasons I believe every student should have a laptop. I hope I have persuaded you to provide a laptop for every student. Thank you for reading my paper.

When students have finished, ask them to share their new endings. You can also share the following example or one you write yourself.

> To receive the education every student deserves, students need to have access to the latest technology in every class, every day in school. As I've shown, a huge amount of money is spent on resources that are out-of-date before they ever enter our classrooms. A laptop, so students can take notes, write papers, access the Internet for research, create charts and graphs, keep scientific journals, work with multiple languages, study art, and read and respond to current affairs as they happen, would save money in the long run. And, today's students would be better prepared to take on more difficult work and more challenging classes by using current resources instead of old ones. A laptop for every student could be the answer to many of the most critical woes of the American education system.

FOCUS LESSON Ending With a Sense of Resolution

By showing students stellar endings from the works of professional writers, you make abstract techniques more concrete. When students see what techniques work and why, they become more inclined to try those techniques in their own writing. Could there be a better reason to use mentor texts? In this lesson, students read and hear strong endings of magazine and newspaper articles about sports, and categorize those endings by type. Then, they try a favorite type in their own writing.

Materials:
- Types of Endings reproducible (page 135 and CD)
- Sample Endings reproducible (pages 136–137 and CD)
- sets of cards featuring the different types of endings, one per card. (Create a set for each student in your class.)
- draft pieces from students' writing folders

What to Do:
1. Ask students if they have a favorite ending from a book, magazine article, movie, TV show, or other source. Discuss why those endings are so good, referring to the Think About on page 133 to guide you.
2. Distribute the Types of Endings reproducible and talk to students about each type. Give common examples such as the tragic ending in some Shakespearean plays in which the main characters die.
3. Hand out the sets of ending cards and tell students you are going to read endings from published nonfiction articles by sportswriters.
4. After you read each sample ending, ask students to sort through their cards and find the type that fits it best.
5. After all students have chosen a card, ask them to hold it up for their classmates to see. If there is disagreement, read the ending again and invite students to stick with their first choice or change it.
6. Come to consensus about each sample's type of ending. If students feel an ending falls into two categories, that's okay, as long as they can defend their argument.
7. Ask students to select the type of ending they like the best. Then have them choose a draft from their writing folder and revise the ending, accordingly.

Lesson Extension
Ask students to gather examples of strong endings from a fiction genre, such as science fiction, realistic fiction, or fantasy. Categorize the endings by type, according to the list on page 135. Post the endings as models to refer to during writing time.

Types of Endings

Nonfiction Endings:

Summary	rounds up the piece's main points
Call-back	refers back to the lead as a reminder of the main point stated at the beginning
Thematic reprise	reflects on the piece's meaning and provides the take-away message
Encouraging message	concludes with a "pep talk," making the reader feel optimistic
Quotation	concludes with a direct statement that sums up the piece's main message or theme
Ta-da!	uses a grand statement that provides the reader with closure: licks the envelope

From *A Writer's Guide to Nonfiction* by Elizabeth Lyon (2003), adapted for middle school.

Fiction Endings:

Epiphany	wraps up the story with a sudden insight by the character
Moral	reveals a lesson for the reader
Image	provides a visual connection to a key point in the story
Irony	notes the incongruity between what the character says and does and how the story turns out
Tragedy	ends on a dark note, prompting the reader to consider how the final events reveal the theme
Surprise	ends with an unexpected turn of events
Hollywood ending	provides the perfect ending, in which everything works out fine

From "How to Write a Strong Ending in Fiction" by Lisa Scott (2008), adapted for middle school.

Sample Endings

From "Someone to Lean On" by Gary Smith (2001)

Summers, though, are still the most difficult time for Radio. Should a traveler ever get lost in upstate South Carolina some July or August day and find himself wandering near the railroad tracks in Anderson and happen to notice an old boarded-up school with a FOR SALE sign planted in the weeds out front, he ought to take a little look at the abandoned McCants Junior High football field just behind it. He might just see a man with sprinkles of white hair gesturing wildly at thin air, screaming, "All wight, tomowwow's Thuhsday, dat's a light day! You wear yo' shorts an' T-shirts, no pads, an' be on da fiel' at four o'cwock on da nose, you got dat, boys?"

Just smile and wave. It's only Radio, living the dream. (p. 98)

ANSWER: Ta-da!

From "Shadow of a Nation" by Gary Smith (2001)

(first paragraph of article) Singing. Did you hear it? There was singing in the land once more that day. How could you not call the Crows a still-mighty tribe if you saw them on the move that afternoon? How could your heart not leave the ground if you were one of those Indian boys leading them across the Valley of the Big Horn? (p. 116)

(last paragraph) He wants to go back to the reservation someday and help kids to take the risk, to see both the beauty and the danger of the circle. But he may never live there again. He rolls down the car window. He listens to the air. There is no singing in the land. There is only a quiet, sad-happy song inside a young man's heart. (p. 138)

ANSWER: Call-back

From "Eyes of the Storm" by Gary Smith (2001)

It's midday in the dead of summer. Amanda starts running and realizes after three laps that she has almost nothing left, and there's only one way to come close to Michelle's seven-minute mile. Her face turns scarlet, her body boils, her stomach turns. Nature screams at her to stop. Instead, she sprints. She sprints the entire last lap.

The watch says 7:05 as she crosses the line. Amanda can't believe she ran that fast, and she laughs as she reels and vomits near the flagpole. She laughs. (p. 181)

ANSWER: Encouraging message

From "As Time Runs Out" by Gary Smith (2001)

"My own team—everybody can join. This is it, baby, my ultimate pregame talk. I **need** this one, **gotta** have it. Gotta have so many people calling my answering machine each day that they can't get through. Gotta have people all over the country opening their windows and shouting it out: 'JIMMY VEEEEEE! DON'T GIVE UP!'" (p. 288)

ANSWER: Quotation

From "An Unknown Filly Dies, and the Crowd Just Shrugs" by William C. Rhoden (2007)

One animal breaks an ankle on national television in a Triple Crown race and sets off a national outpouring of emotion. A four-year-old collapses and dies in full view on a sunny afternoon and not many seem to notice. Or care.

As they say, it's the business.

But what kind of business is this? (p. 83)

ANSWER: Thematic reprise

From "What Keeps Bill Parcells Awake at Night" by Michael Lewis (2007)

What this is, he can't—or won't—specify. But when your life has been defined by the pressure of competition and your response to it, there's a feeling you get, and it's hard to shake. You wake up each morning knowing the next game is all that matters. If you fail in it, nothing you've done with your life counts. By your very nature you always have to start all over again, fresh. It's an uncomfortable feeling, but it's nonetheless addictive. Even if you have millions in the bank and everyone around you tells you that you're a success, you seek out that uncomfortable place. And if you don't, you're on the wrong side of the thin curtain that separates Cyclone Hart from Vito Antuofermo. "It's a cloistered, narrow existence that I'm not proud of," says Parcells. "I don't know what's going on in the world. And I don't have time to find out. All I think about is football and winning. But hey," he sweeps his hand over his desk and points to the office that scarcely registers his presence. "Who's got it better than me!" (p. 180)

ANSWER: Quotation and Thematic reprise

From "Baseball for Life" by Sara Corbett (2007)

I thought back to an earlier conversation we'd had, as Jarrod and Jesse tried to describe all the ways in which they were different from each other, despite being best friends.

"He likes rap and I don't."

"He's neat and I'm messy."

"I hate the Red Sox," Jesse announced.

"I hate the Yankees," Jarrod responded.

Jesse lifted his chin defiantly, "Someday I'm going to hit a home run off of you," he said.

"Ain't gonna happen," said Jarrod. Then both boys started to laugh.

I then asked them what they thought was the best part of playing elite baseball. Jarrod stared at the sky for a moment, appearing to think. Jesse looked sideways at Jarrod, as if seeking permission. "I'm gonna say it," Jesse said. Then he turned to face me. "It's about winning," he said. "But not just about winning—it's fun too. I want to do it for the rest of my life."

He paused and looked to his friend.

"Same as Jess," Jarrod said solemnly. He added, "Baseball for life."

Jesse understood this to be a pact. He looked back at Jarrod. "Baseball for life," he said. (p. 239)

ANSWER: Quotation and Encouraging message

ACTIVITIES Ending With a Sense of Resolution

E-Ticket Ride

The Disneyland story I offered as an example in the focus lesson for the key quality Structuring the Body has an ending that often confuses students. I write, "It's definitely an E-ticket ride." I was referring to the kind of tickets that Disneyland used when they first opened, not an electronic ticket as most students assume. My ending could have been, "It was thrilling and exciting."

Use Internet access to read about the cultural use of "E ticket" on a Web site such as Wikipedia (http://en.wikipedia.org/wiki/E_ticket). Discuss with students how "E ticket" has become a metaphor for an experience that is exciting, thrilling, and spine-tingling. Ask students to write a new story that uses "E ticket" in the ending. Encourage them to use the examples from the Web site for inspiration, such as quoting song lyrics or a line of dialogue from a movie that uses the term. Share and discuss.

Podcast Endings

Ask students to think about a current event about which the public has different opinions, such as the outcome of an election, the development of parkland, or a leash law for dogs. Ask students to create an audio podcast with two different endings—one representing each side's opinion on the issue. (You may want to play a few professional, well-edited podcasts for students as models.) Ask them to record their podcasts and play each one for the class. Then have the class vote on which ending is stronger and discuss why. Directions for recording and posting podcasts are available at http://www.scribd.com:80/doc/2163883/Beginners-Guide-to-Podcasting.

Mentor Texts for Middle School: Organization

The following books capture a full range of techniques authors use to organize their writing. Each one provides a stellar example of how to structure text so the reader remains engaged in the writer's message, from start to finish.

Regarding the Trees by **Kate Klise** (Harcourt, 2005)

Through its witty back-and-forth letters and replies, lists, memos, announcements, and a host of other writing responses, the reader is treated to creative and even bizarre responses to Principal Russ's request for a proposal to trim the trees at Geyser Creek Middle School. This book is a hilarious romp and contains a cornucopia of formats for readers to enjoy: newspaper articles, letters, notes, directions, dialogues, and many others.

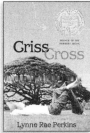

Criss Cross by **Lynne Rae Perkins** (Greenwillow, 2005)

Fourteen-year-old Debbie and Hector must decide what direction to take their lives in this funny and sweet Newbery-winning, multilayered novel. The narrator's voice alternates among Debbie, Hector, and other characters, chapter by chapter, making *Criss Cross* a fascinating study in organization. The author guides the reader forward, through the main story, yet changes point of view in each chapter.

American Born Chinese by **Gene Luen Yang** (First Second, 2006)

Across the country, graphic novels are enticing middle schoolers to read. If you're wondering why, go no further than this book. This book is organized around three separate story lines, each complete on its own. But Yang engineers the plots to converge at the climax, merging the separate stories into one that conveys a powerful message of tolerance and acceptance. The graphic novel format is sophisticated and stunning.

Final Thoughts

Organization may be a thorn in every writer's paw, but when it's working well, there is a grateful reader at the other end. We need to encourage students to discard simple, formulaic structures in favor of more complex, original ones that make their ideas soar. Creating an engaging lead, using sequence and transition words, structuring the body so it flows, and ending with a sense of resolution are all skills students can learn. It just takes time and experience. In the next chapter, I cover a trait that ensures student writing is alive and filled with energy: voice.

CHAPTER 6

Voice:

Anything but Boring!

oring. No critique of writing is worse than that.

Snoopy's dilemma, making his writing interesting

to the reader, is one all writers face. One solution:

focusing on voice. The right combination of the right

words for the right audience creates the right voice.

In this chapter, I share ideas for helping middle school

students understand voice and use it to make their writing

meaningful to the reader. This is the trait that helps writers see the true power of the pen. When writers use voice well, they turn into superheroes. They become faster and more powerful, and can leap tall ideas in a single bound. When they don't use it well, however, they are grounded as if under the influence of some internal form of Kryptonite.

The Voice Trait: A Definition

Voice is the tone and tenor of the piece—the personal stamp of the writer, which is achieved through a strong understanding of purpose and audience. It's the force behind the words that proves a real person is speaking and cares about what is being said. Writers engage the reader with voice, drawing him or her in by making connections between the reader's life and the piece's topic. They have a solid handle on why and for whom they're writing the piece, and choose an appropriate voice—cheerful or melancholy, humorous or serious, confident or uncertain, confrontational or conciliatory, fanciful or authoritative, and so on.

Voice is the heart and soul of the writing—its very life. When the writer is dedicated to the topic, she applies voice almost automatically because she is passionate about what she is saying and how she is saying it. She injects a flavor that is unmistakably her own and that distinguishes her from all other writers. To create strong voice, the writer must apply its key qualities with skill and confidence:

* Establishing a Tone
* Conveying the Purpose
* Creating a Connection to the Audience
* Taking Risks to Create Voice

> **❝** If a book doesn't have voice, it's bad. I like the voice that makes the hairs on your neck stand up or makes your stomach queasy. **❞**
>
> —Jeremiah, grade 7

Why Teachers Struggle With Voice

Voice brings ideas to life in the distinctive style of the writer. In a nutshell, it's the writer's energy. Or, more specifically, it's his electromagnet. If the magnet is activated, the reader enters into the writing. If the magnet is disabled, the reader disconnects and tends to wander.

As important as voice is, however, many teachers confide they don't feel prepared to assess and teach it. At the same time, they can easily spot voice in work that is well written—and quickly detect its absence in work that isn't. As Donald Murray puts it, "Voice is the quality, more than any other, that allows us to recognize excellent writing"

(1985, pp. 21-22). Assessing and teaching this trait is not as hard as many teachers think. The trick is to become skilled at two things: noting and naming voice in the writing students read and create, and choosing model texts and instructional ideas to help students achieve success. I give you starting points later in this chapter.

Interestingly enough, I've found that middle school students are not as intimidated by voice as their teachers are. They are quick to acknowledge that voice engages them and keeps them reading. They know that voice takes many forms and is found in all kinds of print materials, from books to billboards. And most of them can easily note and name it. So, in this section, I turn the tables and lay out some of the reasons teachers, not students, struggle with voice.

We Can't Reach Out and Touch It

Voice is often misrepresented as the "touchy-feely" trait. Writing expert Peter Elbow puts his finger on why: "You are looking for something mysterious and hidden. There are no outward linguistic characteristics to point to in writing with real voice. Resonance or impact on readers is all there is . . . You have to be willing to work in the dark, not be in a hurry, and have faith" (1998, p. 312).

The bottom line is if writing doesn't have voice, we don't enjoy reading it. And if we don't enjoy reading it, the ideas have no impact on us. How can writers bring voice to their work? By slowing down the composing process, working without an exact road map to the destination, and, indeed, having faith that they have something important to say that will become clear. The one thing we teachers shouldn't do is quantify voice because doing that is like trying to hold onto fog. It doesn't work because voice is not like other, more concrete traits. So quit trying. And trust, as Donald Graves does, in the importance of voice: "To ignore voice is to present the [writing] process as a lifeless, mechanical act. Divorcing voice from process is like omitting salt from stew, love from sex, or sun from gardening" (1983, p. 227). The scoring guide, sample papers, and suggested lessons and activities that follow give you tangible ways to capture evidence of voice in your students' writing and guide them when it's absent. However, accepting the fact that voice is abstract is the first step.

We Didn't Learn It in School

When many of us went to school, voice was not part of the writing curriculum. Hard rules certainly were, though—rules that all "good writers" followed like gospel: Never use the first person; Always use complete sentences; and Always provide a thesis statement at the start, offer three supporting details in the middle, and repeat your thesis statement at the end. Imagine!

Times have changed. Voice-filled texts fill today's world. Magazines, newspapers, and high-quality textbooks inform us. Menus, brochures, and Web sites persuade us. And, of course, the literature we provide students engages and enthralls us. Voice is all around us and always has been. Maybe it wasn't called "voice" when we went to school, but good writing has always been infused with it. Thankfully, today's students have a name for it—and it becomes our job, as teachers, to show them how use it skillfully every time they write.

As a member of the National Council of Teachers of English's Standing Committee on Testing and Evaluation from 1996 to 2000, I participated in many spirited discussions about large-scale assessments. Although I and my fellow committee members, made up of classroom teachers, school administrators, and representatives from NAEP, ACT, SAT, and state departments of education, argued frequently, we agreed on one point: students who received the highest scores, regardless of the mode or topic they're given, had one thing in common—voice. If you examine the exemplars each state provides to prepare students for its exam, you will see voice, whether it is named in the rubric or not. The same is true for the NAEP writing test, and the writing component of the SAT and ACT. Regardless of any inexperience we may have, we teachers must embrace the trait of voice if we want today's students to write well for large-scale assessments—and for any other purpose, for that matter.

We Define Voice as Personality

True and false. Every writer has many personalities to draw upon. If that writer is on the receiving end of a good deed, his personality may be defined as grateful. If his choice of presidential candidate loses, it may be defined as aggravated and annoyed. If someone throws him a surprise party, it may be defined as happy and humbled. Each personality reflects how the writer feels in the moment. So which one is his personality? All of them—and others. Many others.

When we write with voice, we take on a specific, temporary personality to fit the purpose and audience of the writing. So when we write a thank-you note for a toaster that we receive as a gift, we use an appreciative voice. But when that toaster burns the bread beyond recognition the first time we use it, we use a completely different voice when demanding a refund from the company that manufactured it. Again, both of those voices are ours. As writers, we need to choose which to use and when to use it.

So although voice often shows itself as the writer's personality, it's *not* the writer's personality. We don't assess personality; we assess how well a student has used voice to meet his purpose for writing and address his audience. Whether he's writing a story about the day five ants crawled up his pant leg or an essay about the mating habits of the fire ant, he should use voice to engage the reader. The story's tone may be personal, expressive, and emotional. And the essay's tone may be more informative, credible, and authoritative. However, in both cases, the writer assumes a personality to create a voice that serves his purpose and audience. Voice is the right amount of energy the writer brings to the piece.

Assessing Student Work for Voice

The following paper by an eighth grader is guaranteed to put you in the spirit to assess student work for voice. As you read it, ask yourself: Is this student's purpose for writing the paper clear? Is there an identifiable tone and/or tenor? Has he taken his audience into consideration? Does he dare to show what he thinks and feels? If you answer "yes" to these questions, the piece has voice.

To hoom ever is unfortunit enough to have to read this.

My topic as you by now proubly know is on trying to talk someone out of doing something. What your about to read is most likely not what your expecting too. I'm going to try to talk you out of reading this papper. Your proubly thinking this kid has eather lost it or is very board. Well, maybe boulth.

Your proubly not getting paid enough so you can stop any time. Whats the matter? Your still reading. Fine keep reading but I'm warning you right now theres proubly something better you would rather be doing. Like feeding your cat. It's proubly setting home right now while you read this starving. Maybe there is a edicational show on T.V. or even an old Western.

I bet your proubly getting hungry about now. Don't you think a nice, big juicy hamberger would taste good. Or even a 12 oz steak done just the way you like it with a little bit of horseradish.

You know that papper right next to you would proubly be much more interesting than this one. It would be easer to grade also.

Buy the way did you know that there are thousands of teachers how die of bordom from reading these? I don't know that but I thought it might happen.

If your still reading this than it looks like I failed or else your really board. Or maybe there just paying you more than I thought.

Now that's voice! The piece may be a little rough in other traits, but it certainly has a lively and engaging voice. Now it's your turn to score the following seventh-grade papers, which represent a wide range of skills in the voice trait. Review the scoring guide on page 147, read each paper carefully, assess it for the voice trait by following the steps on pages 50–51 under "Assessing Writing Using the Trait Scoring Guides," and then read my assessment to see if we agree. Use your own students' writing for further practice.

> ❝ Voice is when the author secretly whispers their idea in your ear. ❞
>
> —Sammy, grade 7

The papers were all written in the expository mode, in response to the prompt "Think of an invention that has been either helpful or harmful and provide an explanation for your choice." Therefore, the purpose of the papers is to inform and explain. If a writer employs elements of narrative writing, such as figurative language, the story of one's past, or a problem to be resolved, it's fine, even worthy of celebration. After all, good writers often use such elements in expository pieces to add voice and make their central idea clear.

Also, beware of personal bias. Sometimes students write voice-filled papers on unpleasant topics. And sometimes, the opposite is true: they choose agreeable topics, yet don't use voice effectively. So be on the alert. Don't score the topic. Score the voice—the way the writer reaches out and connects to you, the reader. Ask yourself, "Does the piece have energy or not?" If it does, ask, "How much does it have and is it appropriate to the purpose of the writing."

Finally, even though I focus on voice, I've scored the papers in all the traits (except presentation, since the papers are typeset) in case you need additional samples to practice scoring or use in instruction.

Scoring Guide: Voice

The tone and tenor of the piece—the personal stamp of the writer, which is achieved through a strong understanding of purpose and audience.

Reproducible on **CD**

6

HIGH

5

EXCEPTIONAL

A. **Establishing a Tone:** The writer cares about the topic, and it shows. The writing is expressive and compelling. The reader feels the writer's conviction, authority, and integrity.

B. **Conveying the Purpose:** The writer makes clear his or her reason for creating the piece. He or she offers a point of view that is appropriate for the mode (narrative, expository, or persuasive), which compels the reader to read on.

C. **Creating a Connection to the Audience:** The writer speaks in a way that makes the reader want to listen. He or she has considered what the reader needs to know and the best way to convey it by sharing his or her fascination, feelings, and opinions about the topic.

D. **Taking Risks to Create Voice:** The writer expresses ideas in new ways, which makes the piece interesting and original. The writing sounds like the writer because of his or her use of distinctive, just-right words and phrases.

STRONG

4

MIDDLE

3

REFINING

A. **Establishing a Tone:** The writer has established a tone that can be described as "pleasing" or "sincere," but not "passionate" or "compelling." He or she attempts to create a tone that hits the mark, but the overall result feels generic.

B. **Conveying the Purpose:** The writer has chosen a voice for the piece that is not completely clear. There are only a few moments when the reader understands where the writer is coming from and why he or she wrote the piece.

C. **Creating a Connection to the Audience:** The writer keeps the reader at a distance. The connection between reader and writer is tenuous because the writer reveals little about what is important or meaningful about the topic.

D. **Taking Risks to Create Voice:** The writer creates a few moments that catch the reader's attention, but only a few. The piece sounds like anyone could have written it. It lacks the energy, commitment, and conviction that would distinguish it from other pieces on the same topic.

DEVELOPING

2

LOW

1

EMERGING

A. **Establishing a Tone:** The writer has produced a lifeless piece—one that is monotonous, mechanical, repetitious, and/or off-putting to the reader.

B. **Conveying the Purpose:** The writer chose the topic for mysterious reasons. The piece may be filled with random thoughts, technical jargon, or inappropriate vocabulary, making it impossible to discern how the writer feels about the topic.

C. **Creating a Connection to the Audience:** The writer provides no evidence that he or she has considered what the reader might need to know to connect with the topic. Or there is an obvious mismatch between the piece's tone and the intended audience.

D. **Taking Risks to Create Voice:** The writer creates no highs and lows. The piece is flat and lifeless, causing the reader to wonder why he or she wrote it in the first place. The writer's voice does not pop out, even for a moment.

RUDIMENTARY

Inventions

When I think of an invention that is really helpful or harmful, I think of guns because they are very, very harmful. If you want to know why guns are incredibly harmful, you should read on.

The American Revolution was the first major war when people actually used guns. They were extremely harmful in the Boston Massacre, not to mention all of the battles. The next time there was a war where a lot of people died was for a pretty long time.

I'm going to skip ahead to World War two. A ton of people died when Japan bombed pearl harbor but the real trouble was when the entire world started shooting, invading, and bombing other countries. Millions and millions of people died because of the weapons in that war.

There hasn't been another massive war since world war two, but when there is, millions of people will die because of guns.

Time to Assess for Voice

When we allow writers to choose their topics, but they wind up choosing topics that don't interest them, they miss an opportunity. This writer, for example, could have chosen any invention to write about—and selected guns. There was a reason for his choice, but we don't know what it is. His piece is a bare-bones response that is in dire need of interesting details and precise words and phrases to bring out his voice. It's not expressive at all, making it difficult for the reader to connect and engage.

Voice	
Score **1: Rudimentary**	
Range	**Low**

Other Traits	
Ideas	1
Organization	2
Word Choice	1
Sentence Fluency	3
Conventions	3

A Establishing a Tone

The writer has produced a lifeless piece—one that is monotonous, mechanical, repetitious, and/or off-putting to the reader.

There is nothing unique about the way this writer approaches the topic. He offers a few general facts, but stops there. The piece is a rote response devoid of knowledge and feeling about the idea.

B Conveying the Purpose

The writer chose the topic for mysterious reasons. The piece may be filled with random thoughts, technical jargon, or inappropriate vocabulary, making it impossible to discern how the writer feels about the topic.

It's not clear why the writer picked guns as a topic. He's general, repetitive, and sure of only one thing: guns kill people in wars. It's a good topic, without doubt, but the writer needs to make his intention for writing the piece much clearer.

C Creating a Connection to the Audience

The writer provides no evidence that he or she has considered what the reader might need to know to connect with the topic. Or there is an obvious mismatch between the piece's tone and the intended audience.

That guns are used in war to kill people is not a new idea or a new spin on an old idea. The point is obvious. The content is flat. The writer's purpose is vague at best.

D Taking Risks to Create Voice

The writer creates no highs and lows. The piece is flat and lifeless, causing the reader to wonder why he or she wrote it in the first place. The writer's voice does not pop out, even for a moment.

Sadly, the piece contains no moment that would allow a teacher to say, "Here is where you begin to show what you really think and feel." It therefore falls squarely into the "boring" category. The reader is left to wonder why the student wrote it.

Invention

The invention that I thought was especially helpful to people was cars, here are four reasons why I think they are helpful.

First they are helpful because they get you where you need to go. For illustration to school, home, work, etc.

Secondly they are used for entertainment such as racing, or to show engines of, paintings, and wheels.

Thirdly they are helpful because they are preferable than riding a bike or riding a horse. Imagine riding a bike or riding a horse all the way from Boise, Idaho to Orlando, Florida. That would take a lot of time and a lot of energy. When you drive a car it doesn't take away energy. It would take forever to walk or ride a bike that far. Disneyworld would probably old and broken down by the time you got there.

Lastly they are helpful because you want have to wait on someone to come, and get you if had somewhere to go, you can just get in your car and go.

In conclusion that why according to, everyday life cars are helpful

Time to Assess for Voice

This piece has "blah, blah, blah" written all over it, with the exception of the third paragraph where the writer provides a glimmer of voice by slowing down, offering some details, and making an important point for the reader to consider. Since the writer applies voice in one paragraph, she should be able to apply it in the others, with encouragement and the right kind of instruction.

Voice	
Score	**2: Emerging**
Range	**Low**

Other Traits	
Ideas	2
Organization	2
Word Choice	2
Sentence Fluency	2
Conventions	4

A Establishing a Tone

The writer has produced a lifeless piece—one that is monotonous, mechanical, or repetitive, and off-putting to the reader.

> *This piece is a good argument against formulaic writing because the formula deadens the voice. The writer needs to expand each paragraph and add voice to make her perspective on the topic clear.*

B Conveying the Purpose

The writer chose the topic for mysterious reasons. The piece may be filled with random thoughts, technical jargon, or inappropriate vocabulary, making it impossible to discern how the writer feels about the topic.

> *Cars may be a helpful invention, but this piece does not sell that idea very well. We get a flash of insight in the third paragraph, but then it fades away.*

C Creating a Connection to the Audience

The writer provides no evidence that he or she has considered what the reader might need to know to connect with the topic. Or there is an obvious mismatch between the piece's tone and the intended audience.

> *Except when the writer acknowledges how tiring walking from Boise to Orlando would be, she doesn't consider the reader. She writes to fill the page, not to communicate.*

D Taking Risks to Create Voice

The writer creates no highs and lows. The piece is flat and lifeless, causing the reader to wonder why he or she wrote it in the first place. The writer's voice does not pop out, even for a moment.

> *One moment of voice quietly reveals itself, and that's it. This piece is a bare-bones outline. I want to know more about why cars are interesting to the writer—after all, she chose cars as a topic. There must be a reason, but it's not discernible in the writing at this point.*

Inventions

Invintions are used all around us. Like T.V.'s, phones, hairdryers, microwaves, all kinds of stuff. But we could not have most Invintions without one main invention, electricity. With the help of Ben Franklin, a kit, and some lightning, we would proble not have electricity today. We have had electricity for quit some time now, and it has been very helpful. From the very first, black and white t.v., to the telephones we use today. Electricity is used every day. I no I use it all the time. For example, when I watch t.v., blowdry my hair, use the microwave, and even when I'm asleep at night. (I use a nightlight!) Besides all the fun stuff I use electricity for like, games, t.v., and such, electricity is very help full in our world today. For example, if somebody has bene in a car acsident and stranded in the middle of no where, they could just take out a cellphone. And call for help. Also even doctors use electricity to save lives. Plus the use of electricity helps people cook there food. You can proble see now why electricity has bene helpful and fun in meny peoples lifes today. I no it helps me. And thats why electricity is so important to people all over the world.

Time to Assess for Voice

This writer achieves voice with varying degrees of success. Clearly, he's tried to create an engaging, conversational piece. An expressive tone pops through here and there, but then retreats. Because the writer doesn't have his voice under control, the reader can't get inside the topic to appreciate fully his point of view.

Voice	
Score	**3: Developing**
Range	**Middle**

Other Traits	
Ideas	3
Organization	2
Word Choice	3
Sentence Fluency	2
Conventions	1

A Establishing a Tone

The writer has established a tone that can be described as "pleasing" or "sincere," but not "passionate" or "compelling." He or she attempts to create a tone that hits the mark, but the overall result feels generic.

The writer gives the reader reasons to engage, but fails to draw him or her in completely. He shows a basic understanding of electricity, but little control over tone. The piece is "voice lite."

B Conveying the Purpose

The writer has chosen a voice for the piece that is not completely clear. There are only a few moments when the reader understands where the writer is coming from and why he or she wrote the piece.

The writer uses a voice that doesn't quite fit the purpose. Explaining the importance of electricity demands a compelling and informed voice. The voice here is chatty.

C Creating a Connection to the Audience

The writer keeps the reader at a distance. The connection between reader and writer is tenuous because the writer reveals little about what is important or meaningful about the topic.

I don't feel distanced from this writer, but I don't feel connected either because the information he presents doesn't seem all that important or meaningful to him. His tone is weak, whereas it should be more commanding.

D Taking Risks to Create Voice

The writer creates a few moments that catch the reader's attention, but only a few. The piece sounds like anyone could have written it. It lacks the energy, commitment, and conviction that would distinguish it from other pieces on the same topic.

When writers speak directly to readers, they're taking a risk. But in this piece, the technique isn't working as well as it could. The ideas, though plentiful, aren't well developed, leaving me feeling that the writer is not committed to the topic.

Helpful or Harmful Inventions

In our society, there are helpful inventions everywhere. There are also very harmful inventions such as the shoelace. Some people find shoelaces beneficial, but I disagree.

Imagine you are riding a rollercoaster, screaming at the top of your lungs. All of a sudden a shoelace hits you in the face, and you start choking on your own saliva from the shock. That is not very helpful. Shoelaces are one of the many harmful household objects that should be banned.

A couple of weeks ago I was walking across the gym, harmlessly trying to get my friend Edward to smell my new lotion. "Hey Ed"—then I tripped. Not only did I trip, but I fell and bruised both knees and elbows. Not to mention I was in front of about 60 people. "What did you trip on?" you may be asking. I tripped on a *shoelace*. A very dangerous shoelace that I had made the mistake of wearing.

I think that shoelaces should be banned from all public places because not only can clumsy people trip on their own, they can trip on your shoelaces too (I also think there should be limits on doormats too. They are also a tripping hazzard). Velcro would be a nice substitute. It's stylish, versitile, and easy to use. It is a bit more difficult to trip on.

For all of these reasons, shoelaces should be banned at least until people like me develop some coordination or balance. We could switch to Velcro, zippers, buttons, or anything that will keep the clumsy people of the world safe.

Time to Assess for Voice

One way to establish voice right off the bat is to say something unexpected. In this case, the writer takes an ordinary innocuous object, a shoelace, and brands it "harmful." As the reader, I'm intrigued by that, and want to read more. Any writer could say, "Shoelaces are dangerous." But this writer gives us reasons why shoelaces are dangerous. Though his argument is far-fetched, I found myself smiling and even agreeing at times as I read. The piece definitely has energy, which helps the voice along.

Voice	
Score	**4: Refining**
Range	**Middle**

Other Traits	
Ideas	3
Organization	3
Word Choice	4
Sentence Fluency	4
Conventions	4

A Establishing a Tone

The writer has established a tone that can be described as "pleasing" or "sincere," but not "passionate" or "compelling." He or she attempts to create a tone that hits the mark, but the overall result feels generic.

> *This piece is humorous and substantive. By taking the position that shoelaces are harmful, the writer sets the reader up for the unusual and unpredictable details that she uses to argue that position. She doesn't disappoint; she has found her voice. Now she needs to use it to persuade the reader, not just entertain.*

B Conveying the Purpose

The writer has chosen a voice for the piece that is not completely clear. There are only a few moments when the reader understands where the writer is coming from and why he or she wrote the piece.

> *Some readers might find this piece unconvincing. After all, shoelaces offer more benefits than risks. The writer's arguments are fun, but not terribly convincing. To pull off a piece like this well, she needs to build a stronger case, which would provide opportunities for her voice to shine. As it is, it teeters between effective and just plain silly.*

C Creating a Connection to the Audience

The writer keeps the reader at a distance. The connection between reader and writer is tenuous because the writer reveals little about what is important or meaningful about the topic.

> *The writer shares two detailed examples to back up her argument—riding the roller coaster and walking across the gym floor. But because they are so lighthearted, it's hard to take them seriously.*

D Taking Risks to Create Voice

The writer creates a few moments that catch the reader's attention, but only a few. The piece sounds like anyone could have written it. It lacks the energy, commitment, and conviction that would distinguish it from other pieces on the same topic.

> *Taking a position that goes against what most people believe is one way to take a risk. Supporting that position with personal examples is another. But in this case, neither goes far enough to convince readers to stop using shoelaces for their intended purpose: to lace shoes!*

Paper!!!

I have never really liked essays. I think everybody will either choose cars, or the light bulb. These both were near the top of my list. Then I had a great idea, I was going to write a essay on what I was writing on. Paper!!! I think paper is one of the greatest inventions of all time.

Okay, for starters, lets say I had to write this essay on stone slabs. I would have to use paint, or a chisel, which are both pretty messy. Plus dipping it in paint or cleaning it every ten secounds would get on my nerves. Now imagine carrying those stone tables around in your backpack. Seriously, a 80 pound backpack, not gonna happen. We wouldn't have a back by age 20.

There's a lot of talk about the environment these days. If we didn't have paper, what about the stone you've already used and don't wan't. Most would give it to the trash man, let him deal with it. Well whats he going to do with it, burn it? Nope because stone won't burn. That leads me into another aspect of paper I like. You can carry alot of it at one time. Isn't that so cool?

That paragraph was on how paper helps, this one is on what you can do with it. For one you can hang stuff up, like posters and signs or things like those. I really don't think that little piece of tape will do holding that big stone block up. Also paper can lead to art. such as Oragami. Paper is pretty cool because it won't tear easily, and yet, it can be folded. Also it can be mass produced, such as in books and magazines.

Now that I have stated why paper is such a good invention, what do you think? Are you ready to help our environment?

P.S. I am going to recycle this paper when I'm done.

Time to Assess for Voice

This piece is dripping with voice—voice that makes the piece delightful and demonstrates the writer's enthusiasm for the topic. The voice really comes alive in the second paragraph. With a little work, the introduction could be just as effective. The voice falters, though, in the conclusion, with its predictable structure—and nothing smothers voice like a predictable structure. The P.S. saves the piece. Without a doubt, the writer is invested in the topic and was full of energy writing about it.

Voice	
Score	**5: Strong**
Range	**High**

Other Traits	
Ideas	5
Organization	3
Word Choice	4
Sentence Fluency	3
Conventions	3

A Establishing a Tone

The writer cares about the topic, and it shows. The writing is expressive and compelling. The reader feels the writer's conviction, authority, and integrity.

The writer is very expressive. He's excited about his topic and it shows. He argues that paper is an important invention and then backs up that claim with some timely, clever examples. I'd encourage more voice in the introduction and conclusion in the next draft—they are not as strong as the body.

B Conveying the Purpose

The writer makes clear his or her reason for creating the piece. He or she offers a point of view that is appropriate for the mode (narrative, expository, or persuasive), which compels the reader to read on.

That paper is lighter than stone slabs and easier to recycle are two good points, presented in a lighthearted yet credible manner. By expounding on the virtues of paper, the writer achieves his goal to inform and explain.

C Creating a Connection to the Audience

The writer speaks in a way that makes the reader want to listen. He or she has considered what the reader needs to know and the best way to convey it by sharing his or her fascination, feelings, and opinions about the topic.

There's little doubt this writer is aware of his reader. He provides several strong, fleshed-out examples, which enable the reader to understand the message completely. He does it all with a humorous tone—not over the top, just lively and fun.

D Taking Risks to Create Voice

The writer expresses ideas in new ways, which makes the piece interesting and original. The writing sounds like the writer because of his or her use of distinctive, just-right words and phrases.

It's risky to think outside the box. But this writer has done exactly that, which, in part, is why the voice is so strong. Comparing paper to stone slabs is a stretch, but he pulls it off. And the idea of recycling stone tablets adds irony. After all, isn't stone a natural substance to begin with? Love the thinking here.

Helpful Inventions

When you hear the word "invention" you probably think of electronics such as TV, Ipod, cell phone, and computers. Alhough it's true these inventions have changed our lives forever, there is another I think that has had an even greater impact: the base ten number system. This amazing number system impacts every part of our daily lives. It's built around the numbers zero through nine and has exponents on a base of ten. It is the number system that most people use and has been used for many centuries.

We use the base ten number system every single day. We use it for money. We use it to tell temperature. We count the days of the year using base ten. It helps us to tell time. We use the base ten number system to measure distance. Numbers allow us to tell the quantity of humans and animals living in the world. Statistics like "the tallest mountain in the world," "the largest ocean," and "the smallest country," are all measured with the base ten number system. Imagine how difficult it would be to use an index or a table of contents if we did not label our book pages with numbers that use this familiar system.

Calculations come out evenly using the base ten number system. One example is the right triangle. Its side lengths are equal to $a^2 + b^2 = c^2$, where "a" equals a side by the right angle, where "b" equals the other side by the right angle, and where "c" is the right triangle's hypotenuse. You probably remember this from geometry class, and wondered why you needed to know a formula like this. My dad's a builder and he taught me about right triangles when I was really little. I use it all the time when I help him now.

The most basic right triangle has side lengths of 3, 4, and 5. Three is "a", four is "b" and five is "c." It fits into the equation perfectly:

$$a^2 + b^2 = c^2$$
$$3^2 + 4^2 = 5^2$$
$$9 + 16 = 25$$
$$25 = 25$$

Such perfection would not occur in number systems other than the base ten number system.

Students must use numbers in the majority of their classes especially in math and science. And even writing. This essay is about base ten so I think that counts. Cashiers must use numbers during money transactions since American money is designed around the base 10 system. Doctors and surgeons must be precise, so they use the base ten number system. Failing to do so might, in serious cases, cause mortality on behalf of the patient. If construction workers did not use the base ten number system, houses may become tilted and eventually fall. Orthodontists must carefully measure the angles of their patients' teeth with the numbers of the base ten number system. Scientists use the base ten number system to record data accurately and precisely.

People all over the world use the base ten number system because it is easy to understand and apply to many situations. When people from different countries meet, they can understand each other when using numbers, even if they speak different languages. The base ten number system provides everyone with a universal method of communication.

The base ten number system has been useful for billions of humans. It has dramatically changed our lives. So, while all the electronic inventions are great, I think the best invention of all is the base ten system. I hope you give me a perfect score for this paper—a 100.

Time to Assess for Voice

You don't have to be a mathematician to appreciate this writer's conviction and authority. An essay about the base-ten number system could be as dry as a desert gully in July. But the writer feels strongly about the system and makes sure the reader understands exactly why. The tone is not cute, sarcastic, or witty. It's thoughtful, passionate, credible, and, therefore, effective. I hadn't given the base-ten number system a lot of thought in the last twenty years, to be honest. But after reading this piece, I have a whole new appreciation for it largely because of the writer's voice.

Voice	
Score	**6: Exceptional**
Range	**High**

Other Traits	
Ideas	6
Organization	6
Word Choice	6
Sentence Fluency	5
Conventions	6

A Establishing a Tone

The writer cares about the topic, and it shows. The writing is expressive and compelling. The reader feels the writer's conviction, authority, and integrity.

> *I don't know anyone who cares more about the base-ten number system than this writer. Do you? I didn't think so! The passion he has for the topic is palpable. There is no question he believes what he is saying, no question at all.*

B Conveying the Purpose

The writer makes clear his or her reason for creating the piece. He or she offers a point of view that is appropriate for the mode (narrative, expository, or persuasive), which compels the reader to read on.

> *Picking an invention and explaining how it has made a difference to people is a rather ho-hum exercise, but this writer rises to the challenge. It's as though he's been waiting for someone to ask about the base-ten number system for 13 years—and now, finally, someone has! His knowledge and enthusiasm are infectious.*

C Creating a Connection to the Audience

The writer speaks in a way that makes the reader want to listen. He or she has considered what the reader needs to know and the best way to convey it by sharing his or her fascination, feelings, and opinions about the topic.

> *Without the energy this writer brings to the topic, this piece could be very bland. But instead, it's fascinating. I felt I knew this writer after I read his piece. I want to tell him to keep going, keep caring, and keep learning with such joy—and start looking into scholarships for MIT, pronto!*

D Taking Risks to Create Voice

The writer expresses ideas in new ways, which makes the piece interesting and original. The writing sounds like the writer because of his or her use of distinctive, just-right words and phrases.

> *The choice of topic is risky. But by taking it on, explaining concepts in an understandable way, and choosing words carefully, the writer pulls it off. The piece is original. I've never read one quite like it.*

Conference Comments

If the piece scores high in voice, 5 or 6, say something like:

> "I have to admit, I never really thought about the base-ten number system as an invention before. But the powerful and consistent <u>voice</u> you use throughout your piece and all your excellent examples changed my mind. You make a good case here. Thank you."

> "Your views about paper were a pleasure to read. You came up with original ideas, which made your <u>voice</u> stand out. I chuckled through it. Your writing is clever and delightful."

If the piece scores in the middle, a 3 or 4, say something like:

> "The <u>voice</u> in your piece is strongest in the middle. You offer some interesting warnings about shoelaces that I could really relate to. If you revise the beginning and ending with as much enthusiasm, this piece will move up the <u>voice</u> scale."

> "Let's go through your piece with a highlighter and mark the lines that have the most <u>voice</u>. My hunch is that we'll find them in the details, where you share examples from your own life. That's the sort of thing I'd like to see more of in your next draft."

If the piece scores low, a 1 or 2, say something like:

> "I really connected to your <u>voice</u> in the third paragraph because you gave me something to think about. Why don't you try to add information to the other paragraphs, keeping in mind how you want your reader to react to your topic?"

> "There's no doubt that the invention of guns has changed the world. Tell me, though, why is the topic important to you? Can you explain more about the impact of guns in another draft? That will make your <u>voice</u> stand out."

Teaching Writing With the Voice Trait

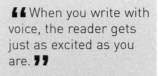

> **"**When you write with voice, the reader gets just as excited as you are.**"**
>
> —Keenan, grade 7

The more energy the writer gives, the more voice the reader gets. Voice creates a romance, of sorts, between the writer and reader. And like any true romance, there is an intangible quality to it. There is, as William Strunk and E. B. White put it, "no satisfactory explanation of style, no infallible guide to good writing. . . no key that unlocks the door, no inflexible rule by which the young writer may shape his course" (2000, p. 66).

I've found that middle school students gravitate naturally toward this trait, knowing that voiceless writing is deadly. It's not hard to convince them that good writing has style, a specific tone, and a clear purpose and audience. Good writing is interesting—even fascinating—to the reader. To help you promote skills in the voice trait, I've organized the remainder of this chapter into sections that correspond to its four key qualities:

* Establishing a Tone

* Conveying the Purpose

* Creating a Connection to the Audience

* Taking Risks to Create Voice

Within each section, you'll find a warm-up exercise, a focus lesson, and two activities, as well as a Think About that lists important questions students should ask themselves in order to bring voice to their writing. (The key qualities and Think Abouts are also included on the CD that accompanies this book.)

Key Quality: Establishing a Tone

It's more than a happy accident when voice works well in a piece of writing. Student writers who think about tone, drafting passages that make a specific connection to the reader, are more successful than those who don't. The voice of the piece is the overall effect of the combination of tones throughout the writing. Writers who use tone effectively figure out that establishing the right tone is essential to connecting to readers. Use the following Think About to expand students' understanding of this fact.

THINK ABOUT:

- Can I name the primary tone of my writing? (For example, happy, frustrated, knowledgeable, scared, convincing)
- Have I varied the tone from the beginning to the end?
- Have I been expressive?
- Did I show that I care about this topic?

WARM-UP   Establishing a Tone

Distribute copies of the Think About and encourage students to revise the following story by establishing a tone that makes the voice stand out.

> Bailey, my cat, had never been gone overnight. I was worried. I went outside and called and called her name. She was gone. I felt bad. I didn't sleep all night. I tried to find her. It made me sad that she was gone.

When students have finished revising the story, ask volunteers to share their work. Share your own revision or, if you wish, this one:

> 11:45 p.m. and I finally crawled into bed after a long day of writing and revising. As I stretched out between the smooth coolness of the sheets, I realized Bailey, my cat, wasn't in her usual spot. She's at least fifteen, and every night since I've had her she's slept with me. I called her name but got no response. I went downstairs; it was very, very still, the kind of quiet that gives you a bad feeling deep inside. My pace quickened as I checked her usual haunts—the linen closet, under the desk, in her corner of the sofa, on the pillow of the guest bed. No Bailey. That bad feeling turned to a sickening, gut-wrenching ache; I realized that somehow, someway, she had slipped outside. And I had no idea how long she had been gone or how far she might have wandered. I threw on my bathrobe and went outside, shaking a can of kitty treats—salmon flavored, her favorite—and called and called her name. I could hear my voice echoing up and down the street: "Here, Bailey. Here, kitty, kitty, kitty. Come here, Boo-Boo." But nothing. An occasional dog barked in the distance, and I heard critters rustling in the bushes, but no Bailey. I fought back the tears as I walked the streets of the neighborhood calling and calling until dawn. Arriving home, alone, I couldn't hold my emotions in check one more minute. I stared at her food bowl and water dish and sobbed.

As a class, name the tones of the revised pieces: frightened, nervous, sad, and so on. Then choose the version with the most voice and discuss how establishing a tone strengthens writing.

(This story has a happy ending, by the way. Five days later, a neighbor recognized Bailey from flyers and told me she thought she saw the end of my cat's striped tail deep in some bushes about a block away. I was overjoyed when I found her—hugging her close to me all the way home, then vowing to strangle her for worrying me so much.)

FOCUS LESSON   Establishing a Tone

The tone of a piece of writing can build. It can begin quietly, setting the scene and providing baseline information, break out boisterously for maximum impact, and end quietly, bringing the piece full circle. In this lesson, students learn that good writing often contains more than one tone, by studying a finely crafted passage from Gary Paulsen's autobiography, *My Life in Dog Years*.

Materials:
- a copy of the passage from *My Life in Dog Years* by Gary Paulsen (page 164 and CD)
- electronic projection system or traditional overhead projector
- copies of the Perfect Tones reproducible (page 165 and CD)
- a draft from each student's writing folder
- pens, pencils

What to Do:
1. Project the passage from *My Life in Dog Years* and read it aloud to students.
2. Tell students that tone is the style or manner in which a writer conveys his or her ideas, which is why establishing it is a key quality of voice. Discuss how Paulsen varies the passage's tone—he goes from informational to personal to insightful.
3. Ask students to pinpoint the specific places in the passage where the tone shifts and name each new tone.
4. Write their responses on the whiteboard.
5. Hand out the Perfect Tones reproducible. Ask students to circle any tones that describe points in the passage and add any that aren't listed.
6. Explain to students that writers often switch tones within the writing to create the voice for the piece overall. For example, Paulsen uses a resigned tone in the first paragraph and a poignant one later, when he describes meeting the man at his book reading. He uses a curious tone toward the end. Each tone, distinctive in its own right, contributes to the overall voice of the passage: heartfelt and nostalgic.
7. Ask students what Paulsen does to create his various tones. Ask how the use of different tones contributes to the piece's overall voice.
8. Ask students to select a piece of writing from their writing folder and pinpoint a passage whose tone could use strengthening. Give them time to revise the piece and then share their originals and revisions with the class.

Lesson Extension

Ask students to go to the library and choose an autobiography. Tell them to read a page or two to a partner and discuss the voice, referring to their Perfect Tones list. Encourage them to add words as they discover new voices in the works of other authors. Create a Perfect Tones bulletin board for students to refer to as they search for the right voice for their own pieces.

From *My Life in Dog Years*
By Gary Paulsen

It seemed like there'd always been an Ike in my life and then one morning he wasn't there and I never saw him again. I tried to find him. I would wait for him in the morning by the bridge, but he never showed again. I thought he might have gotten hit by a car or his owners moved away. I mourned him and missed him. But I did not learn what happened to him for thirty years.

I grew and went into the crazy parts of life, army and those other mistakes a young man could make. I grew older and got back into dogs, this time sled dogs, and ran the Iditarod race across Alaska. After my first run I came back to Minnesota with slides of the race to show to all the people who had supported me. A sporting goods store had been one of my sponsors and I gave a public slide show of the race one evening.

There was an older man sitting in a wheelchair and I saw that when I told a story of how Cookie, my lead dog, had saved my life his eyes teared up and he nodded quietly.

When the event was over he wheeled up to me and shook my hands.

"I had a dog like your Cookie—a dog that saved my life."

"Oh—did you run sled?"

He shook his head. "No. Not like that. I lived up in Twin Forks when I was young and was drafted to serve in the Korean War. I had a Labrador that I raised and hunted with, and left him when I went away. I was gone just under a year; I got wounded and lost the use of my legs. When I came back from the hospital he was waiting there and he spent the rest of his life by my side. I would have gone crazy without him. I'd sit for hours and talk to him and he would listen quietly... it was so sad. He loved to hunt and I never hunted again." He faded off and his eyes were moist again. "I still miss him...."

I looked at him, then out the window of the sporting goods store. It was spring and the snow was melting outside but I was seeing fall and a boy and a Lab sitting in a duck blind. Twin Forks, he'd said—and the Korean War. The time was right, and the place, and the dog.

"Your dog," I said. "Was he named Ike?"

He smiled and nodded. "Why, yes—but how... did you know him?"

There was a soft spring rain starting and the window misted with it. That was why Ike had not come back. He had another job.

"Yes," I said, turning to him. "He was my friend...." (1998, pp. 35–36)

Perfect Tones

silly	resigned
sincere	determined
nostalgic	frustrated
friendly	curious
carefree	calm
poignant	frightened
passionate	
sarcastic	
funny	
deliberate	
anxious	
wise	

ACTIVITIES Establishing a Tone

What's My Tone?

Eighth graders from Oregon chose advertising slogans that capture how they think and feel about themselves, and then wrote papers to explain their choices. Share the two samples below with your students and ask them to brainstorm words that describe the tone of each one.

Paper #1:

I think the slogan "Be all that you can be" is very good for me cause it encourage people to work harder so they live better, and be a better person. People don't work hard enough. If they worked harder life could be so much easiery.

If you think about this slogan it makes sense, and it dosen't. Our basketball team is in second to last, but we have beat the first place team twice. So we haven't been all that we have been.

Paper #2:

On my shirt I would put: "I may be quiet but I listen very loud." As many people know I am a quiet person. Not many people know me very well. Several reasons for this are: I don't need to hear my voice all the time to know I'm alive. I feel and breathe, thus I know I'm around. Another reason is I don't need to monopolize conversations to get attention, or to interrupt people all the time so I can be the center of attention. I know who I am, what I need, and how to get it. I don't need to hurt others to build myself up.

But I do hear well. I hear others cutting "friends" of theirs apart, saying unkind things just to make themselves seem better. I hear people's feelings being hurt by others ignoring them. I hear when no one speaks to me because I choose to be more considerate of others, and not to follow the crowd. I hear tears on faces because they aren't accepted by some because they don't have the right looks, the right clothes, or they are not cool enough to be popular. I hear the lonliness of people sitting in the folding chairs at a school dance because they are not loud enough to be heard.

I plan on listening to my children like my own parents are listening to me. Surprisingly... they were the ones who taught me to listen.

Paper #1 often receives comments such as "flat," "boring," "confusing," "rote," and "distant," whereas paper #2 often receives comments such as "insightful," "wise," "sarcastic," "honest," "worldly," "perceptive." (By the way, teachers who attend my workshops request paper #2 more than any other paper, to share with students as an example of strong voice.)

After brainstorming words to describe each piece's tone, ask students to come up with ideas for improving paper #1. Ask students to revise that paper. To establish the right tone, did they also add ideas, change words, and rework passages? Discuss the impact of other traits on voice.

Your Life as a Soundtrack

Invite students to make a list of key times in their lives, such as losing a tooth, learning to ride a bike, moving from elementary to middle school, participating in a championship game, learning to play a musical instrument, getting a pet, relocating to a new town, or experiencing the birth of a brother or sister. Ask each student to pick the most significant event. Then have them write an explanation of the event and pick an appropriate song to accompany it. Have students read their pieces aloud, with their song choice playing in the background. Ask the class to pick words that describe the tone of the writing and song.

Key Quality: Conveying the Purpose

Before students take a pen to paper or fingers to keyboard, they need to determine the purpose of their writing. Do they want to tell a story? If so, they might write a narrative piece. Inform? If so, they might write an expository piece. Convince? If so, they might want to write a persuasive piece. Once they've determined their purpose, they need to choose an appropriate voice. A narrative piece, for example, might contain an emotional voice—excited, angry, or tense. An expository piece might contain an expert voice, while a persuasive piece might contain a confident, convincing voice. Use the following Think About to expand students' notions about conveying the purpose of their writing.

THINK ABOUT:

- Is the purpose of my writing clear?
- Does my point of view come through?
- Is this the right tone for this kind of writing?
- Have I used strong voice throughout this piece?

WARM-UP   Conveying the Purpose

Distribute copies of the Think About and discuss how one's purpose for writing often determines one's voice in writing. Then ask students to expand one of these sentences, using a voice that is appropriate for the purpose.

I'll never forget going with my father to vote on election day. (*purpose: to tell a story*)

Vote-by-mail is a cost-effective way to manage elections. (*purpose: to explain or inform*)

U.S. presidential campaigns should be shortened to six months. (*purpose: to persuade*)

When they've finished writing, encourage individual students to share their pieces, without revealing their purpose. Then ask the rest of class to guess the purpose. Share your own example or, if you wish, this one:

When elections were first held in the United States, letters with critical information were carried on horseback or stagecoach. It often took weeks or months to get the news or a reply to a letter. Today, information is transmitted every nanosecond, making it possible for all citizens to know what's happening and why at any moment. But, since the election process has not been altered since the 1700s, today's election process is needlessly long and drawn out. A presidential campaign can go on for more than a year, creating voter fatigue and information burnout resulting from news that is broadcast twenty-four hours a day.

In keeping with the times, and with election policies in other countries such as England and Germany, I believe we should shorten the election process to six months. Candidates could win their party's nomination and still have time to campaign in the general election so all citizens could make informed choices. There would be plenty of time to find out all that is important to know but not so much time that we tire of them before they ever take office. After all, shouldn't we be saving their energy (and ours) for when they are elected so they can run the country? (*persuasive*)

FOCUS LESSON   Conveying the Purpose

Finding a topic is where most writers begin. But they can't move forward confidently without knowing *why* they're writing the piece in the first place. Knowing their purpose for writing the piece helps students get started and ensures their finished products will be filled with voice. In this lesson, students choose a writing topic from a list and match it to a purpose—to tell a story, to inform or explain, or construct an argument. From there, they assign an appropriate voice.

Materials:

- a list of purposes for writing

Purposes for Writing
• to tell a story (narrative)
• to inform or explain (expository)
• to construct an argument (persuasive)

- 3" x 5" index cards and a loose-leaf ring for holding them together

What to Do:

1. With your class, brainstorm a list of writing topics such as these:

Topics	
• global warming	• a historical event that changed history
• my favorite Saturday-morning breakfast menu	
• my least favorite school rule	• the most influential man or woman in America today
• steps in cleaning my room	• an invention that would make life easier
• a story I'll never forget	
• the life cycle of the honeybee	• the best excuse ever

2. Provide each student with a list of the purposes for writing (or modes of writing, as they're also known) like the ones provided on page 168.

3. As a class, match a purpose for writing to each topic listed. For example, a purpose for writing about global warming might be to explain how and why global warming is happening (expository).

4. Give pairs of students an index card and ask them to write a topic on one side and a purpose for writing about the topic on the other.

5. Challenge them to think of two additional purposes and write them on the card. For example, for global warming, in addition to writing an explanation of how and why it's happening, they may tell a story about two polar bear cubs separated by melting ice floes (narrative) and construct an argument for reducing air pollution because of its destructive effect on the ozone layer (persuasive).

6. Ask partners to identify an appropriate voice for each purpose and write it on the card. For example, the voice for the expository piece might be informed and authoritative, for the narrative piece it might be scary and creepy, and for the persuasive piece it might be compelling and convincing.

7. Share the results as a class. Put the cards on a ring and leave them in a common place for students to consult when they need ideas for writing.

Lesson Extension

During independent reading, have students look for instances where authors switch modes to support their purpose. For example, authors might tell a story to explain a concept, use facts to make a story more credible, or use anecdotes to make an argument more persuasive. Discuss discoveries with the class.

ACTIVITIES Conveying the Purpose

Mixing Modes

Ask students to select a draft from their writing folder, read it aloud to a partner, determine its primary purpose (or mode), and name the voice. Challenge students to expand their thinking by adding text to create a different voice. For example, if the piece is a story written in a lighthearted voice, ask students to incorporate facts to add seriousness and realism. If the piece is an essay, ask them to incorporate an anecdote to make a key point clear, which, in turn, may add energy. Remind students, however, to remain focused on their original purpose. Read their revisions aloud, and determine whether the voice is stronger.

Purposeful Art

With the class, make a list of different forms of visual and performing arts: photography, painting, dance, pottery, sculpture, printmaking, illustration, music, and so on. Then define art and talk about its purposes. Divide the class into groups and ask each group to pick three forms of art from the list and find examples of them by going online, going to the library, or consulting with the art or music teacher. Once they've gathered their examples, ask groups to write an explanation of the purpose for each one. For example, the purpose of Picasso's *Guernica* is to make a powerful antiwar statement, while the purpose of Munch's *The Scream* is to capture a painful, emotional moment. Display the examples. Collect the explanations and read them aloud, one at a time. Ask students to match each explanation to a piece of art, and discuss their choices.

Key Quality: Creating a Connection to the Audience

When students are composing a piece, regardless of the stage they're at in the writing process, they should never lose sight of who will be reading that piece when it's finished. In other words, they should always keep their audience in mind. When they make good decisions about what the reader needs to know and select appropriate words and phrases, voice emerges. Whether they're using formal or informal language, the King's English or street slang, writers connect to readers by speaking to them in a suitable voice. Use the following Think About to expand students' notions about creating a connection to the audience.

THINK ABOUT:

- Have I thought about the reader?
- Is this the right voice for the audience?
- Have I shown what matters most to me in this piece?
- Will the reader know how I think and feel about the topic?

WARM-UP   Creating a Connection to the Audience

Distribute copies of the Think About and ask students to give voice to the following rules for people visiting the zoo.

Don't throw food.

Don't put your hands or arms inside the enclosure.

Don't make loud noises.

Don't throw trash.

Don't take flash pictures.

When they're finished, ask students to share their work with one another. If you worked along with students, share your piece with them, too, or this one, if you prefer:

Humans: Pay Attention!

Since there are humans out there who don't seem to know how to behave at the zoo, here are some guidelines for you to follow. Most of you know these things (duh!), so thanks in advance. But for those of you who don't, listen up.

We have our own food. It's balanced so we have a completely nutritious diet. So, keep your peanuts and popcorn to yourself. We don't like it and it's not good for us. It's not all that good for you, either. Try some broccoli.

If you insist on sticking your arms and legs inside our enclosure, we might be tempted to bite or yank. It's possible, so if we were you, we wouldn't chance it. You are probably pretty attached to your hands and arms (get it?). Keep it that way.

What's with all those stupid noises? You don't sound like us and it's annoying when we're trying to eat, sleep, or go about our day. Keep your rude sounds to yourself. Or save them for your parents on the ride home in the car.

Nobody likes trash, and we're no exception. There are trash cans all over the zoo use them. When you throw your cups and junk food wrappers in our enclosure it makes a mess that somebody has to clean up. Are you volunteering?

Those bright lights hurt our eyes so please, don't take flash photos of us. Can you imagine what it would be like to have flashes going off every time you look up? It's not fun, so please don't do it. Buy a postcard from the gift shop. Their pictures are better than yours, anyway.

Sincerely,

The Bears: Grizzly, Brown, and Polar

FOCUS LESSON   Creating a Connection to the Audience

Voice is strong when the writer's desire to engage the reader is strong. When the writer puts his or her interest in the idea behind the work, while keeping the intended audience in mind, two things usually result: a strong reader-writer bond and a strong piece of writing. In this lesson, students write "Dear Abby"–style letters. They pose questions and write creative, informative responses, keeping the reader's needs firmly in mind.

Materials:
- examples of "Dear Abby"–style letters
- a list of advice topics (page 172)
- paper, pens, pencils

> **Advice Topics**
> - How to keep a brother or sister out of your room
> - How to avoid doing assigned chores
> - What to do when you accidentally break something that's off limits
> - How to hide a personal item, like a journal, from siblings
> - How to text in class without getting caught
> - How to prepare a parent for a less than perfect report card
> - How to have fun at the school dance when you can't dance
> - What to do when the zipper breaks on your favorite pair of pants
> - How to hide a bad haircut
> - What to do when visiting a friend's house for dinner and the meal is terrible
> - How to listen in on a friend's conversation without being noticed

What to Do:

1. Share the examples of "Dear Abby"–style letters and discuss the format: One person writes and poses a problem and the other writes back with a solution.

2. Give students the list of advice topics. Read and discuss each one. Add items to the list if students offer them.

3. As a class, decide on the name of the person dispensing advice. The most famous advice columnist was Abigail Van Buren, and as a result, the format is often referred to as "Dear Abby," but students can use a different person's name if they wish—it doesn't change the writing format.

4. Form groups of four or five students. Ask each group to pick one of the topics.

5. Have two to three members of each group assume the role of "advice seeker" and have the remaining members assume the role of "advice giver"—or "Abby." Then have them write their questions and responses, based on the topic they chose.

6. Separate the subgroups by positioning the advice seekers in front of a curtain or screen and the advice givers behind that curtain or screen. If the school has a public address system, secure permission for advice givers to use it to answer questions.

7. Invite advise seekers to read their questions and listen for the responses from the advice givers. Note the different answers the same question may generate.

8. Reverse roles, allowing students to select a different topic. Have them write out their questions and responses, and then read them aloud or broadcast them over the PA system.

9. Discuss how the responses to each question were tailored to address the needs of the person asking it. Ask advice givers how the voice in their writing might be different if the person in need was:
   - the president of the United States
   - a police officer
   - the principal
   - a stranger
   - a younger brother or sister
   - a parent
   - a best friend

Lesson Extension

Create a blog called "Dear Abby's Best Advice for Teens" and have students maintain it under your supervision. Have students post question on topics such as how to tell a friend you need some space, tips for persuading a teacher not to assign homework, and how to prepare parents for a progress report that's less than ideal. Then rotate volunteers weekly to play "Abby" and respond to questions.

ACTIVITIES   Creating a Connection to the Audience

Audience and Point of View

Your students won't develop strong voice if you, the teacher, are their only audience. They will focus more on pleasing you rather than capturing on paper what they truly think and feel. Help them build skills in voice by having them assume an unusual point of view about a typical writing topic. If students are writing about their state's history, for example, ask them to assume the role of the flag and brag to other flags about the state's history and how proud they are to represent it. Or if they're studying early explorers, let them assume the role of one of those explorers and document in a journal their observations about new lands they discovered and challenges they faced. When students write from a different perspective, they think about the audience for the writing and adjust their voice accordingly.

Voice Posters

Tell students that other teachers also teach the trait of voice and might want a set of posters to display in their classrooms that define the trait and help their students use voice in writing. Have them design a poster on voice. Explain that the poster should include the key qualities of the trait, which are explained on page 32, and be attractive and useful to middle school writers. Give each student adequate time to complete his or her poster, hang the finished products around the room, and let the class vote on the top five. Have students write a cover letter to teachers who might be interested, explaining that the posters are available and how to obtain them. Students might want to make copies and pass them out to other teachers at their school. They may wish to post an announcement on the intra-district information page that the posters are available and how to get them, or put them online to be downloaded by anyone. (Examples of student-created posters for each trait appear on page 304 and the CD that accompanies this book.)

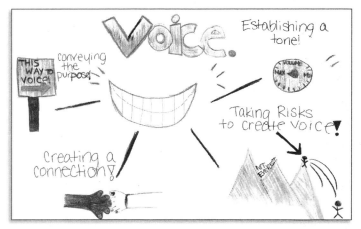

Key Quality: Taking Risks to Create Voice

Whether we're parachuting from a plane, purchasing stocks, or trying out a new writing lesson, risk taking requires confidence. We help student writers gain confidence by making it safe for them to experiment with new techniques—and to keep trying those techniques if they don't work the first time. It may take a leap of faith for middle schoolers to create pieces that are different from everyone else's. As you probably know all too well, fitting in is a huge priority for them. Being an individual isn't always cool. So your students may have to be coaxed into taking risks, but it's worth it. Trust me, you'll be stuck reading a lot of bland, unoriginal writing unless you target voice for instruction. Use the following Think About to expand students' notions about taking risks to create voice.

Reproducible
on CD

THINK ABOUT:

- Have I used words that are not ordinary?
- Is my writing interesting, fresh, and original?
- Have I tried to make my writing sound like me?
- Have I tried something different from what I've done before?

WARM-UP   Taking Risks to Create Voice

Successful businesspeople know how to sell their products and services. They may advertise through the mainstream media, but also through word of mouth, especially when it comes to the teen market. Web sites such as www.iliketotallyloveit.com are devoted to "social shopping," where opinions and comments about products are posted by teens for teens. Distribute copies of the Think About and have students rewrite the following review for breath mints so that middle school students will want to buy them immediately.

> These mints taste good. They don't stain your teeth. They come in a nice container.
> They don't cost too much, and they help with bad breath.

When students have finished writing, allow them to share their work with classmates. If you revised the advertisement along with students, share your work as well or, if you prefer, the following example.

> At last! Sweet Me mints are the answer to every budget- and breath-conscious teen's prayers. These yummy-tasting breath mints are conveniently packaged—you don't need a Ph.D. in physics to open the flat container that slips easily into a back pocket or purse. They are reasonably priced, unlike some of the other best-selling varieties, and they are calorie free. Ever had your friends tease you about having a green tongue and teeth because the dye in a breath mint stained them? This won't happen with Sweet Me. These sweet little mints get the job done using all natural ingredients. Gotta love that!

FOCUS LESSON   Taking Risks to Create Voice

Satire is a humorous way to call attention to people's actions or attitudes, using irony, sarcasm, or even ridicule. When a writer is careful with satire, making sure he doesn't inadvertently hurt anyone's feelings, he makes a powerful point and a lasting impression by changing behaviors and attitudes. Satire is a fun way to help students take writing risks. This lesson will get them started.

Materials:
- a list of how-to topics (below)
- paper, pens, pencils

> ### How-to Topics
> - How to feed your dog or cat
> - How to answer the phone
> - How to set up your MySpace profile
> - How to babysit
> - How to be the best at _____
> - How to grocery shop
> - How to clean your room
> - How to take out the trash
> - How to send a text message

What to Do:
1. Explain that satire is a lighthearted way to make fun of people's actions and attitudes, using irony, sarcasm, or ridicule to make a point.
2. Ask if any students have read David Macaulay's *Motel of the Mysteries* or Tina Ferraro's *Top Ten Uses for an Unworn Prom Dress*. If possible, obtain a copy of both books and share satirical passages with students. (Picture books by Jon Scieszka, such as *The Stinky Cheese Man and Other Fairly Stupid Tales*, *The True Story of the 3 Little Pigs*, *Math Curse*, *Science Verse*, and *Knucklehead*, are excellent models of satirical writing, too.)
3. Discuss situations in which satire might be useful, such as in a political debate, a birthday toast, or a disagreement with a friend.
4. Tell students that one way to apply satire in writing is to say something completely outrageous and unexpected. For example, if students were writing a review of the school lunch menu with the hope of improving it, they might suggest using leftover chicken nuggets as hockey pucks or burritos as doorstops.
5. Put students into pairs, show them the how-to topics, and ask them to choose a topic or come up with one of their own.

6. Discuss the style and tone of a typical how-to explanation—usually a matter-of-fact list of steps or procedures. For example, if the topic is how to grocery shop, the steps might include making a list, selecting items that are the best bargain, picking one special item as a treat, and spending as little time as possible shopping in order to get on to other errands or home to cook.

7. Help students brainstorm ways to approach the topic using satire by writing the opposite of what the reader expects. A satirical approach to some of the topics on the list might include the following:

   • If the writer's goal is to demonstrate good restaurant manners, he or she might write about using fine china and silver to feed a pet on a white tablecloth.

   • If the writer's goal is to demonstrate good phone etiquette, he or she might write about answering the phone by mumbling, yelling, or pretending not to hear the caller clearly.

   • If the writer's goal is to focus on safe driving behavior, he or she might write about smashing down a car's gas pedal, stomping on the brake, or crawling along slower than pedestrians.

8. Tell students they're going to write how-to manuals on their chosen topic, using satire to change their readers' current attitudes about or behaviors related to the topic. Remind students that satire is humorous, but respectful. They should take risks to entertain their readers, but not offend them.

9. Give students time to write their manuals. Encourage them to create illustrations and/or add pictures from magazines to add visual appeal.

10. Display manuals in the classroom. Invite students to read them and enjoy how writers take risks to create a satirical voice.

Lesson Extension

Over the next week, ask students to collect examples of satire they find in books, magazines, newspapers, TV shows, movies, podcasts, song lyrics, and conversations. Make a list of the sources and discuss the different approaches to satire. Ask students to rate the risk factor for each approach. A cartoon poking fun at a popular politician or important news event may be "low risk" because satire like that is so commonplace, but using satire in a confrontation between classmates may be "high risk" because feelings can be easily hurt.

ACTIVITIES   Taking Risks to Create Voice

Voice Signs

In Beaverton, Oregon, my hometown, you'll find traffic signs like these, which are part of a campaign to promote safe driving:

Show these photographs to students and ask if these signs contain more voice than traditional road signs. Most students will say they do. In fact, some students may feel they contain so much voice they're hazardous because they could distract rather than enlighten drivers. Have student pairs choose three traditional traffic signs (yield, school crossing, speed limit, for example) and design new ones with voice to get the attention of drivers. Students might be interested to check the Web site stopredlightrunning.com to see if their city is part of the campaign.

Finding Voice in the Least Likely Places

When you surf the Internet, you probably notice that creators of some Web sites are better than others at drawing you in and maintaining your interest. I've been surprised and delighted by some of the "voicey" sites I've run across, such as Howcast.com, HowStuffWorks.com, and theonion.com. The following excerpt is from the travel site Kayak.com:

Rome

Sure, you can get a taste of Roman life (at least the salacious parts) by turning on HBO ROME, but Kayak members aren't armchair travelers, so walk among the ruins of buildings where Julius Caesar lived, loved, and worked. Visit the Roman Forum, the political and economic center of Rome where Caesar might have watched Russell Crowe battle lions, tigers, and hotel employees, oh my! Finish the day by dining at Ristorante di Pancrazio, a wonderful Italian restaurant situated close to the spot Caesar was assassinated in 44 B. C. Order the Caesar salad.

Read this example to students and talk about taking risks to create voice. Then put them in small groups to research and write similar pieces about a city they have visited or dream of visiting such as Paris, Istanbul, or New York City.

Mentor Texts for Middle School: Voice

So many recent fiction and nonfiction books for middle schoolers scream "voice." The authors really know teens and the importance of offering material to keep them reading. Here is a pitifully short list of favorites (and, oh, how I agonized over making the cuts).

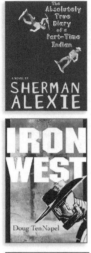

The Absolutely True Diary of a Part-Time Indian by Sherman Alexie (Little, Brown, 2007)

Writing with a sharp, biting sense of humor that draws on raw emotion, Alexie gives us a compelling main character, Arnold Spirit, or "Junior" as he's better know. Junior is guaranteed to be your students' new best friend by the time they turn the last page.

Iron West by Doug TenNapel (Image Comics, 2006)

Take the graphic comic format, set the story in the Old West circa 1898, add bloodthirsty, weapon-toting robots, and you're ready to rumble. This is a book with original voice from beginning to end.

Out of the Pocket by Bill Konigsberg (Dutton, 2008)

Bobby is outgoing, popular, and proud to be the star quarterback of the high school football team—that is, until he is "outed" by an unscrupulous student journalist. I recoiled at the reaction of a few of his teammates and rejoiced at the support of steadfast friends and family members. Bobby's voice needs to be heard by all students, gay and straight.

Final Thoughts

Voice may be the most misunderstood trait, but it may also be the most powerful. It transforms writing from ordinary to extraordinary. Establishing a tone, conveying the purpose, creating a connection to the audience, and taking risks to create voice are teachable skills that give students tools to use every time they write. But to write with voice, students must choose just the right words—words that add energy, enhance clarity, and captivate the reader. The next chapter focuses on just that.

CHAPTER 7

Word Choice:

In Search of the Perfect Union

Our founding fathers knew how to choose words. Before sending the Declaration of Independence to the Continental Congress for approval, Thomas Jefferson revised it 47 times, with feedback from John Adams and Benjamin Franklin. Congress made 39 word changes to the draft—or "draught," as it was called—before it was adopted on July 4, 1776. Members fought bitterly over the language because they knew only the perfect words in the perfect places would capture their vision of the perfect union—the United States of America.

Jefferson's "rough draught" of the
Declaration of Independence

As you can see, there are many word changes on this draft. For example, "sacred and undeniable" was changed to "self-evident" as religion in government was pushed aside in favor of secular authority. The phrase "to arbitrary power" shifted to "under absolute power" and finally to "under absolute Despotism" to challenge the British monarchy's abuse of authority over the colonists. "Fellow subjects" was shortened to "subjects" and finally to "citizens," signaling a new era of freedom. These are but a few of the small but significant word changes to a document that ultimately altered the course of history. To understand our history is to recognize the weight each word brings to the Declaration of Independence.

Your students may not be founding fathers, but they are writers who just might care about their work as much as the authors of the Declaration of Independence did, if we encourage them to use resources, play with language, read books with particularly powerful words, and experiment with words as they write.

Working a draft over, revising sentences until every word fits, is like soothing a distressed child. Indeed, those words are a petulant, attention-demanding brood. Imagine how our founding fathers struggled to calm them. Surely there were many tantrums along the way to the Declaration of Independence we know today. Expect them from your students as well, as they become caregivers of language the way our founding fathers were.

Traits of Writing: The Complete Guide for Middle School

The Word Choice Trait: A Definition

Words are like building blocks. By selecting nouns, verbs, adjectives, adverbs, and every other kind of word carefully, writers construct a message. If that message is solid, the words spark the imagination, create images, and connect—on many levels—with readers. Good word choice brings clarity to the writer's ideas. It also supports organization, since words signal sequence (*then, later, while*) and transitions (*however, furthermore, therefore*), creating a logical flow. It also creates voice, as William Zinsser asserts: "Good writing has an aliveness that keeps the reader reading from one paragraph to the next, and it's not a question of 'gimmicks' to personalize the author. It's a question of using the English language in a way that will achieve the greatest clarity and strength" (1976, pp. 5–6). Word choice is the workhorse trait: it's how writers transform the ordinary into the extraordinary, the mundane into the spectacular. It's how they use language to move, enlighten, and inspire.

When students write expository texts, encourage them to use everyday words as well as content-specific words. When they write narrative texts, encourage them to use lively, fresh, and colorful words that have the power to draw in the reader and create a sensory experience. And when they write persuasive texts, encourage them to use compelling and convincing words to elevate the reader to a new level of understanding about their topic. To accomplish all this, writers must embrace the key qualities of the word choice trait:

* Applying Strong Verbs
* Selecting Striking Words and Phrases
* Using Specific and Accurate Words
* Choosing Words That Deepen Meaning

> **"** The traits saved my writing career. Before I learned them I was a mess. For instance, I didn't know how to use words accurately. I always thought you could just throw in anything to fill up space. **"**
>
> —Destiny, grade 8

Why Students Struggle With Word Choice

Middle schoolers know that, in our culture, words rule. They see the influence of words in sales and marketing. They see how words are used to stereotype characters in movies or on TV. They are consumers of both good texts, such as high-quality literature and well-written magazine articles, and not-so-great texts, such as instant messages and poorly crafted newspaper articles or editorials. That means they're ripe to be taught what works, what doesn't, and why. One of our most important responsibilities as writing teachers is to show them how to power up their word choice—even if it is hard work. Here are some reasons choosing words can be difficult for them.

They Are Immersed in Nonstandard English

Wherever students go—to the mall, to the movies, to a friend's house to watch TV or listen to the radio—they hear and see nonstandard English. In fact, they are deluged by it. Few worry about language accuracy when writing notes or sending e-mails. They speak in nonstandard English, too. When they're talking on the phone or hanging out with classmates, you can bet they are not self-checking for subject-verb agreement and dangling participles.

Take text messaging, for example—or "texting" as it's more commonly known. When students text, they write quickly, very quickly, using the first words that come to mind. They also use shorthand: symbols and partial words that work perfectly well for communicating with friends. And no matter how much we adults fuss about the negative impact of texting on traditional writing, even Don Quixote wouldn't be foolish enough to challenge that windmill. It's here to stay, make no mistake about it. And it can't be all bad—after all, they *are* writing.

Establish boundaries: texting is okay for personal communication outside of school, but for writing in school, using standard English is standard practice. After all, standard English is the content that students study and learn in the English classroom. There may be legitimate circumstances where nonstandard English is acceptable, for example, if you assign a format that lends itself to nonstandard English, such as notes, e-mails, or realistic fiction. But otherwise, final papers should always adhere to standard English—which is, after all, required for English and other subject areas.

Although texting is not the best way for students to learn how to use words well, it does motivate them to write and provides a logical starting point for talking about the differences between standard and nonstandard English and the appropriate places for each of them. Set your boundaries, and then ask students to show you how they communicate with words and symbols when they text. Their knowledge of words may surprise you.

They Think Longer Is Better

When middle school students have trouble coming up with the right words while drafting and revising, they tend to turn to the thesaurus to find the longest word, not the best word. This happens for a number of reasons. First, many of them have been told by teachers that one of the keys to success on the state writing assessment, as well as on the SAT and ACT exams that loom not too far in their future, is to use big words. Second, many of them have endured years of memorizing prefabricated vocabulary lists in almost every subject. But memorizing lists doesn't improve students' writing skills. Reading and writing improve writing skills. So throw away the lists and put books in their hands— books by Sandra Cisneros, Walter Dean Meyers, and Gary Soto. Harper Lee, my favorite author of all time, is a true wordsmith. These writers know that it isn't the length of the word that makes all the difference—it's the rightness of the word. As students marinate in the beautiful language of writers like these, they begin imitating them—and making their way, word by word, to a bigger vocabulary.

Our goal should be to help writers help the reader make meaning—not to encourage them to cram as many big words as possible into a piece. They should follow the good advice of Strunk and White: "The surest way to arouse and hold the reader's attention is by being specific, definite, and concrete" (2000, p. 21). They should draw upon words they know and can use well. An eighth-grade student writing about friendship for the Oregon state assessment knew this when he capped off his sample with this: "P.S. When we were told to write this they told us to 'use the biggest, most complexed words' we could. That's not the way I talk, and shurely not the way I would describe friendship. So I wrote my true feelings and hope that's what you grade and not the way we use the complicated words." Thank you.

They Think They've Nailed It the First Time

First drafts are not about good word choice. They are about getting the idea down so the writer has something to revise. Many tired, overused words such as *good*, *nice*, and *very* abound in student writing because students don't understand that concept. But to get a piece of writing right, students have to revise for the just-right words. They have to try and try again for language that deepens meaning. They have to strive to hear the music of the words. First drafts are not the place for such work.

In his memoir, *On Writing*, Stephen King makes this point clear. He uses adverbs as an example, explaining that although they may abound in first drafts, they should be as scarce as hen's teeth in final products. In fact, he goes so far as to say, "The road to hell is paved with adverbs….They're like dandelions. If you have one on your lawn, it looks pretty and unique. If you fail to root it out, however, you find five the next day. . . fifty the day after that. . . and then, my brothers and sisters, your lawn is *totally*, *completely*, and *profligately* covered with dandelions. By then you see them for the weeds they really are, but by then it's—*GASP!!*—too late" (2000, p. 118).

He's got a point. On a first draft, a student might write, "She slowly walked into the room." But on a second or third pass, she would hopefully chose a more descriptive verb, such as *ambled*, *strolled*, or *meandered*, and ditch the adverb altogether. It may not be what students want to hear, but no writer nails it in the first draft—ever. Ask Thomas Jefferson.

Assessing Student Work for Word Choice

The following sixth-grade papers represent a wide range of skills in the word choice trait. Review the scoring guide on page 185, read each paper carefully, assess the paper for the word choice trait by following the steps on pages 50–51 under "Assessing Writing Using the Trait Scoring Guides," and then read my assessment to see if we agree. Use your own students' writing for further practice.

The papers were all written in the narrative mode, in response to the prompt "Tell about a time you'll always remember." I chose papers written at the same grade level, in the same mode, and to the same prompt so you can focus on the issue at hand, word choice, without other factors serving as distractions. But keep in mind, it's critical for students to develop skills in word choice regardless of the grade they're in, the mode they choose, or the prompt they're given. Their writing should contain well-chosen words all the time. Even though I focus on word choice, I've scored the papers in all the traits (except presentation, since the papers are typeset) in case you need additional samples to practice scoring or use in your instruction.

Scoring Guide: Word Choice

The specific vocabulary the writer uses to convey meaning and enlighten the reader.

Reproducible
on **CD**

6 · **HIGH**

EXCEPTIONAL

A. **Applying Strong Verbs:** The writer uses many "action words," giving the piece punch and pizzazz. He or she has stretched to find lively verbs that add energy to the piece.

B. **Selecting Striking Words and Phrases:** The writer uses many finely honed words and phrases. His or her creative and effective use of literary techniques such as alliteration, simile, and metaphor makes the piece a pleasure to read.

C. **Using Specific and Accurate Words:** The writer uses words with precision. He or she selects words the reader needs to fully understand the message. The writer chooses nouns, adjectives, adverbs, and so forth that create clarity and bring the topic to life.

D. **Choosing Words That Deepen Meaning:** The writer uses words to capture the reader's imagination and enhance the piece's meaning. There is a deliberate attempt to choose the best word over the first word that comes to mind.

5

STRONG

4 · **MIDDLE**

REFINING

A. **Applying Strong Verbs:** The writer uses the passive voice quite a bit and includes few "action words" to give the piece energy.

B. **Selecting Striking Words and Phrases:** The writer provides little evidence that he or she has stretched for the best words or phrases. He or she may have attempted to use literary techniques, but they are clichés for the most part.

C. **Using Specific and Accurate Words:** The writer presents specific and accurate words, except for those related to sophisticated and/or content-related topics. Technical or irrelevant jargon is off-putting to the reader. The words rarely capture the reader's imagination.

D. **Choosing Words That Deepen Meaning:** The writer fills the piece with unoriginal language rather than language that results from careful revision. The words communicate the basic idea, but they are ordinary and uninspired.

3

DEVELOPING

2 · **LOW**

EMERGING

A. **Applying Strong Verbs:** The writer makes no attempt at selecting verbs with energy. The passive voice dominates the piece.

B. **Selecting Striking Words and Phrases:** The writer uses words that are repetitive, vague, and/or unimaginative. Limited meaning comes through because the words are so lifeless.

C. **Using Specific and Accurate Words:** The writer misuses words, making it difficult to understand what he or she is conveying. Or he or she uses words that are so technical, inappropriate, or irrelevant the average reader can hardly understand what he or she is saying.

D. **Choosing Words That Deepen Meaning:** The writer uses many words and phrases that simply do not work. Little meaning comes through because the language is so imprecise and distracting.

1

RUDIMENTARY

One time

One time I got into a fight with my two little brothers 'cuz they make me so mad. They mess around in my bed and break and ruin my stuff. how would they like it if I took all there stuff is what I told them? Then I get them back some how like stolen something valubale to them. then my mom got mad and then my dad got mad because I did that. Its not easy being the bigger brother because I have better stuff than they do like games and other things. We had a fight for about a week. But we arn't mad any more.

Time to Assess for Word Choice

This writer could have provided fascinating insights about his family. Instead, he provides an unoriginal, uninteresting description containing uninspired words and phrases. The piece is an excellent example of a first draft that could, over time, evolve as the writer adds adjectives and nouns that create a picture of his family members, along with verbs that enliven the whole piece.

Word Choice	
Score **1: Rudimentary**	
Range	**Low**

Other Traits	
Ideas	2
Organization	2
Voice	2
Sentence Fluency	2
Conventions	2

A Applying Strong Verbs

The writer makes no attempt at selecting verbs with energy. The passive voice dominates the piece.

> *Even though this is a short piece, the lack of strong verbs is noticeable. Instead of "We had a fight for about a week," the writer could have written, "We fought for a week." Or even better, he could've written, "We ripped and tore into each other for a week."*

B Selecting Striking Words and Phrases

The writer uses words that are repetitive, vague, and/or unimaginative. Limited meaning comes through because the words are so lifeless.

> *Repeating "stuff" three times in a piece this short is not good word choice. The lack of striking words and phrases is problematic because it leaves the reader without a clear picture of what the writer is trying to say.*

C Using Specific and Accurate Words

The writer misuses words, making it difficult to understand what he or she is conveying. Or he or she uses words that are so technical, inappropriate, or irrelevant the average reader can hardly understand what he or she is saying.

> *Sentences such as "Then I get them back some how like stolen something valuable to them" are confusing and force the reader to go back and figure out what the writer means. Reading this sentence aloud would help the writer recognize words that aren't working.*

D Choosing Words That Deepen Meaning

The writer uses many words and phrases that simply do not work. Little meaning comes through because the language is so imprecise and distracting.

> *The words are so common and indistinct ("stuff" and "mad"), the reader gets, at best, a fuzzy picture of the writer's intention for writing the piece in the first place.*

We Won

I couldn't imagine what it would be like if we won this baseball game, it would be wonderful. I would go insane! I would be so happy for the rest of my life because we won. If we just keep our eye on the ball we will probably hit it every time. I hope we keep getting home runs.

We had a big game and our last, when we went to Canada. My dad went up to hit the ball. It was a winning home run. That was the ball that won the game for us. We won the game, finally!

We finally won we have never won a game before, all the years going there. I think we don't practice enough. But that year we did. We are there for one weekend and spending time with our family. I love spending time with my family that I don't see that much.

After the last game we go to a party. If you win the game you can say this is the party for winning. It felt so good to say that to people. I love going to Canada. I will never forget that year we won.

Time to Assess for Word Choice

"Win," "winning," and "won" are repeated so many times in this piece, I found myself scanning ahead to brace myself for their next appearance. When one word keeps popping up like a bad habit, it disrupts the piece's flow. It drags the piece down on the word choice scale.

Word Choice	
Score	**2: Emerging**
Range	**Low**

Other Traits	
Ideas	2
Organization	2
Voice	3
Sentence Fluency	2
Conventions	4

 A Applying Strong Verbs

The writer makes no attempt at selecting verbs with energy. The passive voice dominates the piece.

A few strong verbs, including forms of "to win," dot the piece. But the writer relies too heavily on forms of "to be."

B Selecting Striking Words and Phrases

The writer uses words that are repetitive, vague, and/or unimaginative. Limited meaning comes through because the words are so lifeless.

The repetitiveness of forms of "to win" is so rampant that the reader could miss passages such as "keep our eye on the ball" and "I would go insane." Although these phrases are not all that original, they are stronger than "win," "won," and "winning."

C Using Specific and Accurate Words

The writer misuses words, making it difficult to understand what he or she is conveying. Or he or she uses words that are so technical, inappropriate, or irrelevant the average reader can hardly understand what he or she is saying.

The writer does not misuse words. Rather, he misses an opportunity to use them well. For the most part, his words are general and imprecise. If he didn't use "win," "won," and "winning" so frequently, his piece would undoubtedly receive a higher score in word choice. This is a good piece to save in the writing folder for revision work later.

 D Choosing Words That Deepen Meaning

The writer uses many words and phrases that simply do not work. Little meaning comes through because the language is so imprecise and distracting.

With the exception of a couple of strong moments, especially at the beginning, the piece reads like a first draft. The writer seems to have chosen the first words that came to mind, rather than choosing the best words. As a result, clarity suffers.

My Very Best Friend!

My best friend was one who was kind. She was nice, willing to share, and always came up with good ideas. My best friend from my old house was the greatest friend I've ever had. We would play together almost everday and would see each other at school.

Her grandmother lived very close and we would always go over her house for lunch. We'd watch movies too! We enjoyed the same things, so her grandmother did our hair the same. I think one of the reasons that we were best friends was because our families got along so well.

Since we like the same things we would always agree on one another's ideas. Like riding bikes, playing on the playground, and watching movies. The great things was our older sister's were best friends. So where ever she went, the younger sisters (us) would get to tag along!

I also hope to see my best friend again! I also hope that you have learned a little about my best friend. I wonder how many kids have good best friends that treat them with respect. Do you have a best friend?

Time to Assess for Word Choice

There's not one moment of pizzazz in this piece. Not one place to point to and say, "There! That's it—a beautiful turn of phrase." Strong, striking, and specific words are cast aside in favor of more ordinary ones. As a result, it's not a memorable piece, which is too bad because the writer probably cares about her idea and, most likely, has some delightful, one-of-a-kind details to support it that would make the piece strong.

Word Choice	
Score	**3: Developing**
Range	**Middle**

Other Traits	
Ideas	3
Organization	3
Voice	3
Sentence Fluency	3
Conventions	3

A Applying Strong Verbs

The writer uses the passive voice quite a bit and includes few "action words" to give the piece energy.

"Hope," "wonder," "ride," and "agree" are about as good as it gets in this piece. These verbs combined with even less active ones create a flat tone.

B Selecting Striking Words and Phrases

The writer provides little evidence that he or she has stretched for the best words or phrases. He or she may have attempted literary techniques, but they are clichés for the most part.

The words and phrases in this piece are anything but striking. Though the writer gives examples of how she spends time with her friend, she does not explain them in a way that sets them apart from anyone else's experiences with a friend.

C Using Specific and Accurate Words

The writer presents specific and accurate words, except for those related to sophisticated and/or content-related topics. Technical or irrelevant jargon is off-putting to the reader. The words rarely capture the reader's imagination.

For the most part, the words are accurate, but not specific: "same things," "great things," "great friend," and "best friend." As a result, the writer doesn't give the reader enough information to create a vivid mental image of the friendship—and, after all, that's the writer's job.

D Choosing Words That Deepen Meaning

The writer fills the piece with unoriginal language rather than language that results from careful revision. The words communicate the basic idea, but they are ordinary and uninspired.

This descriptor explains this paper perfectly. The language is all too commonplace. The words are accurate, but not original. Revising with special attention to the words would make a big difference.

Dance Competition

I can remember the cheering crowd, the frowning judges and the loud music. DANCE COMPETITION!!! Starting from years 9-12, I have been doing dance competition at my dance school, until that day I only missed one dance competition. Those wonderful times makes my stomach all bubbly. We were kinda the worst team and kept on getting bad scores. But that never kept us down. Here is my experience.

We all woke up complaining and kicking our feet. On the way to the dance location, we slept hazely in the car. But our energy came flashing back once we saw our dance team. When we started getting ready, our parents dashed on our eye shadow, smoothed on some lipstick, and bopped us with the blusher. Then, the painful hairstyles. They twisted our hair into a tight bun and pinned in some clips that felt like they were gonna go straight into our heads. Then, swish, they sprayed hair spray all over our heads; it made our heads a hard, smooth, plateau. Oh oh, here comes the scratchy, tight costume. Now we are ready for the performance.

We all walked quietly backstage and started stretching. We watched the team before us and started wondering, "Oh my gosh, they are so superb, could we beat them," it was practically impossible. The music suddenly jerked to an end. The dancers did a leap off the stage. They gave the stage to us. We felt like going back to the dressing room and hiding. But too late, we have been pushed to the stage. We all took our poses. We suddenly heard our music play, the lights went up, and all we could do was dance. A kick and a leap here, a turn and a fling there. The stage got hot and the fun had arrived. That is, until we turned around and the judges were right there, frowning, and writing notes. Their look made us want to jump and run. Sweat started to run from our pores and the end finally came. We ran off the stage and into the dressing room, with the judges frowns still clogged in our minds.

More makeup, dash, more hairstyles, slash, then costumes, bam! It's like we were Barbies for our parents. We were ready for a new dance all over again. We repeated this for about 8 times. Then, late at night, it was time for the awards. We were thinking we actually had a chance of getting a good score. The judges called us up, and as usual, we had a bad/sorta ok score. We got silver (in competition, that's sort of bad). We all went home with broken hearts and churned stomachs. By the next day we felt confident and found out why we got those scores: everything from un-pointed feet to no smiles and even bad hand position.

Weird huh, that it never was a bad experience. Most of what I wrote here seems repulsive but it is an admirable, fun thing to do. After 4 years of getting used to it, it's gonna be tougher living without it. I can probably start again next year. Who knows, my dancing and techniques might become better!

Time to Assess for Word Choice

I commend this writer for trying to use striking, specific, and accurate words, but she is off in many places. As I read this piece, I could almost picture the writer scratching out words in favor of bigger or more interesting ones. If she had stopped to read her draft back to herself, she might have caught at least a few of the more problematic words. That said, she knows to avoid settling for the first word that comes to mind, and that's an important skill.

Word Choice	
Score	**4: Refining**
Range	**Middle**

Other Traits	
Ideas	5
Organization	5
Voice	5
Sentence Fluency	4
Conventions	4

A ## Applying Strong Verbs

The writer uses the passive voice quite a bit and includes few "action words" to give the piece energy.

> *There are many forms of "to be" in this piece, such as "was" and "were." But there are many more strong verbs and verb phrases, such as "swish," "frowned," "clogged," "slept hazely," "flashing back," "dashed on eye shadow," and, my favorite, "bopped us with the blusher," which propel the piece past the midpoint in word choice.*

B ## Selecting Striking Words and Phrases

The writer provides little evidence that he or she has stretched for the best words or phrases. He or she may have attempted literary techniques, but they are clichés for the most part.

> *Some passages are awkward and could use revision, such as "We were kinda the worst team," but not many.*

C ## Using Specific and Accurate Words

The writer presents specific and accurate words, except for those related to sophisticated and/or content-related topics. Technical or irrelevant jargon is off-putting to the reader. The words rarely capture the reader's imagination.

> *The words are specific and accurate, but often awkwardly expressed—for example, "Our energy came flashing back" and "Most of what I wrote here seems repulsive but it is an admirable, fun thing to do." The writer is definitely on the right track, but needs to rethink how she's using words.*

D ## Choosing Words That Deepen Meaning

The writer fills the piece with unoriginal language rather than language that results from careful revision. The words communicate the basic idea, but they are ordinary and uninspired.

> *The words in this piece are like wild horses. They are a sight to behold—but they must be reined in and tamed to be useful.*

Darius

I first knew about Darius in February of 1993. I personally was not too sure if I was going to like him or not, my brother on the other hand, was so excited to get to meet him. For me, this meant two brothers and not one sister. How was I going to handle being in the middle of two boys?

He finally came into this world on May 17, 1993, named Darius Nathan Elmore, and my baby brother. He had dark brown curly hair, deep brown eyes, and fair skin. I was actually excited about him, and fought with my older brother, Demetrius, over who got to hold him first. I knew that this was the beginning of what would be a close brother-sister relationship.

As Darius grew up, the curly hair got cut off, skin got darker, front two teeth fell out, and the relationship began to grow. It seems that when those teeth fell out he began to know everything. Then again, he was five, aren't they always right? Like when Darius and my mom would go shopping for new shoes, they would get home and he would be so excited just to put them on. He would put them on, go to the opposite side end of the hallway, and run as fast as he could down it. Darius, believing with all his little heart that he was so much faster in those new shoes. We would all just laugh, and he would swear that now he could beat anyone in a race. We just let him think that, because we knew if we were to argue about it, we would not win the fight.

Darius was also a very sore loser, just like Demetrius neither one of them liked me to beat them, probably because of the fact that I am a girl. One time while visiting our grandparents, when Darius was probably six or seven, we decided to ride our bikes up the street to play on the playground at the elementary school. On the way back, the boys challenged me to a race. I was all for it, I knew I could beat these boys. On your mark, get set, go, and we were off! I was in the lead, peddling as fast as my feet could go. Next thing I knew my bike began to wobble, I looked back only to see Darius ramming his bike tire into the back of mine with a big grin, and a look of determination. I eventually ended up on the ground eating gravel, as he rode off quickly to his victory.

Now that he's almost twelve, standing 5'5, weighing 130 lbs, he has short hair that is soft in texture and thick that would not curl if his life depended on it, and is also very light brown. Darius still has the same deep brown eyes, and his skin is as fair as when he was little. He has started to grow some facial hair, voice has began to crack, and has that teenage mentality, the one where hes never wrong, and anything he says, goes. Now instead of shoes making him faster, when he come back from lifting weights, he claims his muscles have gotten bigger, and he is already stronger. When we tell him it is not possible, he doesn't want to hear it, because he knows what he's talking about, and its his body and he can tell.

Darius has also got all these little sayings that he's picked up from different people; "that's a neck", and "you are too bummy", are the two that you can hear him say on a daily basis. I don't know where he got it from, but every time he hears someone say something that is stupid to him, or doesn't make sense, he will quickly say, "that's a neck", and slap them on the back of the neck, and laugh. The saying "you are too bummy", is one I personally hear quite frequently. If I don't want to do what he wants when he wants, like take him to a friends house, he'll get angry and say "you are too bummy", I guess this is supposed to bother me, and maybe it's supposed to change my mind.

Even though there are some things about Darius that can really make me mad, he also knows how to put a smile on my face, when things just do not seem to be going right. We talk to each other about things that we don't want to talk to our parents about, we sit and cry together as we talk about the death of our Demetrius, and most of all we get on each other's nerves, but isn't that what siblings are for? From that day in February of 1993, when I first heard about him, and was upset because I was wishing for a sister, to now, I wouldn't trade him for anything or anybody in this world. Darius is my little brother—a rascal, no doubt, but loveable, too.

Time to Assess for Word Choice

This writer knows words. She doesn't fall into the "thesaurus trap," favoring instead to use everyday words with thought and care. Her variety of nouns and verbs, adjectives, and adverbs makes the ordinary extraordinary: "I eventually ended up on the ground eating gravel, as he rode off quickly to his victory," "He has short hair that is soft in texture and thick that would not curl if his life depended on it," "Darius is my little brother—a rascal, no doubt, but loveable, too." There's much to admire about this piece. That said, the word choices in first two paragraphs aren't quite as good as those in the third, making them ripe for revision.

Word Choice	
Score	**5: Strong**
Range	**High**

Other Traits	
Ideas	6
Organization	6
Voice	6
Sentence Fluency	3
Conventions	5

A Applying Strong Verbs

The writer uses many "action words," giving the piece punch and pizzazz. He or she has stretched to find lively verbs that add energy to the piece.

There are plenty of strong verbs in this piece, but also weaker ones such as "was" and "has." Revising those words would add energy to the piece and help to pop it up a level on the word choice scale.

B Selecting Striking Words and Phrases

The writer uses many finely honed words and phrases. His or her creative and effective use of literary techniques such as alliteration, simile, and metaphor makes the piece a pleasure to read.

This writer's genuine affection for her brother shines through. Her personal insights and examples, as well as her use of figurative language, bring the siblings' strong relationship to life. The piece's biggest problem is sentence fluency. As the writer revises for that trait, I suspect she will also hone the piece's words and phrases even more.

C Using Specific and Accurate Words

The writer uses words with precision. He or she selects words the reader needs to fully understand the message. The writer chooses nouns, adjectives, adverbs, and so forth that create clarity and bring the topic to life.

I could pick Darius out of a group of children because his sister's description of him is so precise. This is true not only of Darius's physical characteristics, but also of his temperament. This piece is a loving portrait—one that both brother and sister will undoubtedly cherish for years to come.

D Choosing Words That Deepen Meaning

The writer uses words to capture the reader's imagination and enhance the piece's meaning. There is a deliberate attempt to choose the best word over the first word that comes to mind.

Although I felt a bit bogged down while reading the beginning of this piece, I was totally engaged by the time I finished. The words began to sing in the third paragraph, where, I suspect, the writer relaxed and lost herself in her idea. There's so much right about the words in this piece. With just a little more work, it will likely get the highest score.

The Savior of the Chickens

A steel daisy. That is the best image to describe my grandma, Louise J. She was the strongest women I ever met, yet there was surprising gentleness in her. So many of the rich and wonderful memories in my life center on her.

Of course she had to be strong, giving birth to five boys, almost six (one was still born), and the youngest a girl Renee. And my four uncles, Gary, Eddie, Casey, and Mike, and not to mention my dad, Jerry, were a hand full, always getting into fights with each other, and others at school. Just imagine the noise and craziness with five boys in a house. She seemed to be fearless and have a quality that said she had "been there and done that." Once her leg was pinned between two trucks and she lay there forever until they could get her out. Then, she endured a ten-hour operation to insert a metal plate put in her leg, leaving a nasty scar. I think that is why she would never be seen in anything but blue jeans. She wasn't vain, but I think the scar was pretty ugly.

Something very few people can say they have experienced is what she called "the owl incident." She raised chickens for eggs, and one night she heard the chickens just going bezerk! So she rushed out to the chicken coop and found an owl swooping around the chickens trying to snatch one. Without skipping a beat my grandma grabbed a board and started beating the holy "poo" out of the owl until it stopped moving. That's how it always was with Louise J. She grabbed life and took it head-on with full force.

There was a sweet gentleness about her, too. Everyday she cooked a huge breakfast and then a huge dinner. One of her specialties was homemade chicken noodle soup, with noodles made from scratch. This is one of my best memories of her. I will never forget the image of her standing in the kitchen kneading the dough for the noodles, her bent, knotted hands pushing love into it with each movement even though it gave her pain due to her arthritis. Then she cut the flat dough into thin strips and cooked them. And oh, they tasted like nothing else on this earth while they were still steaming hot and served at dinner. She was the best at everything in the kitchen. She made jellies and jam: peach with just a dash of cinnamon picked fresh from the orchard next to the barn, wild blackberry and raspberry from bushes around the farm, and strawberry from her garden—seedless because of her dentures.

Her gentle side was never more evident, though, than when she visited her baby boy in the cemetery. She always brought him flowers, fresh cut from around her garden. She loved everyone in her family but we all knew she had a soft spot in that tough exterior for her lost child.

Everyone was sad to see her go. The worst part of her heart problem, towards the end, was the once active and energetic little, old woman was confined to a wheelchair, unable to cook, garden, or even care for herself. That amazing woman who cared for everyone else had to be cared for herself at the end. But she lived her life to the fullest and though no one wanted to see her go it was what was best, now she has no pain. She had the perfect balance of strength and sensitivity and I hope I am half the woman she was one day.

Time to Assess for Word Choice

This rare and remarkable piece brought me to tears. Sophisticated language and finely crafted details stand out from beginning to end. This writer knows her subject. By capturing memories so carefully, she welcomes us to life with her grandmother. My favorite line is "I will never forget the image of her standing in the kitchen kneading the dough for the noodles, her bent, knotted hands pushing love into it." "Pushing love"—what a lovely thought.

Word Choice	
Score	**6: Exceptional**
Range	**High**

Other Traits	
Ideas	6
Organization	6
Voice	6
Sentence Fluency	5
Conventions	6

A Applying Strong Verbs

The writer uses many "action words," giving the piece punch and pizzazz. He or she has stretched to find lively verbs that add energy to the piece.

Of word choice's four key qualities, the writer needs to work on this one the most. Another pass to add strong verbs would improve the piece, even though it already contains many good ones, such as "raised, "rushed," "kneading," "tasted," and "confined."

B Selecting Striking Words and Phrases

The writer uses many finely honed words and phrases. His or her creative and effective use of literary techniques such as alliteration, simile, and metaphor makes the piece a pleasure to read.

Filled to the brim with striking words and phrases, this piece is a standout. The writer writes from the heart, offering vivid descriptions such as "grabbed life and took it head-on with full force" and "soft spot in that tough exterior."

C Using Specific and Accurate Words

The writer uses words with precision. He or she selects words the reader needs to fully understand the message. The writer chooses nouns, adjectives, adverbs, and so forth that create clarity and bring the topic to life.

Using the right word in the right place is one of the secrets of good word choice. And, without a doubt, this writer is in on that secret. She takes us on a hilarious romp (catching the owl in the chicken coop) and a tragic one (leaving flowers at the baby's grave). She knows how to put the reader in a specific time and place. I could almost taste that jam: "peach with just a dash of cinnamon picked fresh from the orchard next to the barn."

D Choosing Words That Deepen Meaning

The writer uses words to capture the reader's imagination and enhance the piece's meaning. There is a deliberate attempt to choose the best word over the first word that comes to mind.

The piece gave me a glimpse into the life of a remarkable woman. It's a true tribute, one I'm sure Louise J. herself would have cherished had she lived to read it. There is wordsmithery at work here. Couldn't you smell those jams and jellies? Didn't you laugh out loud at the phrase "holy poo"? Didn't you ache over Louise's loss of mobility at the end of her active life? This is word choice at its finest.

Conference Comments

If the piece scores high in word choice, 5 or 6, say something like:

> "Thank you for carefully choosing <u>words</u> to describe your brother. I hope you let him read your piece—I'm sure he'd enjoy it. Your use of verbs is particularly effective in the middle and end. To strengthen your piece, you could replace verbs in the opening two paragraphs with action <u>words</u> as strong as those in subsequent paragraphs."

> "You use <u>words</u> beautifully to describe your grandmother. I love how you write about both funny and serious times you had together, using precise <u>words</u> to create clear pictures in my mind. I feel like I know your grandmother. Thank you."

If the piece scores in the middle, a 3 or 4, say something like:

> "There are so many good things about this piece. In your next draft, will you use <u>words</u> and phrases that are as special to you as your friend is? Try for some that you've never used before."

> "Your love of <u>words</u> really shows! You've reached for <u>words</u> that have sparkle and energy. Good for you. I'd like to help you use them with more accuracy, however. Let's pick one paragraph and work on its <u>words</u> together."

If the piece scores low, a 1 or 2, say something like:

> "I can see your brother really gets on your nerves. Would you share more details about that in your next draft? Try adding some descriptive <u>words</u> to show how he makes you feel and using strong verbs to create action. As you revise, read your piece aloud to hear how the <u>words</u> sound. That always helps me."

> "Your dad sounds like quite a baseball player. In your next draft, you might want to focus on the moment he hit the home run. I know you'll come up with many interesting <u>words</u> to describe that event. What did you hear? What did you see? Your <u>words</u> need to be as exciting as the home run hit itself."

Teaching Writing With the Word Choice Trait

Teaching about words is standard practice in English classrooms. But instead of giving students simple work sheets and canned vocabulary lists, have them read great literature, collect interesting words, and start noticing how words are used (and abused) in the world around us. There's really no end to the possibilities. This trait should bring energy and life, humor and reflection, joy and passion to your classroom. To make your teaching more manageable, I've organized the remainder of this chapter into sections that correspond to word choice's key qualities:

* Applying Strong Verbs

* Selecting Striking Words and Phrases

* Using Specific and Accurate Words

* Choosing Words That Deepen Meaning

Within each section, you'll find a warm-up exercise, a focus lesson, and two activities, as well as a Think About—a list of important questions students should ask themselves as they choose words for their writing. (The key qualities and Think Abouts are also included on the CD that accompanies this book.)

> **66** I never figured reading had anything to do with writing. But now I read everything I can get my hands on about science and the environment. (I love these subjects!) Reading makes it easier to think of words to write. **99**
>
> —Josh, grade 6

Key Quality: Applying Strong Verbs

Verbs power the sentence. To prove it, take a look at these two sentences:

1. When Jared saw the skunk in his living room, he went up the stairs and went under his bed.

2. When Jared spotted the skunk in his living room, he darted up the stairs and disappeared under his bed.

The first one is dull because of its weak verbs—"saw" and "went." The second is more compelling because of its strong ones—"spotted," "darted," and "disappeared." Use the following Think About to expand students' notions about applying strong verbs.

THINK ABOUT:

- Have I used action words?
- Did I stretch to get a better word—*scurry* rather than *run*?
- Do my verbs give my writing punch and pizzazz?
- Did I avoid *is, am, are, was, were, be, being,* and *been* whenever I could?

WARM-UP   Applying Strong Verbs

Distribute copies of the Think About and ask students to rewrite the following paragraph, using stronger, more powerful verbs to give it more energy.

> I am going to the track meet later today. It's going to be fun. My brother is going to be running the 200-meter race. It is a sprint. Sprints are hard because you have to run so fast. He should win.

Once students have revised the paragraph, ask them to share it with a partner, compare verbs, and revise further, as needed. Encourage volunteers to read their new paragraphs to the class, while other students record the strongest verbs. After everyone has had a chance to read, make a list of the most energetic verbs on the board for all to see. Compare the new verbs with those in the original paragraph and discuss. Share the following sample revision, if you wish, and add its verbs to the class list.

> The track meet <u>begins</u> at 4:00 today. My brother <u>trained</u> for months, <u>sprinting</u> up and down the field dozens of times a day, <u>developing</u> the muscles in his legs that will <u>enable</u> him to <u>explode</u> with speed and, hopefully, <u>win</u> the 200-meter race. "<u>Run</u>, Devon, <u>run</u>," I'll <u>shout</u> from the stands. I <u>pray</u> he <u>wins</u>.

FOCUS LESSON   Applying Strong Verbs

In this three-part lesson, students examine the lyrics to a classic rock-and-roll song, "Roll Over Beethoven" by Chuck Berry, and a more contemporary pop tune, "Unwritten" by Natasha Bedingfield, paying special attention to both writers' extraordinary use of verbs. From there, they create "Verbs With Vim, Vigor, and Verve" posters in small groups to consult when writing.

Materials:

- the songs "Roll Over Beethoven" and "Unwritten," purchased on CD or downloaded from a music Web site, along with accompanying lyrics
- posterboard
- markers, pens, pencils
- a thesaurus or synonym finder
- computer and speakers

What to Do:

Part 1

1. Distribute copies of the lyrics to "Roll Over Beethoven" and allow time for students to read them silently.
2. Ask students to read the lyrics a second time and circle the verbs in each line. Students will notice that many lines have strong verbs: "I'm gonna *write* a little letter," "gonna *mail* it to my local D. J.," "The jukebox's *blowin'* a fuse," for example.
3. Divide the class into small groups. Assign each group a stanza for a choral reading.
4. Allow time for each group to practice reading its stanza aloud. Tell students to emphasize the verbs in each line.
5. Ask groups to read their stanzas aloud to the class, in the order Berry wrote them.
6. Discuss the meaning of the lyrics. Point out that Berry uses letter writing as a way to encourage radio stations to play his song to make it popular: "It's a jumping' little record I want my jockey to play." He urges them to think of his song as a new, cool contemporary piece as he shares: "Roll over Beethoven and tell Tchaikovsky the news" and "I got the rockin' pneumonia, I need a shot of rhythm and blues."
7. Discuss the verbs throughout the song lyrics. Students will most likely notice that the verbs are strong.

Part 2

8. Distribute copies of the lyrics to "Unwritten" and allow time for students to read them silently.
9. Ask students to read the lyrics a second time and circle the verbs in each line. Students will notice that many lines have strong verbs: "*Open up* the dirty window," "*Let* the sun *illuminate*," "*Feel* the rain on your skin," and "*Drench* yourself in words unspoken," for example.
10. Divide the class into small groups. Assign each group a stanza for a choral reading.
11. Allow time for each group to practice reading its stanza aloud. Tell students to emphasize the verbs in each line.
12. Ask groups to read their stanzas aloud to the class, in the order Bedingfield wrote them.
13. Discuss the meaning of the lyrics. Point out that Bedingfield uses writing as a metaphor for living life, in lines such as "I'm just beginning, the pen's in my hand, ending unplanned," "Staring at the blank page before you," and "Today is where your book begins." She urges listeners to live a rich and purpose-driven life.

14. Discuss the verbs throughout the song lyrics. Students will most likely notice that the verbs are strong.

Part 3

15. Explain to students that they are going to create posters to display around the school to remind everyone to use strong verbs when they write. Give them the posterboard, pens, and markers. Or have them go to Wordle (www.wordle.net) to create "word clouds" that can be enlarged into posters. (See example below.)

16. Have students title their posters "Verbs With Vim, Vigor, and Verve" and cover them with as many strong verbs as they can fit, using the song lyrics, favorite books, their personal vocabularies, and print and online resources such as thesauruses and synonym finders.

17. Hang the posters around the school or offer them to other teachers to use in their classrooms as reminders to use strong verbs in writing.

Lesson Extension

Play "Roll Over Beethoven" and "Unwritten" for students, encouraging them to follow along on their copies of the lyrics and enjoy it. Play the songs again, and this time, ask students to snap their fingers each time they hear/read a verb. Discuss how the vocal arrangements highlight the songs' verbs. Invite students to share other songs that contain strong verbs.

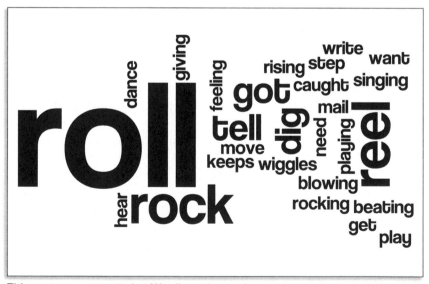

This poster was created at Wordle, using verbs from "Roll Over Beethoven."

ACTIVITIES Applying Strong Verbs

"Said" Is Not Dead

Many teachers would like to eradicate the word *said* from students' writing vocabularies. But, in truth *said* is a potent word. Sure, if it's overused, it can deaden dialogue. But if it's never used at all, students are likely to select unnatural-sounding words to replace it. Share the following dialogue with students and ask them to fill in every blank with *said* and then repeat the process by filling in every blank with a verb other than *said*.

> "It's such a beautiful day today, I think I'll take my car to the car wash," _____ Gerome.
>
> "Hold on a minute," _____ Athan, his little brother. "You promised next time I could come along too," he _____.
>
> "I never _____ that. You are making that up."
>
> "Yes, you did," _____ Athan. "And Marlee was right there. Tell him you heard what he _____," _____ Athan.
>
> "I am not getting in the middle of this fight," Marlee _____. "You two sort it out by yourselves. I mean it," she _____.
>
> "Fine!" Gerome and Athan _____ in unison.
>
> "Tell you what," _____ Gerome. "Why don't you both get busy and wash my car for me *in the driveway*," he _____. "Here's a bucket and a shammy. Have fun!" Gerome _____.

When they've finished, compare the two versions. Students will likely find that neither using *said* nor completely avoiding *said* works. They may even note some instances where no word is needed at all; the speaker is implied. Encourage students to use verbs creatively when writing dialogue, but to use the verb *said* when it is the most natural choice, which is often.

Adverbs, Anyone?

Earlier in the chapter, I talked about Stephen King's disdain for adverbs—how they tend to bog down writing rather than boost it up. He has a point, especially when you consider most middle schoolers' love affair with the adverb. This activity helps them use restraint.

Put students into pairs and give them a list of active verbs such as *jump, fly, eat, sting, approach, think, kiss, hover, dial, grind, smooth, sneeze, write, empty,* and *rehearse.* Allow pairs 15 minutes to write a fiction or nonfiction piece, using as many of the verbs as they can in any tense or form (for example, *fly, flies, flying, flew,* and *flown*) but no adverbs. At the end of 15 minutes, have pairs read their piece to other pairs and score them this way: For each active verb used, award one point. For each adverb used, deduct one point. Play until one pair is left—the pair with the highest number of points. Post the piece with the most active verbs and fewest adverbs for all to enjoy.

Key Quality: Selecting Striking Words and Phrases

Every author has a different style of writing. For example, Eudora Welty's style was poetic and languid, whereas Ernest Hemingway's was spare and forceful. Style and word choice go hand in hand because the type of words, the number of words, and the sound of words writers choose have a tremendous impact on the overall quality of their work—and the reader's response to it. Middle school students can use words to develop their own style. To do that, they need to choose striking words and phrases to light up their ideas. Use the following Think About to expand students' notions about that skill.

Reproducible on CD

THINK ABOUT:

* Did I try to use words that sound *just right*?
* Did I try hyphenating several shorter words to make an interesting-sounding new word?
* Did I try putting words with the same sound together?
* Did I read my piece aloud to find at least one or two moments I love?

WARM-UP Selecting Striking Words and Phrases

Distribute copies of the Think About and ask students to revise the following paragraph by focusing on individual words and phrases. Are they the best words and phrases to convey the idea?

> Homework is terrible. I hate homework. I work pretty hard in school, and so I don't know why I have to do so much at home, too. There is a lot of other stuff I'd rather do than homework. I wish we never had to do it any more.

Share the revision below or write one of your own and read it aloud. Then ask students to read their revisions aloud. Finally, read the original paragraph aloud and discuss what a difference choosing striking words can make.

> No reruns of *Leave It to Beaver*. No Mortal Combat. No toe-tapping tunes from Beyonce. No life. When I get home from school, I don't grab my board to do a goofy-grab or fakey-stance or try for my first air walk. No, I do homework. That sit-in-your-chair-until-it's-done work that never ends, day after day after live-long day. Until Saturday. Then it's my time. But meanwhile, I'm doing my math, studying my science, reading my book, wishing I was free.

FOCUS LESSON   Selecting Striking Words and Phrases

Although it takes more work than settling for the first words that pop to mind, reaching for *just-right* words to express an idea leads to better writing. In this lesson, students engage in e-mail exchanges as characters from fairy tales. They choose a character, a topic, and, of course, the words to express themselves. However, students are not allowed to reveal their identities. Instead, they must use striking words and phrases as clues for their readers.

Materials:

- computers with e-mail software installed—ideally, one for every two students
- e-mail addresses for each pair of students (generated through the school mail service) Note: Traditional pen-and-paper can be used if e-mail is unavailable
- a list of fairy tale characters

Fairy Tale Characters

- Goldilocks
- one of the three bears
- Little Red Riding Hood
- one of the three little pigs
- the wolf in "Little Red Riding Hood" or "The Three Little Pigs"
- Hansel or Gretel
- the stepmother or witch from "Hansel and Gretel"
- Sleeping Beauty
- Snow White
- one of the seven dwarves
- the evil queen in "Sleeping Beauty" or "Snow White and the Seven Dwarves"
- Cinderella
- the wicked stepmother or one of the stepsisters in "Cinderella"
- the prince in "Sleeping Beauty" or "Cinderella"

What to Do:

1. Write the names of fairy tale characters on slips of paper and place those slips in a hat.
2. Ask students to pair up and have one partner draw a slip.
3. Tell pairs to write an e-mail in the persona of their character and send it to another student pair. The e-mail should include these elements:
   - "Guess Who's Coming to Dinner?" in the subject line
   - An introduction revealing where you live (Use just-right descriptions that zero in on the location, such as "a magnificent castle," "a brick house," or "the deep, dark forest.")

- Your favorite things to do (Use compound adjectives to describe personality traits, such as "mirror-gazing time waster," "princess-seeking hopeless romantic," or "evil pig-eating schemer.")
- Your favorite foods and drinks (Use alliteration to describe them, such as "bubbling broth," "pickled pork," or "gooey girl.")
- Your closest friends and family members or people and animals who know you best (Describe what makes you unique from their point of view.)
- A problem that requires the help of the e-mail's recipients (Use italics or boldface to emphasize the deepest part of the problem.)

4. Tell pairs to write messages back and forth until they have figured out one another's characters.
5. If time allows, put the slips back in the hat, have students draw again, and repeat the exercise with different partners and e-mail recipients.
6. When time is up, ask students to tell you some of the striking words and phrases that helped them to identify the character with whom they were corresponding. Discuss which of the required techniques (using just-right descriptions, using compound adjectives, using alliteration, writing from an alternate point of view, or emphasizing key parts) was easiest to do and which was hardest.

Lesson Extension

Ask students to write a story in which two unlikely characters meet in an unexpected location, such as Goldilocks running into one of the seven dwarves at the grocery store or Cinderella's prince meeting one of the three little pigs at a bowling alley. Tell them to use the techniques they used in their e-mails to select striking words for their stories. Read the stories aloud when students have finished.

ACTIVITIES   Selecting Striking Words and Phrases

Thesaurus Overload

Share the following piece of eighth-grade writing with students:

> My friend Allison is a real fun anyone. The reason I say this is because we have been patrons for at least seven years so we recognize a lot on each other. We always do more things together than we do with our other scoundrels. I must say she is my best friend. We like to go skating in the summer. We like doing this because there are a lot of further friends there. We really get inured when we skate.
>
> We are always prudent before we do things and always try to do things just right. We try to be fluent and respective so we can get across to each other on what we are talking about. Actually I think our friendship is very lucrative. She is very gingerly when talking to other people, so they may not get furried.
>
> She would never divulge about me and never has. Sometimes we mimic each other, yet not often. Somethings she likes are totally bizarre than what I like. Sometimes things get very complicating though when trying to explain something.

We eat a lot of food but we never gorge food down at each other's houses. We are also very suave to each other's parents and use a lot of mannerism. Our houses are encased with large fences. Both us get into a lot of financial situations and have to borrow money from each other.

There is always chaos in what we are doing. Like when I was making pudding she said I adjoin too much milk and stuff like that. She is a most memorable friend and I think she is always trying to be so prim. Our friendship will never detract from our lives. We always try to have legible handwriting on our homework because we reckon we will get a better grade.

It is very hard to talk about this subject because you have to think inflexibility about what you are going to write next. I like Allison a lot because she is a very honest friend. I hope our friendship will never disintegrate and distress. She is perpetually a best friend.

Have students get into small groups, choose a paragraph, and revise it, paying particular attention to the writer's misuse of individual words. When groups have finished, reread the piece, revised paragraph by revised paragraph, and discuss how replacing "thesaurus words" with more natural-sounding words can make a big difference in a piece's overall quality.

More Than the Sensational

Read aloud the following passage from Gary Paulsen's book, *Guts: The True Stories Behind the Hatchet and Brian Books*. As you read, ask student to listen for a particular word or phrase that catches their attention.

The other truth—one that Brian came to know, and something that people all over the world have known and spoken of for thousands of years—is that hunger makes the best sauce.

Something that you would normally never consider eating, something completely repulsive and ugly and disgusting, something so gross it would make you vomit just looking at it, becomes absolutely delicious if you are starving. (pp. 118–119)

When you've finished, ask students to call out the word or phrase that caught their attention. Most, of course, will say "vomit." Interestingly, though, I've found that most teachers say "hunger makes the best sauce." Both are good answers. Explain why you chose the word or phrase you chose and why the more sensational words and phrases stood out. Tell them that sensational words like *vomit* are perfectly fine to use in writing, as long as they are used for a clear purpose and effect. Prepare yourself; once you open the door to using sensational words and phrases, students may go a little crazy. But in time, with practice on drafts and exposure to writing like Paulsen's, they will learn restraint.

Key Quality: Using Specific and Accurate Words

For a piece of writing to be strong, the words it contains must not only be striking, but specific and accurate as well. A good rule of thumb is to use precise nouns and verbs to make a complicated idea easy to understand. In her book *Woe Is I*, Patricia T. O'Connor echoes this sentiment: "A good writer is one you can read without breaking a sweat. If you want a workout, you don't lift a book—you lift weights. Yet, we're brainwashed to believe that the more brilliant the writer, the tougher the going" (1996, p. 195). I couldn't agree more. Words should be chosen to ease the reading experience, and not to dazzle the reader. Doing this is not easy, of course. It takes great effort and care to find the perfect words. Use the following Think About to expand students' notions about using specific and accurate words.

Reproducible
on CD

THINK ABOUT:

- Have I used nouns and modifiers that help the reader see a picture?
- Did I avoid using words that might confuse the reader?
- Did I try a new word, and if so, did I check to make sure I used it correctly?
- Are these the best words that can be used?

WARM-UP Using Specific and Accurate Words

Distribute copies of the Think About and ask students to revise the following directions by making its words more accurate and specific.

> To get something from a music Web site just go there and grab the one you want from the store. Put it in a playlist and be sure to get all the right information about it. To see the latest podcasts or RSS feeds, check your music site, too. There's nothing to it.

Encourage students to read their revisions to the class and discuss how using accurate and specific words makes directions much easier to follow. You can share this example with them or write one of your own as well.

> To download a song from an Internet music site such as Rhapsody, Napster, or iTunes, follow these steps:
>
> 1. Make sure your computer has the software for the music site. For example, a free version of iTunes is available at http://www.apple.com/itunes/download/.
> 2. Launch the software application.
> 3. Double-click on the application heading to open and begin browsing for your selection.
> 4. Type the name of the song or the musician you want in the search box.
> 5. Double-click on the song, album, video, or podcast you wish to purchase.

6. Follow the purchasing directions. Your selection will download in a folder and you can move it or file it in a playlist as you wish.

7. Close the applications file. The next time you open it, your new download will be there, ready to enjoy.

FOCUS LESSON   Using Specific and Accurate Words

Signs communicate information for a specific audience. For example, stop signs tell drivers to come to a halt. Construction signs tell pedestrians to use caution. Grocery store signs tell shoppers what's on sale. The amount of information on a sign differs depending on its purpose and audience. In this lesson, students write three exhibit signs for an aquarium animal of their choice for three audiences: a child, an adult, and a marine biologist. Then the class examines each set of signs and determines which ones contain the most specific and accurate words for each audience.

Materials:
- information about marine animals from the library or the Internet
- transparency of aquarium exhibit signs for the pond turtle (page 210 and CD)
- posterboard and paper
- markers, pens, pencils
- small sticky notes
- scissors, tape, glue

What to Do:
1. Discuss different kinds of signs in public places and their purposes. Ask students to comment on how the language of signs differs depending on whether they are written for children, men, women, tourists, or commuters. For example, a sign advertising a restaurant for children might contain only a few big, bold words and show delicious-looking, kid-pleasing food, such as pizza and macaroni and cheese. A sign targeting upscale shoppers might contain lush descriptions and high-quality photographs of designer clothing items, while a sign targeting young athletes might contain action words from a particular sport to entice them to buy equipment necessary to play that sport.

2. Ask students to think about and discuss the language for a sign that would entice tourists to visit a local attraction. Then ask them to do the same for a sign that would alert a commuter to a new bus schedule. Discuss other uses for signs and their audiences.

3. Show students the three aquarium exhibit signs for the pond turtle. Ask them to match each sign to the appropriate audience:
   - a child
   - an adult
   - a marine biologist

Sign #1: Pond Turtles

Pond turtles live on all the continents except Antarctica. They live in fresh water such as rivers, lakes, and ponds. In North America, these pond turtles live mostly in Washington and western Canada. Pond turtles can grow as long as 16 inches! Bugs should watch out. Pond turtles eat them for breakfast, lunch, and dinner. The longest-living pond turtle is forty years old. That's ancient!

Sign #2: Western Pond Turtles

The western pond turtle is one of the most common turtles in the northwestern United States and Canada. They are primarily found in Washington and western British Columbia. Their shell, or carapace, ranges in size from 4" to 16" depending on the age. A few Western Pond Turtles live to the ripe old age of forty. Their low-carbohydrate insect diet is supplemented by small fish, frogs, and plants.

Sign #3: *Clemmys Marmorata*

The *Clemmys marmorata*, also known as *Pseudemydura umbrina*, is best known as the western pond turtle. It is one of two native North American species of the testudines order and the crown group *Chelonia*. Its diet consists mostly of the larvae of caddis flies, dragonflies, and nymphs. Recorded size at 4.7–7.2 in. (12–18 cm). Life expectancy: four decades. Mature at seven. Features a low carapace with shields that have a network of lines radiating from growth centers. Extirpated: British Columbia. Near Extinction: Washington State.

4. Put students in small groups and ask each group to select an aquarium animal other than the pond turtle.

5. Have them gather five categories of information about the animal from books and the Internet:
   - its scientific name
   - its habitat
   - its maximum size
   - its maximum life span
   - its eating habits

6. Ask students to create three exhibit signs for the animal—one for children, one for adults, and one for marine biologists. Remind them to use specific and accurate words in each sign so that it is understandable to the intended audience.

7. Mount the signs on the posterboard and display them.

8. Ask students to walk about and read the signs. Have each student select his or her two favorite signs for each audience (six total) by placing a small sticky note on them.

9. Read the most popular signs to the class and discuss why their words work particularly well for each audience.

Lesson Extension

Take students on a field trip to an aquarium, zoo, museum, or other place where they can examine information-packed signs. Discuss how important it is for sign writers to use specific and accurate words to convey their ideas. When students return to class, ask them to write a thank-you note to the museum staff that includes their thoughts about the signs' effectiveness.

ACTIVITIES   Using Specific and Accurate Words

Valiant Tries at Similes and Metaphors

When writers seek to create a clear visual image in the reader's mind, they often use two forms of figurative language: similes and metaphors. Experienced writers do this well—they create images that ring true. Inexperienced writers, however, usually need practice. Share with students the following examples of bad figurative language:

- Her face was a perfect oval, like a circle that had its two sides gently compressed by a thigh exerciser.

- His thoughts tumbled in his head, making and breaking alliances like socks in a dryer.

- She grew on him like she was a colony of E. coli and he was room-temperature Canadian beef.

- She had a deep, throaty, genuine laugh, like a dog gagging.

- Her vocabulary was as bad as, like, whatever.
- The little boat gently drifted across the pond exactly the way a bowling ball wouldn't.
- Her hair glistened in the rain like a nose hair after a sneeze.
- John and Mary had never met. They were like two hummingbirds who had also never met.
- The ballerina rose gracefully en pointe and extended one slender leg behind her, like a dog at a fire hydrant.
- It hurt the way your tongue hurts after you accidentally staple it to the wall.

(Adapted from the *Washington Post*, "The Style Invitational," March 14, 1999, http://www.washingtonpost.com/wp-srv/style/invitational/invit990314.htm)

After you've shared a few chuckles, ask students to choose one of the examples and revise it, using specific and accurate words to create a more apt image in the reader's mind. If time allows, ask students to illustrate their before and after versions. Display their finished products around the room.

Dumb It Down

Share with students the following passage from Albert Einstein's "What I Believe" and then my simplified version of it:

> The human mind is not capable of grasping the Universe. We are like a little child entering a huge library. The walls are covered to the ceilings with books in many different tongues. The child knows that someone must have written these books. It does not know who or how. It does not understand the languages in which they are written. But the child notes a definite plan in the arrangement of the books—a mysterious order which it does not comprehend, but only dimly suspects. (1930, p. 3)

Simplified version:

> Our minds can only understand a little bit. When you go into a library and look at all the books, you can't know what's in all of them. That would be too hard. But you do notice if they are organized. And that's something.

Discuss the differences in the two versions. The words in Einstein's original essay work perfectly because they are specific and accurate (not to mention simple and elegant), enabling readers to wrap their minds around his beliefs about the human potential. My version doesn't even come close to capturing the enormity of that question. Once you've shared this model, have students find passages from the writings of other great thinkers, such as Carl Sagan, and "dumb them down." In the process, they'll develop an appreciation for the power of words to convey a complicated concept.

Key Quality: Choosing Words That Deepen Meaning

Good writers listen to the sound of their words as they revise. They read drafts closely, striking out boring, repetitious words and replacing them with more exciting, imaginative ones. They play with words until they fit, like a lock's tumblers falling into place. What they *don't* do is use the first words that come to mind. Why? To deepen the meaning of their message. Use the following Think About to expand students' notions about choosing words that deepen meaning.

THINK ABOUT:

- Did I choose words that show I really thought about them?
- Have I tried to use words without repeating myself?
- Do my words capture the reader's imagination?
- Have I found the best way to express myself?

WARM-UP   Choosing Words That Deepen Meaning

Distribute copies of the Think About and the paragraph below. Ask students to get into pairs and read the paragraph aloud, listening for and circling repetitive words, phrases, and details. Then ask them to revise the paragraph to eliminate repetitiveness and express the main idea more cogently.

> I'm the best goalie ever. It's a really, really hard job. Nobody else can do it but me. I'm the best goalie our team has had in like, two or three years, I think. I'm pretty sure that's true. Anyway, I'm a really good goalie. I love playing goalie because it's the best and really greatest position.

When students have finished, ask for volunteers to read aloud the original paragraph and their revised paragraphs, and then share the following revised paragraph or one of your own. Discuss word changes that deepen the piece's meaning.

> Heads up! Here they come, thundering down the field right at me—twenty girls bearing down, and ten hoping to catch me unaware. My heart starts to race and I position myself in front of the goal anticipating their forward's signature move of passing the ball to her wing for a quick goal. There it is... *ka-thump.* Ah, I caught it. *What a laugh. Nice try, ladies,* I think to myself as I draw the ball in close, willing it not to pop out of my arms. Now, look out. I'm going to kick it so far they'll never get back down to this end again. There it goes, *thwack...* far across the field, landing right at the nimble feet of one my own players. Sweet!

FOCUS LESSON   Choosing Words That Deepen Meaning

All writers have a tendency to fall back on words and phrases they've used again and again. But to grow as writers, we must always stretch for the best word. We must choose words that deepen the meaning of our message and give the reader a clear picture of what's going on. In this lesson, students pair up to write scary stories, but they're not allowed to use words and phrases typically used in scary stories, such as *fear*, *fright*, and, indeed, *scary*. As a result, they're forced to push their descriptive limits and come up with truly original work.

Materials:
- copies of the Forbidden Words reproducible (page 215 and CD)
- paper, pens, pencils

What to Do:
1. Brainstorm with students a list of ideas for a scary story. Help them come up with a plot, characters, settings, and a problem to be resolved.
2. Tell students they will be writing a one-page scary story with a partner, using the ideas they brainstormed. The story can be real, imagined, or a combination of both.
3. Have students choose a partner and give them ten minutes to decide on the plot, characters, setting, and a problem to be resolved.
4. After partners know what they want to write, hand out the Forbidden Words reproducible. Explain to students that they are not to use any of the words on the list, in any form. For example, not only is *scare* off limits, but so are *scary*, *scared*, and *scaring*.
5. Give students 20 minutes to test their descriptive limits by drafting their scary stories.
6. When they've finished, ask volunteers to read their stories. After each reading, ask listeners to note one word or phrase from the piece that surprised them and/or worked well. Make a list of these on the board or a chart.
7. After all volunteers have had a chance to read, ask all students to revise their stories, incorporating words and phrases from the list you just made.
8. Discuss what students learned about deepening meaning by limiting access to familiar word and phrases.

Lesson Extension

Ask students to make lists of words that are commonly used to express other emotions such as happiness, sadness, and anger. Challenge them to write another story without using any of the words they brainstormed. Share their stories with other students in the school. You may even want to consider creating a blog so that students can post and discuss their stories online.

Forbidden Words

afraid	scare
alarm	shock
creep	spook
dread	startle
fear	surprise
flesh	sweat
fright	terrify
panic	terror
petrify	unbelievable

ACTIVITIES Choosing Words That Deepen Meaning

Where Did That Come From?

The English language is riddled with idioms, such as "once in a blue moon" and "raining cats and dogs," whose origins are a mystery to most of us. Wordsmiths have collected these interesting word-choice treasures over the years and put them onto Web sites and into books. Brainstorm common idioms with students and consult resources, such as *The Dord, the Diglot, and an Avocado or Two: The Hidden Lives and Strange Origins of Common and Not-So-Common Words* by Anu Garg, to explore their histories. You may be surprised by what you find. Students will delight in some of the dark, humorous, and downright wacky stories behind everyday language. I guarantee the words and phrases that catch their imagination most will find their way into their next piece of writing.

Wordplay Every Day

Writing is hard work. Unless you incorporate ways to make it enjoyable, students will get discouraged. I suggest wordplay. Don't let a day go by without engaging in some form of it. Here are some favorite wordplay techniques to spice up your writing classroom:

Palindromes: words and phrases that are spelled the same way backward and forward, such as *mom*, *dad*, and—get this—"Rats live on no evil star."

Anagrams: a pair of words or phrases that contain the same letters in a different order, for example, *Motley Crue* and *me cruel toy* or *Elvis* and *lives*.

Onomatopoeia: words that are spelled the way they sound, such as *shhh*, *buzz*, and *moo*.

Spoonerisms: a phrase in which the initial syllables of two of its words have been swapped, for example, "Go shake a tower" from "Go take a shower."

Oxymorons: the juxtaposition of two contradictory words, such as "minor crisis" and "original copies."

Experimenting with these techniques helps students recognize the delightful way the English language works—and have fun in the process. If you have a writing center, focus on one technique a week. Ask students to leave examples for other students to create a lengthy list by the week's end. Or, if you wish, have students add one or two examples per week to a wordplay section in their writer's notebooks. Examples might come from materials they're reading or their own imaginations.

Mentor Texts for Middle School: Word Choice

The following books are by authors who are especially skilled in word choice. Share them with your students and point out examples of word choice's key qualities as you encounter them.

The Blue Star by **Tony Earley** (Little, Brown, 2008)

This coming-of-age story picks up where Earley's *Jim the Boy* left off. In *Jim the Boy*, Earley introduces us to Jim Glass, a smart, self-conscious boy, growing up with his mother and uncles in the rural South. Now Jim is in high school—and no longer a boy. Set during the early years of World War II, this sweet story explores Jim's crush on Chrissie Steppe, a girl he's known most of his life, but suddenly sees in a whole new light. Earley captures teenage angst using gentle language—a perfect match for the quieter, simpler time in which the story is set.

The Color of My Words by **Lynn Joseph** (HarperCollins, 2000)

Twelve-year-old Ana Rosa Hernandez is the central figure in this story set in the Dominican Republic, a country where writing is discouraged and words are feared. But she hungers to write. Although she knows the danger she may face if she does so, she and her family find scraps of paper and then a notebook, and Ana begins to work. Her writing brings the spotlight to her family, which leads to tragedy. Nonetheless, Rosa realizes she has a great gift, and vows to transform her world with her words.

Tasting the Sky: A Palestinian Childhood by **Ibtisam Barakat** (Farrar, Straus and Giroux, 2007)

In this powerful, expressive, and well-crafted memoir, Barakat tells her story of living through war, separating from her family, and becoming a refugee. Her language is poetic, and she uses simple words with grace. I found it heartening that Barakat believes language is the best tool we have to make sense of the world—or at least as much sense as the world makes during terrible times.

Final Thoughts

Unlike Thomas Jefferson, who waited days for feedback on the Declaration of Independence, our students need feedback daily. We can fill up our classrooms with writing resources and read aloud great literature so students steep in the language of master writers. We can show them verbs that work in a piece of writing—and verbs that don't. We can show them how to use accurate and specific words to make their ideas crystal clear. Fortunately, instruments with which we write have come a long way since Thomas Jefferson's time. We don't have to rely on quill pens, parchment, and candlelight. But the hard work remains the same: adding words, removing words, moving them around, and trying new ones until the writing sounds just right. There's no shortcut for good word choice, just trial and error—and reading. Lots and lots of reading.

Words and phrases alone, however, don't create meaning. They need to be assembled into carefully constructed sentences. The next chapter provides guidelines for showing students how to do just that.

CHAPTER 8

Sentence Fluency:
Hearing Is Believing

The Sound of a Sentence

A sentence can poke turtle-like on a page.
It can leap like an antelope playing.
It can vary from short to the lengthier sort,
Depending on what you are saying.

When you read with your eye and hear with your ear,
Your readers will love what you're writing.
A balance of turtle and antelope sentences
Helps make your piece exciting.

"He screamed!" is a sentence both short and direct.
It grabs us. It holds our attention.
But *where* he screamed and *why* he screamed
Deserve more than two words to mention.

So vary the patterns and go with the flow
And polish the lines 'til they glisten.
To learn if you've done what you set out to do,
Read it aloud, and listen.

—David L. Harrison

When David Harrison writes a poem, he relies on his ear just as much as his eye. He constructs lines that contain just the right number of syllables to create a rhythmic flow. The words sing. I marvel at his ability to create poems that read so smoothly and communicate so clearly.

David and I met at a conference back in 2005. We became instant friends and e-mail buddies. We share tidbits about our lives regularly, from the mundane (such as our evening's dinner menu) to the critical (such as our latest writing project). There's nothing like the comforting words of another writer when the words won't come—or when they come, but don't fall together quite right. When I hit a roadblock, David often counsels me to read my rough draft aloud. As a writer himself, he knows firsthand that writing needs to sound right, whether it's poetry or prose. And since writing is as much a mental act as a physical one, it only makes sense to think about how words sound as we commit them to paper.

I struggled to find the right words to ask (read: beg) David to write the opening poem for this chapter. After all, offering e-mails of support is one thing, but writing a poem for publication is another. To my delight, he agreed. He worked on the poem for a long time, honing each line to capture a vivid definition of sentence fluency. And I couldn't be more pleased with the result. We continued our regular correspondence during this period, but instead of discussing how our days were going, we discussed this complex trait. We talked of the importance of creating rhythmic flow, but also of matters of grammar. We talked of sentence fluency's connection to the other traits.

I used to think creating fluent sentences was simple. All writers needed to learn was grammar. But I was wrong. Sentence fluency is about much more than that. It's about the way sentences sound in isolation and in combination with other sentences, whether they're grammatically correct or not. A first grader may write:

> I use the computer. I can jump. I can read. I can draw.

Although each of the sentences is grammatically correct (which, for a first grader, is admirable), the piece is repetitive and monotonous. If correctness were all that mattered, this student would receive a perfect score in sentence fluency. However, when we factor in the sound of those sentences—their rhythm, cadence, and tempo—she wouldn't. She still has a great deal to learn about crafting and combining sentences. As readers, students wouldn't select texts like this one because they would be dreadfully dull. So, as writers, why do they often create such texts? We know middle school students are capable of much more. Indeed, by sixth grade, most students can write far more complex pieces— pieces like "I've learned how to use a computer, write, and read, but the one activity I love doing the most is drawing. Give me a paper and pencil and I'm good to go. I feel alive." Better, agreed? We should expect nothing less of middle school students.

Achieving sentence fluency is anything but simple. It takes patience, practice, and good instruction, which is what the remainder of this chapter is all about.

The Sentence Fluency Trait: A Definition

Sentence fluency is about how words and phrases flow through a piece of writing. It is achieved when the writer pays close attention to the way individual sentences are crafted and groups of sentences are combined.

Writing may seem like a silent act, but it isn't. When true writers read their drafts, they hear passages that sing out and those that don't. They check for natural starting and stopping points. They listen for the way the words sound as they flitter and flow within and among sentences. And when passages don't sing out, when starting and stopping points don't seem natural and words don't sound quite right, they know there is work to be done. They might weed out unnecessary words, vary the length and structure of sentences, or try a literary technique such as alliteration or assonance. That is why I call sentence fluency the auditory trait. True writers "read" for it with the ear as much as the eye.

One way writers create fluency is by employing different types of sentences within a single piece. They might use compound sentences to add detail, immerse the reader in information, and reinforce a point. They might use short, declarative sentences to drive that point home. And fragments? Writers might use them to isolate an important thought and make the reader stand up and take notice of it. Just as a musician creates a beautiful song, a writer creates a fluent piece of writing by varying sentence structures and lengths, and paying very close attention to how those sentences sound when they're brought together.

Writing fluently is not simple because it requires the writer to conjure up everything he or she knows about language—how it works, how it looks, how it sounds, how it touches the person receiving it—in order to find the best approach for the piece. In other words, he or she must apply the following key qualities, with skill and confidence:

* Crafting Well-Built Sentences

* Varying Sentence Types

* Capturing Smooth and Rhythmic Flow

* Breaking the "Rules" to Create Fluency

> **"**Always write and read with the ear, not the eye. You should hear every sentence you write as if it was being read aloud or spoken. **"**
>
> —C. S. Lewis, 1959

Why Students Struggle With Sentence Fluency

As I said earlier, writing fluent sentences can be difficult for students to master. It is a complex process that requires knowledge about language and practice in writing, one that presents challenges for many students. In this section, I discuss three reasons why.

They Don't Hear the Music

It's a common cry among us teachers: students don't read enough good literature. As a result, they aren't exposed to the language patterns that make that literature good and they struggle to create sentences that sing. We can teach grammar and syntax until we're blue in the face. But a writer does a lot more than apply grammar and syntax to create sentence fluency. He moves words around until they fit together like the pieces of a jigsaw puzzle. He revisits sections he's assembled. He listens for the "click" that tells him he's found the right the combination of interlocking pieces.

When students read and hear models of fluent writing repeatedly, they become curious about how that writing was created and develop a repertoire of strategies for their own writing. They develop a reader's ear that tells them, yes, that's exactly how my writing should sound—or, no, that's not it at all. This awareness, of course, leads to rich classroom discussions about author's craft. Once the subject is raised, it's a perfect time to teach students about grammar and syntax, logically linking their reading to their writing. When students ask questions like, "Why doesn't this sentence work?" it's akin to waving the checkered flag at a NASCAR race; such questions are the *go* signal, letting us know they want to understand the relationship between sentence structure and the impact of grammar and syntax on the reader. Then and only then is it appropriate to teach specific craft elements about grammar.

Students who don't read extensively may come to understand grammar and syntax, but they'll never develop the instinct that tells them whether their writing is perfect or still needs work. There's no substitute for reading. In today's task-driven world, where students gallop from class to class and subject to subject, reading can move them faster and further toward fluency than any lesson or activity—even those in this book.

> **"** When I checked my sentences, I found one that was 59 words long. I couldn't even breathe when I read it aloud. I turned it into three shorter sentences— much better! **"**
>
> —Diego, grade 6

They Are Happy With Their Sentences the Way They Are

Getting students to revise for fluency can feel like giving a cat a bath. After all, putting those initial sentences onto the page is a tremendous accomplishment for most of them. And trimming out unnecessary words and phrases, moving words and phrases around, replacing words and phrases require a lot of elbow grease. Why bother? I can't say I disagree. Revision is no ride at Six Flags.

Part of the problem may be that revising for fluency is counterintuitive to what students think makes them successful writers: filling up the page. Most students don't have too much trouble getting their ideas down. But that's only the beginning. Once a student has a draft, he or she must take a second, third, and even a fourth look and listen. And that means getting a weed whacker and eliminating all things repetitive and/or unnecessary. We must give students the time and space to mess with their drafts, play with words, phrases, and sentences—transplant them, pull them out, and separate and regroup them. And, of course, they must be exposed to excellent models of fluent writing. They'll be pleasantly surprised by the impact all that has on their writing—and so will you.

They Don't Have a Solid Grasp of Grammar and Syntax

Most middle school students have been taught a thing or two about grammar and syntax, but only through isolated skills practice. They can identify and define parts of speech, for instance, but are woefully unprepared to use that knowledge to construct and combine well-built sentences. Take heart, though. When we teach students to think about how sentences work and how they should sound once they're written, they're more likely to create fluent work. They begin by reading. Then they practice in their own writing what they've learned. The value of applying new skills to one's own writing—including grammar and syntax skills—is well documented in the first chapters of this book.

Once they've mastered the basics of grammar and syntax, students can begin to play around with them. They can, for example, try a fragment, cut an unnecessary prepositional phrase, or move a clause from the beginning of a sentence to the end. These moves involve important decisions. Without a solid understanding of grammar and syntax, writers are at a loss for options, often settling for the simplest of sentences because that's all they can write correctly. We need to teach them grammar and syntax, but only because these serve to make strong sentences. We need to encourage students to try all kinds of sentences in their writing, confident they will eventually be able to craft and combine them effectively because we've taught them the rules of the road—where to yield, where to accelerate, where to stop.

Assessing Student Work for Sentence Fluency

The following eighth-grade papers represent a wide range of skills in the sentence fluency trait. Review the scoring guide on page 225, read each paper carefully, assess the paper for the sentence fluency trait by following the steps on pages 50–51 under "Assessing Writing Using the Trait Scoring Guides," and then read my assessment to see if we agree. Use your own students' writing for further practice.

The papers were all written in the persuasive mode, in response to the prompt "You are the author of a short story or book. Convince someone to choose your work as they browse the shelves at the local library or bookstore." The writers' challenge was to take a position, argue their position, and tell stories and anecdotes related to their position, among other methods for meeting the purpose for writing: to persuade.

I chose papers written at the same grade level, in the same mode, and to the same prompt so that you can focus on the issue at hand, sentence fluency, without other factors serving as a distraction. But keep in mind, it's critical for students to develop skills in sentence fluency regardless of the grade they're in, the mode they choose, and the prompt they're given. Good sentence fluency should be applied to all writing, all the time. Even though I focus on sentence fluency, I've scored the papers in all the traits (except presentation, since the papers are typeset) in case you need additional samples to practice scoring or use in your instruction.

Scoring Guide: Sentence Fluency

The way words and phrases flow through the piece. It is the auditory trait because it's "read" with the ear as much as the eye.

Reproducible on **CD**

6

HIGH

EXCEPTIONAL

A. **Crafting Well-Built Sentences:** The writer carefully and creatively constructs sentences for maximum impact. Transition words such as *but*, *and*, and *so* are used successfully to join sentences and sentence parts.

B. **Varying Sentence Types:** The writer uses various types of sentences (simple, compound, and/or complex) to enhance the central theme or story line. The piece is made up of an effective mix of long, complex sentences and short, simple ones.

C. **Capturing Smooth and Rhythmic Flow:** The writer thinks about how the sentences sound. He or she uses phrasing that is almost musical. If the piece were read aloud, it would be easy on the ear.

D. **Breaking the "Rules" to Create Fluency:** The writer diverges from standard English to create interest and impact. For example, he or she may use a sentence fragment, such as "All alone in the forest," or a single word, such as "Bam!" to accent a particular moment or action. He or she might begin with informal words such as *well*, *and*, or *but* to create a conversational tone, or he or she might break rules intentionally to make dialogue sound authentic.

5

STRONG

4

MIDDLE

REFINING

A. **Crafting Well-Built Sentences:** The writer offers simple sentences that are sound but no long, complex ones. He or she attempts to vary the beginnings and lengths of sentences.

B. **Varying Sentence Types:** The writer exhibits basic sentence sense and offers some sentence variety. He or she attempts to use different types of sentences, but in doing so creates an uneven flow rather than a smooth, seamless one.

C. **Capturing Smooth and Rhythmic Flow:** The writer has produced a text that is uneven. Many sentences read smoothly, while others are choppy or awkward.

D. **Breaking the "Rules" to Create Fluency:** The writer includes fragments, but they seem more accidental than intentional. He or she uses informal words, such as *well*, *and*, and *but*, inappropriately to start sentences, and pays little attention to making dialogue sound authentic.

3

DEVELOPING

2

LOW

EMERGING

A. **Crafting Well-Built Sentences:** The writer's sentences, even simple ones, are often flawed. Sentence beginnings are repetitive and uninspired.

B. **Varying Sentence Types:** The writer uses a single, repetitive sentence pattern throughout or connects sentence parts with an endless string of transition words such as *and*, *but*, *or*, and *because*, which distracts the reader.

C. **Capturing Smooth and Rhythmic Flow:** The writer has created a text that is a challenge to read aloud since the sentences are incomplete, choppy, stilted, rambling, and/or awkward.

D. **Breaking the "Rules" to Create Fluency:** The writer offers few or no simple, well-built sentences, making it impossible to determine whether he or she has done anything out of the ordinary. Global revision is necessary before sentences can be revised for stylistic and creative purposes.

1

RUDIMENTARY

Tell Tale Heart

One day a man came in & wanted to buy a book at the library & so I suggested That I take him over to see the book that just came out that I wrote Hey why don't I show you my new book it's a very good book I said. The man said okay sure, whats the book called The Tell Tale heart and he said whats It about and then I said a little kid is walking in the rain and then he goes for shelter and a guy said you can stay here until the rain stops and the little boy said ok and then he started to look around the factory.

One day it was raining and a little boy was walking in the rain and he went into the factory and there was a old man there that he had made his home so the old man asked him if he would like to stay until the rain stopped and the boy said yea so the boy just started looking around in the factory and then three teenagers came in and were asking where the old man was and then the old man and the little boy started to hide and the three teenagers just started tearing everything apart just to look for treasure that the old man had and hid from the three teenagers that would take it from the old man and then when once the three teenagers were gone the old man showed the little boy what his treasure was but it wasn't that valueable to the little boy but it was to the old man.

Once the rain has stopped the boy didn't want to go home because he was having fun with the old man.

Time to Assess for Sentence Fluency

Sentence Fluency	
Score **1: Rudimentary**	
Range	Low

Aside from the fact that the writer set out to sell us on "The Tell Tale Heart" and then wrote about a completely different story, he's forgotten to stop and take a breath. Run-on sentences and excessive use of the word *and* are rampant. They make the piece impossible to read aloud and comprehend. It feels as if the writer was so caught up in what he wanted to say, he forgot to create sentences. I'm thrilled his idea excited him so much, but his lack of sentence fluency is a fatal problem for me, the reader.

Other Traits	
Ideas	1
Organization	2
Voice	1
Word Choice	2
Conventions	2

A Crafting Well-Built Sentences

The writer's sentences, even simple ones, are often flawed. Sentence beginnings are repetitive and uninspired.

> *It's possible to extract simple sentences. For example, the beginning contains four possible sentences: "One day a man came in and wanted to buy a book at the library. So I took him over to see the book that just came out that I wrote. 'Hey, why don't I show you my new book? It's a very good book,' I said." But the writer didn't parse the beginning that way and failed to apply that strategy in the remainder of the piece.*

B Varying Sentence Types

The writer uses a single, repetitive sentence pattern throughout or connects sentence parts with an endless string of transition words such as *and*, *but*, *or*, and *because*, which distracts the reader.

> *This writer goes on a run-on binge. In revision, at the very least, he should try replacing the conjunction* and *with a period, and begin a new sentence.*

C Capturing Smooth and Rhythmic Flow

The writer has created a text that is a challenge to read aloud since the sentences are incomplete, choppy, stilted, rambling, and/or awkward.

> *This piece needs clearly defined sentences. When I read it aloud, I struggled to determine where the sentences begin and end. The bulk of the piece isn't fluent at all.*

D Breaking the "Rules" to Create Fluency

The writer offers few or no simple, well-built sentences, making it impossible to determine whether he or she has done anything out of the ordinary. Global revision is necessary before sentences can be revised for stylistic and creative purposes.

> *There is no evidence this writer understands how to create sentences. It would take more than editing (adding periods, capitalizing letters, and so forth) to make the piece flow. It would take extensive revision.*

The monkies paw

I think you should read *my* story instead, because it is mystery/suspence. My story is better to read because it is a very interesting story. The story was about a husband and a wife, they get a *mysterious* monkies paw that grants them 3 wishes. They get their wishes and much more. You should read it to find out what happens next.

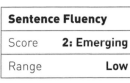

Time to Assess for Sentence Fluency

With its short, repetitive sentences, this piece is a prime example of bare-bones sentence fluency. Nothing very interesting caught my ear. This writer has not stretched her sentence-composing muscles at all. In fact, she's scarcely warmed up—and has a long way to go before she'll be running laps. But she'll get there.

Sentence Fluency	
Score	**2: Emerging**
Range	**Low**

Other Traits	
Ideas	1
Organization	1
Voice	1
Word Choice	2
Conventions	2

A Crafting Well-Built Sentences

The writer's sentences, even simple ones, are often flawed. Sentence beginnings are repetitive and uninspired.

Bingo! This descriptor matches the piece perfectly. Unfortunately, this piece is made up of nothing but flawed, simple sentences.

B Varying Sentence Types

The writer uses a single, repetitive sentence pattern throughout or connects sentence parts with an endless string of transition words such as *and*, *but*, *or*, and *because*, which distracts the reader.

There is little to no variation in the construction of the sentences. And because the piece is so short, there isn't much to assess. This writer might be capable of better work, but the piece provides no evidence to prove that.

C Capturing Smooth and Rhythmic Flow

The writer has created a text that is a challenge to read aloud since the sentences are incomplete, choppy, stilted, rambling, and/or awkward.

The sentences are clearly defined, but poorly crafted. Even if the writer were to punctuate them correctly, they'd still be choppy.

D Breaking the "Rules" to Create Fluency

The writer offers few or no simple, well-built sentences, making it impossible to determine whether he or she has done anything out of the ordinary. Global revision is necessary before sentences can be revised for stylistic and creative purposes.

There is nothing out of the ordinary about these sentences. To make the piece flow, the writer needs to break out and try something different.

The Monkey's Paw

Do you believe in wishes coming true? Have you ever wondered what it would be like to have three wishes? If so, I have written a book that you would find most fascinating. This book is about a magical artifact that grants wishes.

In my story, three characters gain an item called the monkey's paw. The characters are told that this paw can grant you three wishes. Will these characters wish for fame or fortune? With three wishes you could get anything you want.

Then again, the monkey's paw could be a thing of dread. Just imagine wishing for money then finding out your sibling is dead and you will receive a large amount of money for their death. What if you tried wishing that person back to life? Sure, he would come back, but he would be a zombie. The monkey's paw will bring you no happiness, only horror.

Well, are you interested yet? If you are, then buy my book full of magic, wishes, horror, and dread. I guarantee you will like it. If it doesn't haunt you forever.

Time to Assess for Sentence Fluency

This writer knows how to construct sentences correctly, but not necessarily fluently. Some might find the repetitive use of questions distracting. But the piece contains strong sentences nonetheless, such as "The monkey's paw will bring you no happiness, only horror." Ending the piece with a fragment works well because the writer left me with a quick warning to ponder. For these reasons, I give this piece a strong 3, with its balance of sentences that are in need of revision and those that aren't.

Sentence Fluency	
Score	**3: Developing**
Range	**Middle**

Other Traits	
Ideas	3
Organization	3
Voice	3
Word Choice	3
Conventions	4

A Crafting Well-Built Sentences

The writer offers simple sentences that are sound but no long, complex ones. He or she attempts to vary the beginnings and lengths of sentences.

> *Despite all the questions, the writer has varied his sentence beginnings. He has also included simple and more complex sentences throughout, particularly in the third and fourth paragraphs.*

B Varying Sentence Types

The writer exhibits basic sentence sense and offers some sentence variety. He or she attempts to use different types of sentences, but in doing so creates an uneven flow rather than a smooth, seamless one.

> *The artificial tone that all the questions creates makes it difficult to assess this writer's sentence sense. Perhaps he used a question as an introductory line because his teacher asked him to. After all, that is a technique good writers commonly use and good teachers commonly recommend. But he should have stopped there.*

C Capturing Smooth and Rhythmic Flow

The writer has produced a text that is uneven. Many sentences read smoothly, while others are choppy or awkward.

> *The abundance of questions makes the piece feel forced. One question would be fine, but five questions are just too many. They overshadow the other well-crafted sentences.*

D Breaking the "Rules" to Create Fluency

The writer includes fragments, but they seem more accidental than intentional. He or she uses informal words, such as *well*, *and*, and *but*, inappropriately to start sentences, and pays little attention to making dialogue sound authentic.

> *The fragment at the end is perfect. I'd be interested to find out from the writer if using it was a deliberate move—and if it was not, I'd point out why the fragment works well.*

Twilight

Suspenseful books are great to read, and really get your emotions going. They make you want to read on, unlike those other genres that can be completely boring. You should read my suspenseful book <u>Twilight</u>, so you can experience your emotions and mood for the book.

<u>Twilight</u> is a very exciting story. There are always surprises throughout the book. For example, say you fall in love with a vampire. He tries to scare you, but you are not afraid. The vampire gets frustrated, and wants to drink your blood. But he refuses, because he loves you, and cares about you. This book has lots of excitement and surprises!

<u>Twilight</u> has a lot of suspense in it. What if you were lost down a dark street, all by yourself, and you notice some guys stalking you? That makes you want to see what happens next.

<u>Twilight</u> will get you wanting to read more. There may be a time when you think something will happen, but it doesn't. Or a terrible thing is about to happen, and then, in the blink of an eye, the problem is solved, but how? You'll then want to know what happens next, I can guarantee.

I hope you will choose to read my book, because it is filled with loads of suspense. You'll be wanting to read <u>New Moon</u>, after <u>Twilight</u>, followed by <u>Eclipse</u>, and then <u>Breaking Dawn</u>.

Time to Assess for Sentence Fluency

This piece scores a 4 in sentence fluency because it contains many sentences that work well alone and in combination with others. The first paragraph is typical for a middle schooler, but the writer gathers momentum in the following paragraph, kicking the piece's flow into gear. Here rhetorical questions such as "Or a terrible thing is about to happen, and then, in the blink of an eye, the problem is solved, but how?" and declarative statements such as "You'll then want to know what happens next, I can guarantee" stand out. The piece loses steam at the end, however. So I would advise this writer to revise the beginning and ending and then ask her to read the new draft aloud to identify opportunities to create more complex sentences throughout. Doing this would raise the piece's fluency even higher.

Sentence Fluency	
Score	**4: Refining**
Range	**Middle**

Other Traits	
Ideas	3
Organization	3
Voice	3
Word Choice	3
Conventions	4

A Crafting Well-Built Sentences

The writer offers simple sentences that are sound but no long, complex ones. He or she attempts to vary the beginnings and lengths of sentences.

As is often the case with papers that score in the middle range, this paper contains a combination of strengths and weaknesses. It has some terrific sentences, but has others that need work. For instance, the beginning sentence of each of the middle three paragraphs is stilted but is often followed by a better one, such as "There may be a time when you think something will happen, but it doesn't" from the fourth paragraph.

B Varying Sentence Types

The writer exhibits basic sentence sense and offers some sentence variety. He or she attempts to use different types of sentences, but in doing so creates an uneven flow rather than a smooth, seamless one.

This piece is strong in this quality. The writer varies sentences, particularly in the middle, creating a nice flow.

C Capturing Smooth and Rhythmic Flow

The writer has produced a text that is uneven. Many sentences read smoothly, while others are choppy or awkward.

Most of the sentences work, but a few don't, particularly those at the beginning and end. The middle flows nicely, with its combination of simple and complex, complete and incomplete sentences.

D Breaking the "Rules" to Create Fluency

The writer includes fragments, but they seem more accidental than intentional. He or she uses informal words, such as *well*, *and*, and *but*, inappropriately to start sentences, and pays little attention to making dialogue sound authentic.

When the writer breaks the rules, interesting sentences emerge, such as "Or a terrible thing is about to happen, and then, in the blink of an eye, the problem is solved, but how?" In a conference with her, I would confirm whether such sentences were intentional or fortunate mistakes. I would also ask her to read the piece aloud, listening for opportunities to revise the punctuation to enhance the rhythm.

Twilight

I spotted a customer across the bookstore. From what I could see, she was looking at love stories, and having a hard time settling on one. She methodically selected a book, glanced at the back cover, skimmed through the pages, and then placed it back on the shelf. A frustrated, yet disappointed, look flicked across her face every time. I approached her slowly, "Found anything that you are interested in?" She looked up, startled. Then deciding I looked friendly enough, she answered.

"Well, not really. Every one of these seem the same to me," she sighed. Putting down yet one more book, she looked up at me with hopeful eyes, "Do you have any suggestions?"

Ah, my favorite question! I smiled. Of course I did. "Come with me," I said. We weaved between shelves until I found the book I was seeking. I handed it to her with careful hands.

"Twilight," she read out loud. She looked at it curiously; it's a thick book with a dark, intriguing cover. "What makes this different than the others?" she asked.

"Do the others tell a story about a girl that falls in love with something other than a human?" answering her question with a question. But I knew the answer. That did it. She was curious, I could tell, but not convinced. "Not to mention the twists and turns and the great review." She looked at the book more closely, thumbing through the pages as I added "Truly, a love story with a bite."

"I'll try it," she finally decided giving me a little smile. I walked with her towards the front of the store so she could make her purchase.

"Trust me," I winked. "No one knows the story quite like me."

Time to Assess for Sentence Fluency

Although I wish this writer had devoted more space to explaining why *Twilight* is the perfect selection, I can't criticize the sentences. She creates a pleasing rhythm by incorporating natural-sounding dialogue into the body of the piece. In fact, she shows impressive control over dialogue, a difficult skill. If she read the piece aloud, she'd surely find places to revise, such as "I handed it to her with careful hands," which is as much a word choice issue as it is a sentence fluency issue. Therefore, the piece deserves a 5, strong, in sentence fluency.

Sentence Fluency	
Score	**5: Strong**
Range	**High**

Other Traits	
Ideas	4
Organization	5
Voice	5
Word Choice	4
Conventions	6

A Crafting Well-Built Sentences

The writer carefully and creatively constructs sentences for maximum impact. Transition words such as *but*, *and*, and *so* are used successfully to join sentences and sentence parts.

> *The writer treats the reader to many carefully and creatively constructed sentences. And rather than relying on traditional transition words, she intersperses internal and external dialogue to make clear connections from one sentence to the next.*

B Varying Sentence Types

The writer uses various types of sentences (simple, compound, and/or complex) to enhance the central theme or story line. The piece is made up of an effective mix of long, complex sentences and short, simple ones.

> *A close examination of this piece reveals many different types of sentences. This writer knows when to make a short statement and when to let the idea roll along for a while. Nicely done.*

C Capturing Smooth and Rhythmic Flow

The writer thinks about how the sentences sound. He or she uses phrasing that is almost musical. If the piece were read aloud, it would be easy on the ear.

> *Passages like this one are beautiful: "A frustrated, yet disappointed, look flicked across her face every time. I approached her slowly, 'Found anything that you are interested in?' She looked up, startled." A nice, smooth blend of description and dialogue.*

D Breaking the "Rules" to Create Fluency

The writer diverges from standard English to create interest and impact. For example, he or she may use a sentence fragment, such as "All alone in the forest," or a single word, such as "Bam!" to accent a particular moment or action. He or she might begin with informal words such as *well*, *and*, or *but* to create a conversational tone, or he or she might break rules intentionally to make dialogue sound authentic.

> *With its short and long sentences, dialogue, and description, this piece flows well. The writer has no trouble creating text that is pleasing to the ear when read aloud. Her use of dialogue is particularly strong, and certainly enhances the piece's sentence fluency.*

The Tell-Tale Heart

Why, good day, my young fellow! You look like you are in need of a book—yes, a mystery or suspense, I believe. Why a mystery, you ask? A mystery throws back the veil on the unknown elements, the deepest, darkest secrets brought into the light. Are we truly mad? Is there really nothing to fear but fear itself?

My literary works are not like those boring, predictable, realistic works of fiction, or those exhausting romances. Fantasy? Life is not about magic powers or mystical beings, boy. Life is cruel and polluted with the sickly. Everyone must accept these harsh realities, not gallop away on some horned steed.

"The Tell-Tale Heart," one of my newer pieces, is not as predictable as some of those people like to call "great accomplishments." Humph! In most books you could guess the entire book before the first chapter was complete! My stories will keep you up well into the solemn hours of the night, chewing your fingers on the disturbed, worm-like thoughts wriggling around uncomfortably in the soil of your head.

Still not convinced, I see. What of the characters? I find it quite tiresome that the main character is always such a cherub. Are any of us really saintly? Of course not. So you can never honestly know what the characters will be like. Who is innocent? Who is guilty? As the reader goes on through the story, it begins to knit itself together into a tight knot, eventually tying up at the end with a twisted, contorted mass.

So, here—take this book, "The Tell-Tale Heart." I trust you are at least mildly engaged by such stories, judging by your expression. But remember this bit of advice: check under your floorboards, the backs of your closets, the farthest reaches of your attic. You can never be sure what may be lurking behind the most benign, unthreatening objects.

Time to Assess for Sentence Fluency

What else can I say but "Bravo!" It's hard enough to write fluently in one's own voice, let alone in Edgar Allan Poe's, but this writer pulls it off with style and creativity. His piece is a remarkable accomplishment. Using both sentence fluency and word choice to persuade, he's got Poe's writing style down, for sure. I suspect his teacher shared some of Poe's work beforehand. She may've shown how Poe used sophisticated words within a combination of simple sentences, complex sentences, and every kind of sentence in between. Middle school students never seem to tire of Poe. Though reading his works can be challenging for them, they delight in his dark themes. Kudos to both student and teacher.

Sentence Fluency	
Score	**6: Exceptional**
Range	**High**

Other Traits	
Ideas	6
Organization	6
Voice	6
Word Choice	6
Conventions	6

A Crafting Well-Built Sentences

The writer carefully and creatively constructs sentences for maximum impact. Transition words such as *but*, *and*, and *so* are used successfully to join sentences and sentence parts.

> *Each sentence is crafted, not just thrown together. It draws you into the idea, almost seductively—in the style of the "master of macabre" himself.*

B Varying Sentence Types

The writer uses various types of sentences (simple, compound, and/or complex) to enhance the central theme or story line. The piece is made up of an effective mix of long, complex sentences and short, simple ones.

> *Just about every type of sentence is present. I especially enjoyed the one-word exclamations, followed by complex sentences.*

C Capturing Smooth and Rhythmic Flow

The writer thinks about how the sentences sound. He or she uses phrasing that is almost musical. If the piece were read aloud, it would be easy on the ear.

> *After I read this piece silently, I read it aloud to see if it was as good as I thought it was. It was. It's as smooth as a piece of writing can be—an easy ride and delightful treat.*

D Breaking the "Rules" to Create Fluency

The writer diverges from standard English to create interest and impact. For example, he or she may use a sentence fragment, such as "All alone in the forest," or a single word, such as "Bam!" to accent a particular moment or action. He or she might begin with informal words such as *well*, *and*, or *but* to create a conversational tone, or he or she might break rules intentionally to make dialogue sound authentic.

> *Interjections, fragments, and phrases, along with eloquent complete sentences, add up to a stellar piece of writing—one I'd share with students over and over again as an example of powerful sentence fluency*

Conference Comments

If the piece scores high in sentence fluency, 5 or 6, say something like:

> "You lead the reader through the piece with a variety of <u>sentences</u>, making it an exceptional example of <u>fluency</u>. You also capture Poe's voice by using the word choice and <u>sentence fluency</u> traits with great skill. Very impressive. Can you emulate other authors' styles this way? Try Steinbeck's. His <u>sentence structure</u> is quite different from Poe's."

> "The use of dialogue in your piece heightens its <u>fluency</u>. When I read it aloud, it sounded natural. The <u>sentences</u> flowed together seamlessly. How about adding more information about *Twilight*? Keep the <u>sentences</u> flowing as you have here, but develop the content."

If the piece scores in the middle, a 3 or 4, say something like:

> "You have some very <u>fluent</u> passages in this piece, especially in the middle. Try revising the <u>sentences</u> at the beginning and end to flow as smoothly and rhythmically as 'What if you were lost down a dark street, all by yourself, and you notice some guys stalking you?' That's a nicely written, natural-sounding <u>sentence</u>."

> "Your ending really worked for me. I love how you used a fragment to leave your reader thinking. As you consider revising the rest of the piece for <u>sentence fluency</u>, try changing several of your <u>sentences</u> from questions to long and short statements. Too many questions in one short piece can distract the reader from your central idea."

If the piece scores low, a 1 or 2, say something like:

> "You've covered a few fundamentals of <u>sentence fluency</u> in this piece. I can see you have simple <u>sentences</u> down. I'd suggest trying some more complex <u>sentences</u> on the next draft. Think about varying the length and structure of your sentences, and see what happens."

> "You have a lot to say, which is great. But, as hard as I tried, I couldn't tell where your <u>sentences</u> begin and end. Would you read the piece to me? I bet we can find natural places to punctuate and capitalize <u>sentences</u>. From there, we can look at your <u>sentence structures</u> and work on flow. Finally, is this piece really about 'The Tell Tale Heart'? You might want to double-check your title."

Teaching Writing With the Sentence Fluency Trait

Sentence fluency demands a lot. To create it, writers need to be able to construct sentences that are not only correct, but also creative. They must be able to apply the hows and whys of grammar and usage. They must be able to combine words and phrases effectively. They must be able to string sentences together smoothly. And they must do all this in a way that makes it seem effortless to the reader. The extent to which a writer applies these skills can help or hinder the writing he or she produces. To get this challenging trait under control and master it, students need to be taught two principles: construction and flow. So I've organized the remainder of this chapter into sections that relate to those principles and correspond to sentence fluency's key qualities:

> **❝**I know that one thing I need to do is make my sentences shorter. Run-ons and I are best friends. We need to break up.**❞**
>
> —Jessica, grade 7

* Crafting Well-Built Sentences

* Varying Sentence Types

* Capturing Smooth and Rhythmic Flow

* Breaking the "Rules" to Create Fluency

Within each section, you'll find a warm-up exercise, a focus lesson, and two activities, as well as a Think About—a list of important questions students should ask themselves to bring sentence fluency to their writing. (The key qualities and Think Abouts are also included on the CD that accompanies this book.)

Key Quality: Crafting Well-Built Sentences

The first step toward sentence fluency is crafting sentences that contain all the right parts. Naturally, a solid understanding of grammar and usage will help students take that step. How else will they be able to follow rules and break rules intentionally to make their sentences interesting and clear? Teaching grammar and usage within the context of students' own writing, rather than relying on decontextualized work sheets and drills, makes perfect sense. And so does studying the work of other, more able writers, as you'll see in this section. It all leads to better sentence fluency, which is, of course, the ultimate goal. Use the following Think About to expand students' notions about crafting well-built sentences.

THINK ABOUT:

- Do my sentences begin in different ways?
- Are my sentences of different lengths?
- Are my sentences grammatically correct unless constructed creatively for impact?
- Have I used conjunctions such as *but*, *and*, and *so* to connect parts of sentences?

WARM-UP Crafting Well-Built Sentences

Distribute copies of the Think About and ask students to revise the following paragraph by improving the quality of its sentences.

> I wanted to get an iPod. I asked my dad for one. I asked over and over. I wanted an iPod very badly. I wanted it for my birthday. I waited until my birthday. I didn't get an iPod that day. I was disappointed.

When they've finished, ask students to share their revision with a partner and talk about how they used ideas from the Think About. Then share with the class the following revision or one that you create.

> I wanted an iPod so badly it was all I could think about, day and night. Imagine being able to tune out the world and listen to your music any time, anywhere. Sweet. I asked my dad if he'd get me one for my birthday, but I knew it was a longshot. Money has been tight, so I was pretty sure it wouldn't happen. I was right. My birthday came and went, and no iPod. I tried not to act disappointed, but my dad said, "Charlie, I know you really want that iPod. Come to the office with me the next three Saturdays and help out. I'll pay you. And I'll match what you save so you might get that iPod sooner than you think." It wasn't a lot of fun working on Saturdays when my friends were outside playing, but in the end, it was worth it. It took a month, but I now have my new iPod. It's even better than I imagined.

FOCUS LESSON Crafting Well-Built Sentences

Beginning sentences in different ways and creating sentences of different lengths are strategies writers use to build grammatically correct sentences. In this lesson, students examine the sentences in a paragraph written by Gary Paulsen and chart their findings, learning an important lesson in how a master craftsman creates sentences that not only are well-built but sound fluent as well. They then glean information from the chart and use it to revise a paragraph of their own.

Materials:
- copies of the excerpt from Gary Paulsen's *Winterdance* (page 242 and CD)
- copies of the Think About for Crafting Well-Built Sentences (on the CD)
- paper, pens, pencils

What to Do:
1. Ask students what they think writers do to makes their sentences grammatically correct. Invite discussion about beginning sentences in different ways, varying sentence lengths, using conjunctions to join sentence parts. You may wish to discuss how punctuation marks such as end marks, commas, and semicolons can be used to make sentences grammatically correct as well.

2. Give students a copy of the Think About for Crafting Well-Built Sentences. Compare the ideas in it with those students shared.

3. Tell students you are going to read a paragraph from Gary Paulsen's book *Winterdance*, a nonfiction account of the Iditarod sled-dog race. Ask them to listen for how the sentences sound so they can discuss their beginnings, their lengths, and the way they're constructed.

4. Give students a copy of the *Winterdance* reproducible and read Paulsen's paragraph aloud.

5. Direct students to the chart that follows the paragraph and fill it in together.

6. Ask students what they notice about the sentences, based on information from the chart. They will likely notice that one of the sentences is short, two are long, and one is extremely long. They will also notice that the sentences begin in different ways. Save discussion about information from the fourth column, the last word in each sentence, for the end of the lesson.

7. Tell students to create the same chart on a separate sheet of paper. Then ask them to choose a draft from their writing folder, and fill out the chart for their draft. If their piece is long, tell them to choose a passage from it that's six or seven sentences long. What patterns do they notice in their own sentences? Do their sentences begin differently? Are they of different lengths?

8. Point out that the last word in each of Paulsen's sentences has only one syllable. Tell students that, although it's not a hard-and-fast rule, ending many sentences with single-syllable words can create a sound that signals a final thought.

9. Ask students to replace one or more of the final words in Paulsen's sentences with synonyms of two or more syllables. For example, they might change "wait" in sentence #2 to "linger." Read both versions aloud and compare. Studying how sentences end may help students learn about the key quality Capturing Smooth and Rhythmic Flow.

10. Have students note on their draft changes they want to make to their sentences when they revisit the piece.

From *Winterdance: The Fine Madness of Running the Iditarod*
by Gary Paulsen

Caught up in anxiety, not wishing to cause problems with the race, I harnessed my dogs too soon, way too soon, and tied the sled off to the bumper of the truck. The difficulty with this was that I had pulled number thirty-two and with the dogs tied on the side, harnessed, and ready to go, waiting to go, crazy to go—every team going up to the chutes had to be taken past my team—they had to wait. Dogs do not wait well. An old Inuit belief states that dogs and white men stem from the same roots because they cannot wait, have no patience, and become frustrated easily, and it showed mightily then. (p. 141)

Sentence Grid for Gary Paulsen's Paragraph:

Sentence Number	Number of Words	First Two Words	Last Word
1.			
2.			
3.			
4.			

Lesson Extension

Have students browse textbooks, novels, magazines, newspapers, and other publications, and pick a paragraph that has at least four sentences. Then have them create a chart like the one in the lesson to capture how each sentence begins, how it ends, and how many words it contains. When they've finished, share paragraphs and data from the charts with the class and ask students to discuss how the information might influence their writing.

ACTIVITIES Crafting Well-Built Sentences

Change It Up

Sometimes students get stuck in a rut, writing the same old simple sentences in piece after piece. This activity gives them a swift kick in the sentence fluency pants! Put students in groups of four or five and ask each member to write a sentence on any topic. Tell each member to pass his or her sentence to the member on the left. That member must add a sentence to develop the topic. But here's the rub: The new sentence cannot begin with either of the first two words of the original sentence, nor can it have the same subject or a pronoun form of that subject. For example, if the first student writes, "Mary went to the store," the second student cannot write, "Mary bought some eggs," nor "She bought some eggs." But he could write, "Riding there on her bike took about fifteen minutes."

When all group members have successfully written a second sentence, ask them to pass both sentences to the member on the left. Continue the process until all four or five papers return to the member who originated them. Then have students share the completed papers with the group. Discuss which was harder, changing the sentence beginnings or changing the subject of each sentence.

Four Words Longer/Four Words Shorter

This activity is great for students who tend to write sentences of average length—and only sentences of average length. Ask students to write a sentence on a topic of their choice and then give it to a partner. Have the partner develop the topic by adding a sentence that is at least four words longer or shorter than the original one. Ask students to pass the papers back and forth, adding sentences of different lengths, until each piece contains ten sentences. Read each piece aloud and discuss how well-built sentences affect fluency. Have students select the sentence they feel is the strongest and explain why.

Key Quality: Varying Sentence Types

Writing that is fluent usually contains a variety of different types of sentences—simple, compound, complex, and compound-complex. However, it's all too easy for middle school students to get stuck writing the same type of sentence in paper after paper. So it's important to teach them different sentence types and offer practice opportunities to use them in their own writing. Use the following Think About to expand students' notions about using varying sentence types.

THINK ABOUT:

- Do I include different kinds of sentences?
- Are some of my sentences complex?
- Are some of my sentences simple?
- Did I intermingle sentence types, one to the next?

WARM-UP Varying Sentence Types

Distribute copies of the Think About, reminding students that there are four basic types of sentences: simple, compound, complex, and compound-complex. Review these sentence types as needed, using the reproducible on page 247 as a guide. Then ask students to revise the following paragraph, which is made up of only simple sentences—sentences with a subject, predicate, and, at most, a prepositional phrase—by bringing more sentence variety to it.

> Snow is supposed to be great. I've never seen it, though. I wish I could see snow. I'd lie in the snow. I'd make a snow angel. I'd make snowballs. I'd throw snowballs at all my friends. I wouldn't eat yellow snow. No, I wouldn't do that.

Discuss the changes students make. Ask them to look at their revised paragraphs and count the number of simple, compound, complex, and compound-complex sentences. Invite questions about how to differentiate among these sentence types. Then share the following revised paragraph or one that you create.

> I hear snow is great. Of course, I wouldn't know from personal experience since I've never seen the stuff. But if, by some miracle, it snowed here, I'd lie in it and roll around. I'd create an angel in the fresh snow by flapping my arms up and down. And I'd make a whole bunch of snowballs to throw at my friends. Even though I've never seen snow, I know enough not to eat it when it's yellow. I would not ever do that! If it snowed a lot, I'd finally get a snow day from school so I could relax and sleep in. Ah, that would be the best of all.

FOCUS LESSON   Varying Sentence Types

Bringing a beautiful, natural sound to writing can be difficult, especially to nonfiction writing, given all the facts and figures it typically needs to contain. But some authors make it look easy. Nicola Davies is such an author. Her picture books about animals are stunning for many reasons, including their sentences. Davies mixes long, elegant sentences with short, more declarative ones, providing students with models of how to write nonfiction that is every bit as fluent as good fiction.

Materials:
- *Bat Loves the Night* by Nicola Davies
- transparency and copies of the Types of Clauses/Types of Sentences reproducible (page 247 and CD)
- copies of the Sentences Inspired by *Bat Loves the Night* reproducible (page 248 and CD)
- paper, pens, pencils

What to Do:
1. Review the two basic types of clauses (independent and dependent) and four basic types of sentences (simple, compound, complex, and compound-complex) by projecting the transparency of the Types of Clauses/Types of Sentences reproducible and giving each student a copy.

2. Read aloud *Bat Loves the Night*. When you've finished, ask students to discuss its level of fluency. Most of them will give it high marks—the sentences are graceful and flow smoothly from start to finish.

3. Give each student a copy of the Sentences Inspired by *Bat Loves the Night* reproducible.

4. Have students work with a partner to combine Part 1's simple sentences into several compound or complex sentences. They should create at least one of each kind—more if they enjoy the challenge. For example, they could combine the simple sentences "Birds rule the air by day" and "Bats are the monarchs of the night" into a compound sentence "Birds rule the air by day, but bats are the monarchs of the night." Or they could create a complex sentence from several simple ones, Here's an example:

> They live in every habitat.
> There is the subarctic tundra habitat.
> There is the tropical forest habitat.
> There is the desert habitat.

These simple sentences could become:

> "They live in every habitat, including subarctic, tropical, and desert environments."

5. When they're finished, ask students to share their new sentences with another pair of students. From there, ask each pair to share a favorite compound or complex sentence with the whole class.

6. Reread the first half of Davies's book and compare its sentences with the sentences students produced. Discuss the similarities and differences.

7. Have the same partners combine Part 2's simple sentences into compound and complex sentences.

8. Reread the second half of Davies's book and compare its sentences with the sentences students produced. Again, discuss the similarities and differences.

9. Encourage students to look at a piece of their own writing, checking to see if they use a variety of sentences that are easy on the ear when the piece is read aloud.

Lesson Extension

Have students find five well-written nonfiction books at the library. Ask them to write a fluent passage from one of the books on the whiteboard and have classmates label its various sentences types. If students can't identify a sentence type, remind them of the four definitions. Ask students to read the passages aloud for fluency, listening for the various sentence types.

Types of Clauses:

A **clause** is a sentence part that contains a subject and verb.

An **independent clause** can stand alone as a grammatically correct sentence:

> "She began the new book…"

A **dependent clause** cannot stand alone:

> "When she began the new book…"

Types of Sentences:

Simple: A sentence made up of one independent clause that may contain a direct object or prepositional phrase:

> "The students chose a book."
>
> "The students raved about the book."

Compound: A sentence made up of two or more independent clauses, which are joined by a conjunction such as *and*, *but*, or *or*:

> "The students raved about the book, and the author was delighted to receive their complimentary e-mails."

Complex: A sentence made up of an independent clause and at least one dependent clause:

> "When the author learned how much the students liked her work, she decided to write more books."

Compound-Complex: A sentence made up of two or more independent clauses and at least one dependent clause:

> "When the author announced she was writing more books, the students were delighted, but she surprised them by writing about a different subject than they expected."

Sentences Inspired by *Bat Loves the Night*

PART 1: Combine these sentences inspired by the first half of the book

Bats are mammals.
They can really fly.
They are very successful at surviving because they fly.
There are more than nine hundred bat species.
They live in every habitat.
There is the subarctic tundra habitat.
There is the tropical forest habitat.
There is the desert habitat.
Birds rule the air by day.
Bats are the monarchs of the night.

PART 2: Combine these sentences inspired by the second half of the book.

Bat is waking.	She shakes her fur.
She's upside down.	Her fur is thistledown.
She usually hangs upside down.	She unfurls her wings.
She hangs by her toenails.	Her wings are made of skin.
Her eyes are beady.	The skin is fine.
Her eyes are open.	The bones show through.
Her pixie ears twitch.	The bones are like fingers.

ACTIVITIES Varying Sentence Types

Selling Sentences

In order to become skilled writers, students need to feel comfortable crafting all types of sentences—simple, compound, complex, and compound-complex. The more practice you allow them, the more fluent their writing becomes. One way to ensure that is to ask students to create an advertisement for each sentence type. Put students into groups of four and ask each member to design a poster that "sells" one sentence type. Their posters should include these elements:

- the name of the sentence type
- a definition of it
- examples of it
- a statement convincing readers that the sentence type is important—in fact, the most important of all the sentence types

Writing Like "Prose"

Song lyrics, like poetry, are usually written in phrases, not complete, connected sentences the way prose usually is. Ask students to choose a favorite song (that you approve) and download the lyrics from the Internet. Then have them turn those lyrics into prose, by using as many different sentence types as possible. For example:

"Waiting on the World to Change" by John Mayer

Me and all my friends
We're all misunderstood
They say we stand for nothing and
There's no way we ever could

Now we see everything that's going wrong
With the world and those who lead it
We just feel like we don't have the means
To rise above and beat it

Revised as prose:

The world does not understand me or my generation. They believe that we don't stand for anything and that we never will. But it's not quite like that. We see what's wrong with this world and the leaders who have not worked out. We just don't know how to change it right now. We're not the ones with the power to make things better.

Discuss the differences in fluency between the two versions.

Key Quality: Capturing Smooth and Rhythmic Flow

Just as playing scales helps a pianist to create melodies, experimenting with sentence types helps writers create pieces that flow. Writers typically revise sentences over and over until they get them right. Their goal? Creating smooth sentences that are pleasing to the ear. Use the following Think About to expand students' notions about capturing a smooth and rhythmic flow.

Reproducible on CD

THINK ABOUT:

- Is reading the entire piece aloud easy?
- Do my sentences flow, one to the next?
- Do individual passages sound smooth when I read them aloud?
- Did I thoughtfully place different sentence types to enhance the main idea?

WARM-UP Capturing Smooth and Rhythmic Flow

Distribute copies of the Think About and the brief paragraph below. Have students find a partner, read the paragraph aloud, and discuss how it sounds. Are the sentences smooth? Do they glide across the page? Students will likely answer no. Ask them to revise the paragraph to capture a smooth and rhythmic flow.

> Tuesday I would find out if I made it onto the basketball team. I really wanted to be chosen. Basketball is fun. Many of my friends tried out, too. I hoped we all made it. I will wait outside the P.E. teacher's office until the list is posted. If my name is on there, I'll be very happy.

Have students share their revisions with their partner. Then ask volunteers to share their revisions with the class and discuss how listening to the sound of writing leads to better sentence fluency. Share the following revised paragraph or one that you create.

> Ticktock, ticktock. The hands on the clock seemed to crawl as I stood anxiously waiting to find out if I'd made the basketball team. I'd been outside the coach's office many times in the past, but this time it felt different. I fidgeted; I hopped from one foot to the next; I chewed on my lower lip. 9:15 AM. Coach promised he'd have the list posted by then. Seven more minutes. I hardly noticed the other boys also waiting impatiently to see if they'd made it. *What are they worried about,* I thought. *They're awesome players. They didn't miss a pass or a basket in any of the tryouts.* I was not a shoo-in, but if hard work, steady improvement, and a good attitude count for anything I just might have a chance. Ah, there it is. The list is finally posted. I shoved my way through the small crowd to the front and saw the list of names! My heart stopped….

FOCUS LESSON Capturing Smooth and Rhythmic Flow

It's important for students to develop the ability to hear a sentence and know if it sounds right. At first, all sentences will probably sound the same to them. But over time, with experience reading their own work and the work of others, big and little problems will begin to stand out. Hearing high-quality writing read aloud will speed up this process, especially for English-language learners who are used to the rhythms and cadences of their first language. In this lesson, students read a sentence repeatedly. First, they construct a long sentence, word by word, reading along as they go. Then, they deconstruct the sentence, one word at a time, creating a new, shorter sentence with each subsequent reading—and developing an ear for fluency in the process.

Materials:
- copies of two-sided word cards for building sentences (page 252 and CD)
- paper, pens, pencils

What to Do:
1. Hand out the 13 word cards to 13 randomly chosen students.
2. Ask the four students who have the cards "Is," "Brown," "Dog," and "My" to come to the front of the class and arrange themselves in an order that makes a complete sentence. Since the cards show each word capitalized on the front and lowercase on the back, be sure students use the correct side, depending on where their word falls in the sentence: "My dog is brown."
3. Ask the class if the word cards make a sentence. If the answer is yes, read the sentence aloud together and ask a student to tell you what type of sentence it is: simple, complex, compound, or compound-complex (see page 247 for definitions). If the answer is no, ask the four cardholders to rearrange themselves until they make a sentence.
4. Ask another student to join the sentence, read his or her word aloud, and take a place among the cardholders to expand the sentence—for example, "My wet dog is brown." Allow the new cardholder to change the order of the words already in play. Read the expanded sentence aloud. If the class deems the sentence correct, ask a student to identify what kind of sentence it is.
5. Continue adding cards, reading the expanded sentences, and identifying their types until all the cards have been used. If two cards must be added at the same time for the sentence to work, such as "and" and "gives" (the conjunction and the second verb), that's okay because students will see that the conjunction may turn the sentence from simple to compound.
6. Read the final sentence aloud and ask a student not holding a card to tell you what kind of sentence it is—most likely compound, for example, "My dog is fuzzy, mocha-colored, chocolate brown and gives warm, wet, slobbery kisses."

Standing Sentences

Directions for Creating Cards:

1. On pieces of card stock large enough to be read easily from the back of the room, write each of the words below—capitalized on the front and lowercase on the back.

2. For the lesson extension's punctuation mark cards, use an ink color that's different from the one you use for the word cards. (Use these cards once the sentence is fully assembled and students wish to edit it.)

3. Laminate the cards and clip them together for long-term use.

Words for Standing Sentence:

my	and
dog	gives
is	warm
fuzzy	wet
mocha-colored	slobbery
chocolate	kisses
brown	

7. Reverse roles and deconstruct the sentence. Ask students not holding cards to *remove* words, while leaving the sentence intact. As students not holding cards call out words, cardholders take their seats. If you reach a point where two cards must come out at the same time for the remaining cards to create an intact sentence, that's fine. Read each new sentence aloud every time a word card is removed. Tell students the goal is to whittle the sentence down to the shortest one possible that is different from the sentence they started with. For example, they may wind up with "My dog kisses." Or "Kisses is my dog."

8. At the end of the lesson, discuss the importance of listening to the sound of sentences to determine whether they are complete or not. Remind students to read their own sentences aloud as they write to ensure they make sense and have rhythm and flow.

Lesson Extension

The longer sentences get, the more punctuation marks they'll need to make sense. So make a set of cards with commas, periods, exclamation marks, dashes, ellipses, and other punctuation marks on them. Give them to students to add to the sentence as it expands, and remove as it contracts. Discuss punctuation's role in making sentences read smoothly.

ACTIVITIES Capturing Smooth and Rhythmic Flow

Choral Reading: *The Ghost Dance* by Alice McLerran

Some picture books are written so beautifully, they cry out to be read aloud. *The Ghost Dance* by Alice McLerran is one of them. It's about the Paiute Indians' aspiration to restore what's been lost in the natural world—and to maintain what hasn't been. Ask small groups of students to read aloud passages from the book sequentially, until they reach the end. Then ask students if McLerran taught them anything about sentence fluency. They will likely respond that to read in harmony with other students, they had to decide when to raise and lower their voices, how to pace themselves, where to take a breath, and what words to emphasize. Tell them that those skills build oral fluency and can be transferred to their writing.

Reverse Revision

One of the best ways to understand a complex concept like sentence fluency is to give students a strong piece of writing and ask them to weaken it. That's right, weaken it. After all, for students to know what to change, they must have a solid understanding of what is fluent. To get you started, distribute the following piece by an eighth grader, which scored a 6, exceptional, in sentence fluency, and ask students to turn it into a 1 or 2. When they're finished, discuss their "reverse revisions." How did diminishing the piece's sentence fluency affect its overall quality? How did it affect other traits?

> Have you ever read a book that was so interesting you couldn't put it down, even though you wished you had never opened that dreary thing in the first place? Well, that's my specialty. The name is Edgar Allan Poe and I write scary stories for a living. One of my favorites is "The Tell-Tale Heart" in which you step into the body of a killer and hear his every thought, and even more disturbing, his motive.

Don't wander over to the comics section because I'm telling you this book is ASTOUNDING! In my short story, the killer is trying to justify his reasoning for murdering a poor, old, defenseless man while also trying to prove his sanity. As the tale progresses, you find this murderer is anything but sane because the man he killed has done nothing to harm or offend him. Would you kill someone for something they had absolutely no control over, like a cataract in their eye? Well, the narrator in this story does exactly that. You would never find anything like this in a comic book or a mooshy gooshy love story. Can you say BORING?

Understand, I am not trying to deprive you as a reader, but to engage you in a better book. Comics will just leave you empty inside and bore you. Love stories will simply break your heart and lead you to believe that there are always happy endings. A "Tell-Tale Heart" gives you the facts and makes you aware of disturbed people in this world. Wouldn't you much rather be on the edge of your seat DYING to turn the page and read more?

Key Quality: Breaking the "Rules" to Create Fluency

Breaking the rules of standard English, or at least bending them for a specific, desired effect, makes sentence fluency one of the most creative traits. Incorporating fragments, repeating phrases, starting sentences with conjunctions, and using everyday, grammatically incorrect dialogue are just a few of the techniques writers commonly use that stretch the boundaries of correctness. We want students writing outside the box when it helps them to meet their purpose for writing and is appropriate for their audience. It makes for more interesting, more honest work. Use the following Think About to expand students' notions about breaking the rules to create fluency.

Reproducible on CD

THINK ABOUT:

- Did I use fragments with style and purpose?
- Do I begin a sentence informally to create a conversational tone?
- Does my dialogue sound authentic?
- Did I try weaving in exclamations and single words to add emphasis?

WARM-UP   Breaking the "Rules" to Create Fluency

Distribute copies of the Think About and the following dialogue. Have student revise the dialogue by breaking the rules to make it more authentic, meaningful, and, in the process, fluent.

"I am bored," said Justin.

"I am bored, too," said Dimitri.

"Let's go outside," said Justin.

"Yes, let's go outside," said Dimitri.

"Let's throw the football," said Justin.

"Okay, let's throw the football," said Dimitri.

Later, "That was fun," said Justin.

"I agree," said Dimitri.

"Now I'm hungry," said Justin.

"Me, too," said Dimitri.

When students are finished, ask them to read their revisions to the class. Have the class use the Think About to identify "rules" that each writer breaks to create fluency. Then share the following revision or one that you create.

> "It's so boring around here today," whined Justin, "I'm almost desperate enough for something to do that I might do my homework."
>
> "Oh no! Not that," laughed Dimitri. "I'm sure we can find something to do that's better than homework. Hey! Why don't we go outside and throw the football around. We need the practice; tryouts are next week."
>
> "Fine!" replied Justin. "I'll get it from my room. You go outside and mark off some distances. Let's see who can throw the farthest and straightest. The loser has to do the other guy's homework before class on Monday."
>
> "You are on," Dimitri said, pointing his index finger at Justin. "If I lose, it's no big deal to do your homework. You always get them all wrong anyway.
>
> "Ha-ha. Very funny wise guy. Let's see who's still laughing in an hour. And get ready. I'm going to throw like you've never seen before."
>
> "Bring it on, baby!" said Dimitri as he strutted out the door.

FOCUS LESSON Breaking the "Rules" to Create Fluency

Although fragments, or incomplete sentences, were once forbidden by most teachers and editors, writers today sprinkle them into their work for style, interest, and variety—and to create fluency. Skilled writers use them sparingly and purposefully. The perfect fragment at the perfect point can hammer the message home. But too many fragments used carelessly and for an unclear purpose only create confusion. In this lesson, students write a character sketch using fragments—and only fragments. Their challenge is to reveal everything they can about the character in as few words as possible. In the process, they learn to distinguish complete sentences from fragments. They also learn that overusing fragments can lead to underwhelming work.

Materials:
- model writing (page 256)
- Character List reproducible, if desired (page 257 and CD)
- paper, pens, pencils

What to Do:

1. Discuss the fact that a fragment is different from a complete sentence because it doesn't contain the two essential elements of a complete sentence: a subject and a verb. Ask students if teachers in other classes allow fragments. What are the advantages and disadvantages of using fragments in writing?

2. Ask each student to find a book, magazine, or newspaper passage that contains a fragment. Then have them turn that fragment into a complete sentence.

3. Have students read their original passages (containing the fragment) and their revised passages (containing the complete sentence) to the class. Which passage sounds better? Discuss.

4. Tell students they will be writing character sketches, using fragments and descriptive language. Project and read to them the following model:

Failed System
by Daniel Kimzey, Polson, Montana

Jackie rolls tough. He thinks. Others think. Old guys see punk thug. Hat cocked. Baggies hangin' dangerously low. Service-station shirt. Buzz cut. That's how he rolls—with 50 Cent on a stolen iPod—strutting. Never giving much, nods slight. Cold eyes shade lost soul's windows. Dropped out of school the day he turned sixteen. Wasn't really there before. Didn't reveal much. Oozed through the cracks. Jackie didn't read in school because he didn't learn to. Tight secret. Didn't matter anyway. No warning labels cautioning user that huffing harms. Sweet diversion. From what? From a wasted brain. No goal. No path. No desire. Except to escape. Slide back on a wood pallet in the greasy stench of a restaurant alley and slip into nothing. No satisfaction. This time.

5. Share the list of characters with students and ask them to choose one—or create one of their own. Remind them that they must use only fragments in their sketches, and the most descriptive language possible.

6. Allow students time to write their character sketches. Be sure they include physical and emotional qualities of the character, likes and dislikes, details about his or her daily struggles and joys, and so on. Have them read their drafts to a partner as they go.

7. When students are finished writing, ask them to read their sketches to the class, *without naming the character.* After each sketch has been read, have the rest of the class guess the character.

8. Discuss when fragments work in writing—and when they don't. Ask students to think of reasons writing complete sentences might be preferable to only writing with fragments. Discuss with students that using fragments can add a stylistic element to writing, but they should be used sparingly to maximize that effect. Students may wish to look at a piece of their own work to see if a fragment is just what they need to add energy.

Character List

A very old man or woman

A newly elected politician

An expectant mother or father

A successful businessperson

An overworked airline pilot

An experienced plumber

A wildly creative Web designer

A professional athlete

A frustrated teacher

An always-late pizza delivery person

Lesson Extension

Ask pairs of students to revise "Failed System" (or any other fragment-filled paragraph that you find) by transforming all the fragments into complete sentences. When students are finished, put their revisions and the original piece side by side on posterboard and hang them around the room in prominent locations. Ask students to vote for the best revision by signing their name underneath their choice. When the results are tallied, discuss the winner and how it compares to the original piece.

ACTIVITIES   Breaking the "Rules" to Create Fluency

Single-Syllable Sounds

Did you know that the 50 most common words in the English language contain only one syllable? Challenge your students to write a short story or essay using only single-syllable words. Here is a grand example from *Writing!* magazine: "Big words can make the way dark for those who read what you write and hear what you say. Small words cast their clear light on big things—night and day, love and hate, war and peace, and life and death. Small words are the ones we seem to have known from the time we were born, like the hearth fire that warms the home" (Lederer, 1991, p. 4). Ask students to read their pieces aloud and discuss how they sound. Did writing this way increase or decrease sentence fluency?

Sure Sounds Like It

Ask students to brainstorm a list of attitudes for story characters, such as fussy, demanding, relaxed, strident, worried, confident, angry, confused, disappointed, encouraging, whiny, and easygoing. With a partner, have them pick two opposite attitudes from the list, such as angry and relaxed. Then have them come up with a situation in which two characters would exhibit those attitudes. From there, have students write a short scenario, containing dialogue that enables the reader to identify each character's attitude. When students finish, ask them to act out their scenarios before the class. Then have audience members identify each character's attitude.

Mentor Texts for Middle School: Sentence Fluency

High-quality books, magazines, and newspapers can provide powerful models of fluency—models that can help students make their own writing fluent. Hearing the language of books, magazines, and newspapers is critical to understanding fluency from the inside out. So, please, read them aloud. Seize every opportunity to get well-crafted language into the ears and minds of students. By doing this, you not only expose students to powerful models, but also give them the courage to read their own work aloud, which is important for writers of all ages. As Peter Elbow puts it, "When you and your class read your writing out loud, you often hear things in it that you do not experience any other way" (1998, p. 82). I couldn't agree more. The following books are excellent models of sentence fluency, in my estimation. The author of each one has poked, prodded, and polished her sentences to make them sing.

The Forbidden Schoolhouse by Suzanne Jurmain
(Houghton Mifflin, 2005)
In 1833 Miss Prudence Crandall had the courage to welcome 19-year-old Sarah Harris, a talented African American student, to the classroom of her elite, all-white private school. Although this book reads like a great novel, every bit of it is true. It's a finely written, fluent memoir.

The Hunger Games by Suzanne Collins (Scholastic, 2008)
This first installment in a trilogy of futuristic survival stories will keep you and your students up all night. It's that suspenseful. In fact, Collins provides a model for using sentence fragments to build suspense and emphasize key moments that lead to a stunning climax. *The Hunger Games* is definitely one of my favorite books in recent years. The second book, *Catching Fire*, is just as well written. The third one will be as well, I'm sure. Can't wait.

The Tequila Worm by Viola Canales (Wendy Lamb Books, 2005)
Canales is a real storyteller. She paints life in the barrio with a combination of smooth, descriptive sentences and authentic-sounding dialogue. Her book is about 14-year-old Sophie, her family, and her difficult decision to leave her comfortable, comforting home to pursue an education at an elite school. Its fluency runs like a quiet river beneath a powerful, thoroughly enjoyable story line.

Final Thoughts

Traveling through a piece of writing should be effortless. But all too often, sentences create speed bumps and even roadblocks. Well-crafted, original sentences move the reader along with ease. Poorly crafted, uninspired ones make the trip go on forever, prompting the reader to ask, "Are we there yet?" As we leave sentence fluency, the last of the revision traits, in the rearview mirror, we cross the border into editing country and visit conventions and presentation, where I share ideas for helping students take their writing public.

PART THREE
The Editing Traits

I devote the final two chapters of this book to the editing traits: conventions and presentation. I call these the editing traits because they cover what copy editors do as they prepare text for publication: check each word, sentence, and paragraph carefully to make sure they follow the rules of standard English and are a breeze to read.

Editing for conventions is the final big step of the writing process, after the writer has drafted and revised for ideas, organization, voice, word choice, and sentence fluency. The writer cleans up the piece in preparation for the reader, so that errors in spelling, capitalization, punctuation, paragraphing, and grammar and usage don't disrupt the reading experience.

But conventions are more than a list of dos and don'ts. When creatively applied, they can sharpen ideas, boost voice, and add complexity to sentences. Focusing on them helps the writer use standard English to make meaning clear and comprehensible. A strategically placed punctuation mark, for example, can be used to hammer a point home. Nonstandard grammar can be used to create authentic dialogue. Ideally, students learn basic rules, such as capitalizing the first word in a sentence, and move on to more sophisticated skills, such as knowing the right words to capitalize in a title. From there, they learn to break those rules with creativity and intention, when the writing calls for it. And since conventions comprise four broad, very robust editing zones—spelling, capitalization, punctuation, paragraphing, and grammar and usage—there is something new for every student to learn, regardless of his or her skill level.

Presentation is also a part of editing. Once a student has checked conventions thoroughly and is ready to create the final copy, he or she must figure out what the piece should look like, by asking questions such as How wide should I make the margins? Should I single- or double-space the text? Where should I place headings and bulleted lists? What's the best way to integrate charts and graphs so they are easy to read? In other words, the student thinks about how visual elements may affect the reader's ability to follow and understand the piece.

CHAPTER 9

Conventions:

Reader Ready

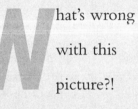

What's wrong with this picture?! Conventions cover capitalization, punctuation, paragraphing, grammar and usage, and, yes, spelling. Whether a popular novelist or city worker, writers use standard English conventions so readers can read what they create, plain and simple. Without conventions, we would be sunk. Each writer would spell words as he or she saw fit. Capitalize any old word on a whim. Stick a period in the middle of a sentence simply because it looks pretty there. Chaos! The word *school* is spelled "s-c-h-o-o-l" for good reason. Any other spelling is just plain wrong and confusing to the reader.

That said, it's important to remember that English is a living language. What was standard when I was in junior high may not be standard today. Ending a sentence with a preposition, splitting an infinitive, dangling a modifier, and using the passive voice, for example, were all crimes in Miss Spellacy's class, punishable by red pen. In today's writing world, however, they're not. In fact, writers often commit these writing acts deliberately, depending on their purpose and audience for the writing. In some ways, teaching and learning conventions is more complicated than ever because students not only need to know the rules, they need to know when it's okay to break them—and when it isn't. Having that skill is the mark of a true writer.

The Conventions Trait: A Definition

> **❝** I've learned a lot about conventions this year. None of it ever stuck before. But this year, I think I get it. I still need to get better in spelling, though. **❞**
>
> —Nicholas, grade 8

Conventions are the editing standards we apply to a piece of writing to make it mechanically correct and, therefore, easy to read. They consist of spelling, capitalization, punctuation, paragraphing, and grammar and usage. Each of these conventions has its own set of rules—rules a copy editor follows to prepare text for publication. Rules that must be taught to middle school students so they can apply them with accuracy and consistency to their writing.

We edit for conventions because we care about our reader. Whether our reader is a teacher, a peer, or the general public, we want him or her to be able to follow our writing effortlessly and become immersed in our ideas, which can only happen if he or she is not bogged down by unintentional errors. There are standard conventions to which we must adhere, unless we depart from them for a clear purpose. To show strength in conventions, the writer must skillfully and confidently apply these key qualities:

* Checking Spelling
* Punctuating Effectively and Paragraphing Accurately
* Capitalizing Correctly
* Applying Grammar and Usage

Why Students Struggle With Conventions

When I travel by plane for business, I sometimes wind up sitting next to a person who asks what I do for a living. I am often tempted to make up a story, because if I reveal what I really do—write books and conduct workshops to help teachers help students become better writers—I usually get a lecture on how, in *his day*, he and his classmates were drilled in grammar, spelling, and cursive handwriting until their writing was "perfect." And when I ask how he feels about writing now, the answer is always—and I mean *always*—the same: "I hate it."

Connecting their disdain for writing to the methods by which they were taught writing is usually a real eye-opener for my fellow passengers. While many of them feel children today are not receiving a good writing education because they are not being subjected to the same outdated methods, they acknowledge that those methods didn't work and never will. As we fly over the country, I'm gratified to see the relief on their faces when I explain that writing instruction has moved on, that we have better ways to teach our nation's children that include grammar, spelling, handwriting, and so much more—and don't lead them to hate writing as adults. Frankly, by and large, we're better at teaching writing than teachers of the past, but most adults don't know that. So it's up to us to teach them, too.

In the meantime, many adults will continue thinking that writing is nothing more than conventions and presentation—and actually inhibit their own children's growth in writing by nagging them about things like spelling and handwriting on a regular basis. Kids tune out when parents hold such a narrow view of writing. We'd do well to remember that, along with the following reasons students typically struggle to master the conventions trait.

They Count On the Teacher to Point Out Errors

Here's the best advice I can give you about conventions: Stop editing papers for students—at least on simple tasks they can and should be doing on their own. Remember, the person holding the pen is the one who's learning. If you are your students' sole editor, congratulations; you are probably getting very good at spotting and correcting problems in conventions. However, more than likely, your students aren't. And the only way for them to get good at editing is for you to start demanding it.

Here's an example of how you might start: Hold a class meeting and create a "No Excuses" list by asking students to name one simple skill in each convention (spelling, capitalization, punctuating, paragraphing, and grammar and usage) they feel they can handle on their own. Start simple, for example:

- Spell *because* correctly.

- Punctuate the end of every sentence.

- Start a new paragraph if you shift ideas.

- Always capitalize the pronoun *I* and the first word in the sentence.

- No text messaging symbols or abbreviations. Use complete words and sentences.

Write out the list and display it prominently. Give students a copy for their notebooks. Tattoo it on their forearms, if necessary!

Add more challenging editing skills to the list over time, but I highly recommend beginning with basic editing skills like these. By holding students responsible for what you *know* they can do, you teach them *how* to edit.

Once the "No Excuses" list is established, let students know they are responsible for everything on it. That means that each time you collect their papers, you should scan them to be sure students have followed all the rules on the list. I have a two-second policy: I look at each piece quickly, focusing on the conventions from the "No Excuses" list. If I see a violation, I hand the paper back to the student and ask him or her to edit it before turning it in again, without pointing out the violation. If I do that—"Sawsan, you spelled *because* wrong here. Please correct it"—the student doesn't learn to spot problems and fix them on her own. Instead, I'd say, "Sawsan, it doesn't appear that you've edited your piece yet. Please check it over and then put it on my desk before you begin something else." If the student seems frustrated, I may give a clue—"It's a spelling problem"—to give her a heads-up. But I never provide all the missing information because I'm trying to teach the student how to spot problems on her own.

They Are Surrounded by Writing That Is Flawed

Take a look at the billboards, menus, brochures, advertisements, Web sites, and other print and nonprint media that surround you and your students—and notice their serious flaws in conventions. There's a sign near my house, for example, that reads "Aloha Hi School" instead of "Aloha High School." Ouch! Middle school students aren't the only ones who struggle with homonyms. Adults do, too. And spelling problems like this can obscure meaning, as you can see by trying to read this sentence: "The knew banned was band from playing won song at there new club." You probably had to translate as you read, which no doubt made understanding my message tricky.

It's fun to find mistakes in the media. It makes us feel smart. And it makes kids feel smart, too. So encourage your students to be on the lookout for examples of poorly used conventions in the world around them and provide a place in the classroom for them to post their discoveries. Over time, they'll develop a proofreader's eye and become better editors of their own work.

They Aren't Taught Grammar in Context

In 1963 a report commissioned by the National Council of Teachers of English entitled *Research in Written Composition* by Braddock, Lloyd-Jones, and Schoer, or the Braddock Report, as it came to be known, concluded that "the teaching of formal grammar has a negligible or, because it usually displaces some instruction and practice in actual composition, even has a harmful effect on the improvement of writing" (pp. 37-38), proving that, for almost half a century, we have known that students learn grammar not by dissecting decontextualized sentences written by some stranger, but by writing their own sentences within a context that matters to them.

Sure, students need to understand grammar. They need to develop control over standard English. They need to learn the purposes of verbs, nouns, adjectives, adverbs, pronouns, prepositions, conjunctions, interjections, and other kinds of words in a sentence. They need to learn how to use language correctly, showing skill in grammar (the study of words and their syntactical relations and functions) and usage (the customary manner in which a language is written), but only as it relates to their writing and how their sentences work. Researcher George Hillocks, Jr., says it best: "School boards, administrators, and teachers who impose the systematic study of traditional school grammar on their students over lengthy periods of time in the name of teaching writing do them a gross disservice which should not be tolerated by anyone concerned with the effects of teaching good writing" (1986, p. 248). Hear, hear.

Have people ever told you that they didn't understand English grammar until they learned another language? That's because learning a second language provides a purpose for understanding how English works. We study English constructions right along with those of the new language we're learning. We're working in context, in other words—the secret to success in conventions, as well as most every other aspect of writing.

Assessing Student Work for Conventions

The following sixth-grade papers represent a wide range of skills in the conventions trait. Review the scoring guide on page 267, read each paper carefully, assess the paper for the conventions trait by following the steps on pages 50–51 under "Assessing Writing Using the Trait Scoring Guides," and then read my assessment to see whether we agree. Use your own students' writing for further practice.

The papers were all written in response to the prompt "Think of an invention that has been either helpful or harmful and provide an explanation for your choice." Because they were all written in the expository mode, the purpose of the papers is to inform and explain. If they contain elements of narrative writing such as figurative language and a problem to be resolved, it's fine—even worthy of celebration. After all, good writers often use such elements in expository pieces to add voice and make their central idea as clear as possible.

I chose papers written at the same grade level, in the same mode, and to the same prompt so that you can focus on the issue at hand, conventions, without other factors serving as a distraction. But keep in mind, it's critical for students to develop skills in conventions, regardless of the grade they're in, the mode they choose, and the prompt they're given—and apply those skills all the time. Even though I focus on conventions, I've scored the papers in all the traits (except presentation, since the papers are typeset) in case you need additional samples to practice scoring or use in your instruction.

Tips for Scoring Conventions

Without a doubt, spelling is the queen bee of conventions. As a result, raters often score for spelling first, and then give lip service to the other conventions. If the spelling is handled well, the piece tends to score high in all conventions. But if it isn't, the piece tends to score low. Very low. But to arrive at an accurate and defensible score in conventions, the rater must take into account *all* conventions equally. As you read the sample papers that follow, ask yourself what is working well in conventions right along with what needs work. If the punctuation and capitalization are strong, the paragraphs break in the right places, and the grammar is well handled, but the spelling clearly needs work, don't overreact. If the score plummets based solely on spelling, it does not communicate to the writer how well he or she understands and applies other important conventions.

Here's a quick way I check the accuracy of my scores after I assess papers for conventions. I ask myself, how much editing (all of the conventions) would need to be done to make this piece ready for its intended audience?

- If I answer, "A lot—this piece has many distracting conventions errors of all sorts, making it difficult to read," the piece scores low, a 1 or a 2.

- If I answer, "Some—it has a few errors in different conventions, not just one. It would take a moderate amount of editing," the piece scores in the middle, a 3 or 4.

- If I answer, "Hardly any—just a little touch-up here and there," the piece scores high, a 5 or 6.

You can fine-tune the score using the details from the scoring guide, once you identify the range.

Here's another scoring tip: If the piece is well edited, but the writer has attempted nothing difficult, such as punctuating complex sentences correctly or spelling challenging words correctly, do not give it the highest score, a 6. To earn a 6, students must demonstrate skill in a wide range of conventions. A simple piece that contains capital letters at the beginning of each sentence, a period at the end of each sentence, new paragraphs in all the right places, and correctly spelled basic words might get a 5. But to earn a 6, it has to show evidence of control over difficult conventions such as punctuating complex sentences, spelling challenging vocabulary words, and nailing the subject-verb agreement.

Scoring Guide: Conventions

The mechanical correctness of the piece. Correct use of conventions (spelling, capitalization, punctuation, paragraphing, and grammar and usage) guides the reader through the text easily.

Reproducible on CD

6

HIGH

EXCEPTIONAL

A. **Checking Spelling:** The writer spells sight words, high-frequency words, and less familiar words correctly. When he or she spells less familiar words incorrectly, those words are phonetically correct. Overall, the piece reveals control in spelling.

B. **Punctuating Effectively and Paragraphing Accurately:** The writer handles basic punctuation skillfully. He or she understands how to use periods, commas, question marks, and exclamation points to enhance clarity and meaning. Paragraphs are indented in the right places. The piece is ready for a general audience.

C. **Capitalizing Correctly:** The writer uses capital letters consistently and accurately. A deep understanding of how to capitalize dialogue, abbreviations, proper names, and titles is evident.

D. **Applying Grammar and Usage:** The writer forms grammatically correct phrases and sentences. He or she shows care in applying the rules of standard English. The writer may break from those rules for stylistic reasons, but otherwise abides by them.

5

STRONG

4

MIDDLE

REFINING

A. **Checking Spelling:** The writer incorrectly spells a few high-frequency words and many unfamiliar words and/or sophisticated words.

B. **Punctuating Effectively and Paragraphing Accurately:** The writer handles basic punctuation marks (such as end marks on sentences and commas in a series) well. However, he or she might have trouble with more-complex punctuation marks (such as quotation marks, parentheses, and dashes) and with paragraphing, especially on longer pieces.

C. **Capitalizing Correctly:** The writer capitalizes the first word in sentences and most common proper nouns. However, his or her use of more-complex capitalization is spotty within dialogue, abbreviations, and proper names (*Aunt Maria* versus *my aunt*, for instance).

D. **Applying Grammar and Usage:** The writer has made grammar and usage mistakes throughout the piece, but they do not interfere with the reader's ability to understand the message. Issues related to agreement, tense, and word usage appear here and there, but can be easily corrected.

3

DEVELOPING

2

LOW

EMERGING

A. **Checking Spelling:** The writer has misspelled many words, even simple ones, which causes the reader to focus on conventions rather than on the central theme or story line.

B. **Punctuating Effectively and Paragraphing Accurately:** The writer has neglected to use punctuation, used punctuation incorrectly, and/or forgotten to indent paragraphs, making it difficult for the reader to find meaning.

C. **Capitalizing Correctly:** The writer uses capitals inconsistently, even in common places such as the first word in the sentence. He or she uses capitals correctly in places, but has no consistent control over them.

D. **Applying Grammar and Usage:** The writer makes frequent mistakes in grammar and usage, making it difficult to read and understand the piece. Issues related to agreement, tense, and word usage abound.

1

RUDIMENTARY

Telephon

For me the telefon was real usful to me. Because it allows me to talk on the fon, with my Dad whin I cant see him. I can call my Dad and ask him on it if he could help me on my hommework. I can call almst anbody I want on the fone with some ones you can put in fon fon numbers. I can evean call my familly to see how they are. I can call my bro to see on were he is at

Time to Assess for Conventions

This piece contains a number of spelling mistakes and some capitalization problems. Furthermore, punctuation marks are missing and the grammar needs work. Since the piece is short, each issue feels particularly serious. I have to say, this writer does not display even an average level of skill in any convention.

Conventions	
Score	**1: Rudimentary**
Range	**Low**

Other Traits	
Ideas	2
Organization	1
Voice	1
Word Choice	1
Sentence Fluency	2

A Checking Spelling

The writer has misspelled many words, even simple ones, which causes the reader to focus on conventions rather than on the central theme or story line.

Since "Telephon" is the title and subject of the paper, it is the most obvious and troublesome misspelling. The writer's spelling of when *("whin") is also troubling since it is a word that most middle school students have been spelling correctly since the early elementary grades.*

B Punctuating Effectively and Paragraphing Accurately

The writer has neglected to use punctuation, used punctuation incorrectly, and/or forgotten to indent paragraphs, making it difficult for the reader to find meaning.

Several missing and misplaced periods suggest that this writer needs to go back and proofread for end punctuation. Although the piece is one short paragraph, a second paragraph could begin at "I can call almst anbody I want…" since the writer shifts from talking about calling his father specifically to calling a range of people.

C Capitalizing Correctly

The writer uses capitals inconsistently, even in common places such as the first word in the sentence. He or she uses capitals correctly in places, but has no consistent control over them.

The writer deserves credit for capitalizing the pronoun I. *But did he do that because he knows that sentences always begin with a capital letter or because he knows that pronoun* I *is always capitalized? It's unclear.*

D Applying Grammar and Usage

The writer makes frequent mistakes in grammar and usage, making it difficult to read and understand the piece. Issues related to agreement, tense, and word usage abound.

Simple constructions are for the most part correct. His subjects and verbs tend to agree, for example. The writer, however, needs to maintain consistency with tenses. I'm not wild about ending the piece with the word at *since it's unnecessary—and awkward at best.*

Invention

An invetion that is harmful to us in this life time are Drugs. Some people say that drugs are ok, but thay really aren't. Drugs can really hurt you. If you want to know what they can do to you keep reading & I will tell you. There are many types of drugs out theyre. There is Tobacco is one and Smoking. These kinds of things can harm you & your body. That is why I don't know why people want to do them. I'm going to tell you what tobacco can do to you. Tobacco can really mess up your teeth. Tobacco can make your teeth & your breath really yellow & stinky. Tobacco is not the worst drug but it is still harmful.

The next harmful Drug is Smoking. I don't know why people would want to smoke. When people start smoking they mess up there insides & there outsides. If you start to smoke at an early age then it will be really hard for you to stop. What people don't get is that when they start smoking the mess up there whole life. Some people say that they can stop smoking if they wanted but you cant because you are adicted. I have seen some of my family members suffer from smoking so i would never do it. When i see people doing drugs I just say that I hope that they will stop because they aint ding nothing but messing up there life.

So all i have to say is that I would never mess up my life doing drugs. If you think about it most of the people are dying because of the drugs. If you have a whole life in front of you don't do the drugs. What Im saying is that if I was you I wouldn't think about doing drugs. if you know what you want in your life then don't do them. If a frend ask you to do drugs with them then tell them that you are crazy because I have a life planed for me.

Time to Assess for Conventions

I admire the sheer amount of writing this student has done, but his piece is riddled with conventions problems. The errors feel random, as though the writer drafted the piece quickly and never reviewed it for spelling, capitalization, punctuation, paragraphing, and grammar and usage issues. Before scoring this piece for any other traits, I would definitely hand it back to the writer and ask him to edit it.

Conventions	
Score	**2: Emerging**
Range	**Low**

Other Traits	
Ideas	2
Organization	2
Voice	3
Word Choice	2
Sentence Fluency	2

A Checking Spelling

The writer has misspelled many words, even simple ones, which causes the reader to focus on conventions rather than on the central theme or story line.

"Invention" is spelled correctly in the title, but not in the first line. Other spelling problems such as "thay," "realy," "ding," "adicted," and "frend," also need attention. However, most words are spelled correctly. I feel the writer has a relatively solid handle on spelling, given the large amount of text he provides.

B Punctuating Effectively and Paragraphing Accurately

The writer has neglected to use punctuation, used punctuation incorrectly, and/or forgotten to indent paragraphs, making it difficult for the reader to find meaning.

The writer puts periods at the ends of sentences but omits apostrophes in a few of the contractions. And since the sentences are so simple, he doesn't use more sophisticated forms of punctuation, making it impossible for me to assess the piece for those forms. The writer attempts nothing difficult. Paragraphing is spotty. There should be more than three paragraphs. The second paragraph, for example, could be broken into two, at "Some people say that they can stop smoking."

C Capitalizing Correctly

The writer uses capitals inconsistently, even in common places such as the first word in the sentence. He or she uses capitals correctly in places, but has no consistent control over them.

The writer uses capitals where they belong, such as at the beginning of sentences, but also where they don't, such as in the middle of sentences, on the words "Drugs" and "Smoking." He also failed to capitalize I in the second and third paragraph.

D Applying Grammar and Usage

The writer makes frequent mistakes in grammar and usage, making it difficult to read and understand the piece. Issues related to agreement, tense, and word usage abound.

In spite of awkward constructions, the sentences are grammatically correct. In the last sentence, the verb "ask" should be asks to agree with the subject, "friend." However, the writer struggles with usage—especially when it comes to the homonyms there, their, and they're.

Cellphones

In a world where communication is a need. Where people are constantly talking, spreading the word and gossip. They need something fast and easy to use. Something that you could carry to everyday locations and still be able to contact the world around you. The solution to their problems. The answer to their questions. It's something small enough to fit in the tiny pockets of everyday jeans. It slides, it flips, it runs up the phone bills it's the cellphone! The cellphone is a keystone in the history of communication. It is useful in many ways and are commonly seen in public. Many features have been added to this wonderful piece of technology. With the cellphone, you can do much more than call and receive calls. You can also text, take pictures, videos, sound recordings, and share them all with friends and relatives. Internet access is also available on most cellphones. Buying games, ringtones, and even music downloads are possible. More new features are adding up every year. With all the features and benefits from this amazing device, it has attracted many generations. teenagers enjoy texting, games, music, and the ease of the cellphone, while adults like the contacting system as well as the extra features that make the cellphone fun. The cellphone is widely used by many ages. The cellphone has definitely impacted the modern society and has changed lives around the world. Without its help the world may be in total chaos.

Time to Assess for Conventions

Upon reviewing this piece, I couldn't help thinking about conventions and sentence fluency simultaneously. Did the writer intend to use fragments or complete sentences? It's not clear. So I had to ask myself, "Do the sentences work?" And my answer was, "No, not really." Transforming the fragments into complete sentences would require the writer to use more capitalization and punctuation, which would allow me to assess this piece on those fronts more confidently. And, the piece needs paragraphs—desperately.

Conventions	
Score	**3: Developing**
Range	**Middle**

Other Traits	
Ideas	3
Organization	3
Voice	3
Word Choice	3
Sentence Fluency	3

A Checking Spelling

The writer incorrectly spells a few high-frequency words and many unfamiliar words and/or sophisticated words.

The spelling is well handled. Aside from spelling cell phone *as one word throughout, the writer does a good job in this department.*

B Punctuating Effectively and Paragraphing Accurately

The writer handles basic punctuation marks (such as end marks on sentences and commas in a series) well. However, he or she might have trouble with more-complex punctuation marks (such as quotation marks, parentheses, and dashes) and with paragraphing, especially on longer pieces.

Periods and one exclamation point are placed where they belong, at the ends of sentences, as are series commas: "Buying games, ringtones, and even music downloads..." The piece is in dire need of paragraphing, though. I see at least three logical breaks.

C Capitalizing Correctly

The writer capitalizes the first word in sentences and most common proper nouns. However, his or her use of more-complex capitalization is spotty within dialogue, abbreviations, and proper names (*Aunt Maria* versus *my aunt*, for instance).

Most but not all sentences begin correctly with capital letters. However, since no other words in the piece require capitalization, it's hard to know what the writer knows about this convention.

D Applying Grammar and Usage

The writer has made grammar and usage mistakes throughout the piece, but they do not interfere with the reader's ability to understand the message. Issues related to agreement, tense, and word usage appear here and there, but can be easily corrected.

The phrase "are commonly seen" should be "is commonly seen." There are some awkward wordings as well, such as "teenagers enjoy texting, games, music, and the ease of the cellphone, while adults like the contacting system as well as the extra features that make the cellphone fun." I would encourage the writer to recast that sentence, among others, in a more pleasing, grammatically correct way.

Let Your Voice Be Heard

When you think about it, microphones have helped us tremendousely in more ways than one. Microphones were made to project your voice without straining it But that is not the only way they have helped us.

When you're on stage, with nerves flipping in your stomach, the last thing you would want to do, is have to scream so that everyone can hear you. So, with the help of technology, microphones can now do many things. Echo, for instance, was made to add effect for a big crowd. Volume has played a big part in the mic. Depending on the environment, people can now adjust their volume to fit the type of the event.

Looking back to how the mic used to be, microphones now are pretty high tech. There are portable mics, that can let you freely walk around without getting tangled in a stringy cord. A portable mic has helped people express themselves, without the hassle of being limited to a tiny space. And if you happen to join the Secret Service, an ear piece comes in handy. It makes getting a more privete messages a lot easier.

Microphones have helped people in so many ways. They are very much appreciated. So whether it's a public speech, an amazing solo, or the secret service, microphones are a great way to let your voice be heard.

Time to Assess for Conventions

This straightforward piece doesn't need much editing. The writer tries to accomplish more with conventions than the writers of the first three pieces, and he has most of the basics under control. However, he needs to try more-complex sentences with appropriate punctuation, add titles or proper nouns (such as "Secret Service") to show advanced capitalization skills, and/or attempt to spell challenging words in order to receive a higher score.

Conventions	
Score	**4: Refining**
Range	**Middle**

Other Traits	
Ideas	4
Organization	4
Voice	4
Word Choice	4
Sentence Fluency	5

A Checking Spelling

The writer incorrectly spells a few high-frequency words and many unfamiliar words and/or sophisticated words.

> *Tricky words such as* tremendously, scream, *and* private *are misspelled, but others, such as* stringy *and* hassle, *aren't.*

B Punctuating Effectively and Paragraphing Accurately

The writer handles basic punctuation marks (such as end marks on sentences and commas in a series) well. However, he or she might have trouble with more-complex punctuation marks (such as quotation marks, parentheses, and dashes) and with paragraphing, especially on longer pieces.

> *There is one missing period, but other than that, the piece is punctuated well. The writer has a good sense of where paragraphs should begin and end as well.*

C Capitalizing Correctly

The writer capitalizes the first word in sentences and most common proper nouns. However, his or her use of more complex capitalization is spotty within dialogue, abbreviations, and proper names (*Aunt Maria* versus *my aunt*, for instance).

> *Capitalization is handled well in this piece. All sentences begin with capital letters except for one. However, with the exception of "Secret Service," the writer attempts no sophisticated forms of capitalization, making it hard to know the extent to which he understands the rules of capitalization.*

D Applying Grammar and Usage

The writer has made grammar and usage mistakes throughout the piece, but they do not interfere with the reader's ability to understand the message. Issues related to agreement, tense, and word usage appear here and there, but can be easily corrected.

> *The writer demonstrates nice control over subject-verb agreement throughout. Pronoun-antecedent agreement is handled successfully.*

Invention

What do you think of when someone says the word "Invention"? Like the majority of people, you probably think of a telephone, car, computer, or a television. The wheel, albeit much less complex, has probably played the biggest role in where we are today.

The wheel has been very helpful in creating the lifestyle we live in. Wheels are not only used for cars, but also play a role in our food. Farmers use tractors and plows to cultivate our food and then they have to ship it in a truck. If it weren't for the wheel, we wouldn't have nearly as much food as we do now because tractors, plows and trucks all require wheels. Wheels even go beyond farming; just think of what you did last weekend? Did you maybe go to the movies? If it weren't for the wheel, there would probably be no such thing as a movie. The film is wrapped around a wheel, and while the wheel spins, the movie plays.

Without wheels, we'd have no form of transportation except by horseback and by boat. Everyone would have to ride a horse because without wheels, there wouldn't even be a horse carriage. Fun things like bikes, skateboards, and roller skates would also be non-existent.

The invention of the wheel was definitely one of the most beneficial inventions. With complex new inventions such as iPods and navigation systems, we forget to look back and appreciate what makes our lifestyle today so complex, yet so easy.

Time to Assess for Conventions

As I read this piece I thought, "If all middle school students used conventions this well, our country would be filled with happy English teachers." I enjoyed reading this piece in part because the writer used conventions to guide me—which is exactly what conventions are supposed to do. There are a few places where the writer really shows off what she can do, such as "With complex new inventions such as iPods and navigation systems, we forget to look back and appreciate what makes our lifestyle today so complex, yet so easy." She demonstrates an excellent use of punctuation to set off the phrasing. This piece is strong from beginning to end.

Conventions	
Score	**5: Strong**
Range	**High**

Other Traits	
Ideas	4
Organization	5
Voice	4
Word Choice	4
Sentence Fluency	5

A Checking Spelling

The writer spells sight words, high-frequency words, and less familiar words correctly. When he or she spells less familiar words incorrectly, those words are phonetically correct. Overall, the piece reveals control in spelling.

The writer's spelling is excellent. However, she uses very basic vocabulary made up of words that are easy to spell, with the exception of "cultivate." In the next draft, I'd encourage her to use more sophisticated words, which might reveal spelling concerns to address.

B Punctuating Effectively and Paragraphing Accurately

The writer handles basic punctuation skillfully. He or she understands how to use periods, commas, question marks, and exclamation points to enhance clarity and meaning. Paragraphs are indented in the right places. The piece is ready for a general audience.

This piece is punctuated superbly. The writer uses commas to set off phrases and clauses especially well.

C Capitalizing Correctly

The writer uses capital letters consistently and accurately. A deep understanding of how to capitalize dialogue, abbreviations, proper names, and titles is evident.

The writer has strong capitalization skills. In the first sentence, "Invention" should not be capitalized, but it's easy to understand why the writer made that mistake—she uses the word in the title. There are capitals at the beginnings of all sentences. However, with the exception of "iPod," the writer uses no proper nouns, which makes it difficult to determine whether she knows that proper nouns should be capitalized.

D Applying Grammar and Usage

The writer forms grammatically correct phrases and sentences. He or she shows care in applying the rules of standard English. The writer may break from those rules for stylistic reasons, but otherwise abides by them.

Grammar and usage are strong in this piece. The sentences work well and are well formed. Nicely done

Hair Straightener

Imaginative people come up with new ideas to satisfy our every want and need. A very popular and helpful invention today is the hair straightener. Although used by women for the most part, it is gender-neutral. Everyone can use it. This marvelous invention has changed the way American teens want to look; they are a huge influence on popular culture. Trust me, I wouldn't go anywhere without mine!

As most people know, the "straight hair" look is popular and trendy in today's world. If you have naturally wavy or curly hair attaining the right "look" becomes a daily dilemma. So, to satisfy the needs of we "curly heads," an inventor came up with the hair straightener. It's an inch-wide flat iron with a hard plastic covering around it. There are temperature settings: high, medium, and low. The amount of heat needed varies according to the type of hair being straightened. Curlier hair takes a hotter iron and a lot of patience. Operation is simple. In order for the straightener to work, plug it into an electrical outlet and wait a few seconds for it to heat up. Presto! You are ready to get to work.

I use a straightener every day. It turns my wavy locks straight and gives me confidence in the way I look. The hair straightener can also help give your hair a variety of looks. Not only can you straighten your hair so it hangs perfectly, the straightener allows you to flip the ends of your hair—in or out. Hair straighteners not only give hairstyle options, they can also fight back frizz in your hair. No one wants frizz, so hair straighteners can be the solution to that hair problem, too.

Personally, I'm glad someone came up with this great invention! Liking the way your hair looks is important, and with the straightener you can control your hair. When you get ready to go to school or out with your friends, you can look in the mirror and say, "You are ready for the world, girl. Go make it yours." It gives you confidence and allows you to not have to worry constantly on the way your hair looks. As far as important contemporary inventions go, the gotta-have-it-hair-straightener has my vote, hands down.

Time to Assess for Conventions

This is an exceptional piece in every trait, including conventions. The writer's capitalization, paragraphing, and grammar and usage are very strong, but her spelling and punctuation are worthy of celebration. She not only has conventions under control, but applies them creatively and effectively. For example, she creates a whole new hyphenated word, *gotta-have-it-hair-straightener*, to emphasize how vital this product is in her life.

Conventions	
Score	**6: Exceptional**
Range	**High**

Other Traits	
Ideas	6
Organization	6
Voice	6
Word Choice	6
Sentence Fluency	6

A Checking Spelling

The writer spells sight words, high-frequency words, and less familiar words correctly. When he or she spells less familiar words incorrectly, those words are phonetically correct. Overall, the piece reveals control in spelling.

Although the spell-checker doesn't like the word "straightener," the writer spells it correctly and consistently throughout. I love how she not only takes on words we would expect to see spelled correctly, but also riskier ones such as "imaginative," "dilemma," and "confidence."

B Punctuating Effectively and Paragraphing Accurately

The writer handles basic punctuation skillfully. He or she understands how to use periods, commas, question marks, and exclamation points to enhance clarity and meaning. Paragraphs are indented in the right places. The piece is ready for a general audience.

The writer shows skill in basic and advanced punctuation, such as the semicolon, the colon, and quotation marks. Commas are used effectively, guiding the reader through some complex sentences. The flow is natural.

C Capitalizing Correctly

The writer uses capital letters consistently and accurately. A deep understanding of how to capitalize dialogue, abbreviations, proper names, and titles is evident.

Since the writer doesn't use proper nouns (except for the name of her invention and the word "American") or the pronoun I, she only needed to capitalize the first word in each sentence, which she did well. I would need to check other pieces by her to determine whether she has other capitalization skills under her belt.

D Applying Grammar and Usage

The writer forms grammatically correct phrases and sentences. He or she shows care in applying the rules of standard English. The writer may break from those rules for stylistic reasons, but otherwise abides by them.

The writer has standard English under control. The one line of dialogue "You are ready for the world, girl. Go make it yours," gives the reader an authentic, delightful glimpse into a teen's vernacular. Other than that, the grammar is correct and proves the writer is skilled in it.

Conference Comments

If the piece scores high in conventions, 5 or 6, say something like:

"Your skillful use of <u>conventions</u> led me through this piece. It allowed me to relax, follow along, and think about your original, well-considered topic. I didn't get distracted by <u>editing</u> issues. Thanks for giving me such an easy and enjoyable piece to read."

"I really appreciate the time you took to go back over your piece and <u>edit</u> it with the reader in mind. Your careful attention to basic <u>conventions</u> such as <u>spelling</u>, <u>capitalization</u>, and <u>punctuation</u> paid off. On your next piece, try some challenging words and/or more complex sentences to give your <u>conventions</u> muscles an even tougher workout."

If the piece scores in the middle, a 3 or 4, say something like:

"With the exception of a few words such as *tremendousely*, *screem*, and *private*, you've <u>spelled</u> words correctly in this piece. With a little more overall <u>editing</u>, the <u>conventions</u> will be even cleaner. Your piece will be in perfect shape for the reader."

"I think you picked a winning topic. Without doubt, cell phones have changed the world. Now, as you prepare the piece for the reader, think about where sentences start and stop. Do you want fragments or complete sentences? Once you've made your decision about each sentence, revise it as necessary to make it as strong and effective as possible. And don't forget about <u>paragraphing</u>. You skipped that <u>convention</u> on this draft. Finally, is *cell phone* one word or two? You might check that <u>spelling</u>."

If the piece scores low, a 1 or 2, say something like:

"You've written a lot here, which tells me you're interested in your topic. Good for you. Now let's get your piece ready for the reader by working on the <u>conventions</u>. See how many <u>spelling</u> words you can correct first. Then, let's talk about <u>punctuation</u>."

"The world would be a different place without telephones, wouldn't it? Let's prepare your piece for someone else to read by taking a close look at <u>conventions</u>, beginning with the <u>spelling</u> of *telephone*. Are there other <u>spelling</u> words I can help you with? And while you are rereading, think about <u>capitalization</u> and <u>punctuation</u>. I'm sure you can fix some of those problems without my help. This is a draft, so go for it!"

Teaching Writing With the Conventions Trait

When many of us were young, learning how to write meant learning how to use conventions. Period. We filled in countless work sheets to develop skills in capitalization, punctuation, and grammar. We memorized spelling lists for Friday's test. We diagrammed sentences. But, ironically, what we didn't do was write enough to master conventions. And the little writing we did do was edited by our teachers, not by us, so we never had the opportunity to practice editing our own work.

It's different today. Increasingly, middle school teachers are teaching conventions as part of the writing process, not as an isolated subject. This shift is exciting, but with it come new challenges. To make teaching conventions more manageable, I've organized the remainder of this chapter into sections that correspond to its key qualities:

* Checking Spelling

* Punctuating Effectively and Paragraphing Accurately

* Capitalizing Correctly

* Applying Grammar and Usage

Within each section, you'll find a warm-up exercise and three activities, as well as a Think About—a list of important questions students should ask themselves as they edit their writing for conventions. I round out the chapter with an activity called "Challenge: Before and After," which requires students to combine individual conventions, providing a more authentic writing experience. These exercises, activities, and Think Abouts will help you create confident, capable middle school editors. (The key qualities and Think Abouts are also included on the CD that accompanies this book.)

> **"** Blank pieces of paper understand me better than anyone, especially when they are no longer blank. The paper understands my problems, so don't be too quick to mark it up. Give it time to show me first. **"**
>
> —Enepay, grade 8

Key Quality: Checking Spelling

Here it is, the Queen of Conventions, spelling. All other conventions combined don't seem to carry the same weight as this one. As such, we teachers are always in search of the best way to teach it, but there is no silver bullet. However, educational researcher Shane Templeton's research summary, "Synthesis of Research on the Learning and Teaching of Spelling," provides insights about spelling instruction:

1. Spelling is a process of abstracting patterns, not a rote memory task.

2. Examining words should be conducted at an appropriate instructional and developmental level.

3. Exploring words within the context of writing should be active and engaging.

4. Learning to spell in the context of writing is effective if students write often.

5. Focusing on morphology—the interrelationships between spelling and vocabulary knowledge—is recommended at the intermediate level and above. (1986, p. 77)

What does this mean to a middle school English/language arts teacher? The weekly spelling test is out, and learning to spell words based on what they mean and how they are used is in. Templeton's summary gives us good footing to move forward with sound spelling instruction that includes having students create individual word lists composed of words they are using and need help learning, spending time teaching about vocabulary and its connection to how words are formed, and designing instructional plans based on students' developmental levels and needs. Thank goodness. Teaching spelling needn't be difficult or time-consuming if you teach it wisely.

What follows are activities to help you get started or continue the good work you're already doing. Although there is great variety among the activities, they all have one thing in common: they require the student, not the teacher, to find and correct spelling errors. It's important for students to learn to spot errors and choose from a variety of methods to correct them. The more we do that for them, the more dependent they become on us. And, of course, our goal is to ensure that our students spell well on their own. Use the following Think About to expand students' notions about checking spelling.

Reproducible on CD

THINK ABOUT:

- Have I used standard English spelling unless I chose not to for a good reason?
- Have I checked words with *ie* and *ei*?
- When adding suffixes to words, have I changed *y* to *i*, doubled the final consonant, or dropped the silent *e* when necessary?
- Have I checked my work for words I have trouble spelling?

WARM-UP Checking Spelling

Distribute copies of the Think About and the Rules to Remember for Spelling reproducible on the CD that accompanies this book. Write the following sentence on the chart or project it and ask students to find and correct the 11 spelling errors in it.

> I beleive that ether Maya or Franklin stoped the ball from goying over the fense 'cuz no body els was cloze enuf to cach it.

Corrected version:

> I believe that either Maya or Franklin stopped the ball from going over the fence because nobody else was close enough to catch it.

Then ask students to examine a sentence of their own to ensure they've followed the rules. If they edit the sentence, have them share it with a partner for an accuracy check.

ACTIVITIES Checking Spelling

Back to Front

While editing a piece of writing, it's easy to get caught up in the message rather than the mechanics. But to really check for spelling, it's important to resist that impulse and look closely and objectively at each word. One way to help students do that is to encourage them to read their pieces backward. That is, start with the last word and gradually move to the beginning. That way, students focus on the words, not the ideas, and will be able to spot spelling errors more efficiently.

Learn It by Singing!

The three songs on the next page are from Becca Gilman, a teacher at Mt. Lake Middle School, in Newman Lake, Washington. They address perennial spelling problems related to adding suffixes to words, such as dropping the silent *e* and changing *y* to *i*. Becca reports that her students' spelling improved noticeably when they learned the songs as a group. As her students are writing on their own and encounter a spelling problem, they sing the appropriate song to themselves to refresh their memory about the rule it teaches.

Your students might also have fun teaching the songs at a local elementary school to help younger students with spelling. (See the CD that accompanies this book for reproducibles of the spelling songs.)

Your Old Friend, Silent e
(Sung to the tune of "Old Time Rock & Roll" by Bob Seger)

You've got your old friend, silent e
What do you do with it
What can it be?
When you add a suffix to a word
You drop that e off
Haven't you heard?

You want to make MOVE, MOVING...
You want to make GROOVE, GROOVING...
You've got to get that e out of the way
Just drop that e off
Hear what I say!
(repeat first verse)

Double Down the Ending
(Sung to the tune of "Pop Goes the Weasel")

If you want to use a one-syllable word
And you have to add an ending
If the words ends with a consonant
Double it—add the ending
Like -er, -ed, -est, -ing
Or other similar endings
If the word ends with a consonant
Double it—add the ending.

Taking y and i to the Ball Game
(Sung to the tune of "Take Me Out to the Ball Game")

Change the y to an i
Before the ending goes on
Like -es, -ed, -er, -est
But never -ing
Change the y to an i
Before the suffix goes on
Every time the y follows a consonant
Just CHANGE IT!

Personal Spelling Lists

Help students keep a personal spelling list—in a notebook, on a separate sheet of paper—made up of words that give them trouble when they write. Help them begin their lists by asking them to each name five words they feel uncertain about when they write. Write those words on the whiteboard so the class can see the range of words. Cluster the words according to family or spelling issue, where possible, and discuss those that are most challenging. The family -*ough* for instance, shows up in words that sound quite different from each other: *thought*, *tough*, *thorough*, and *enough*. Silent letters can create tricky spelling issues as well: *gnat*, *listen*, *island*, *knuckle*, *pneumonia*. Discuss the meaning of the words and their origins. Tell students to be on the lookout for these troublesome words as they write. Be sure to encourage them to add typical spelling demons to their lists as well, such as *Cincinnati*. I never know if it's one *t* or two, one *n* or two, or some combination—it definitely goes on my personal spelling list so I can refer to it easily.

Ask students to add two new words to their lists each week, which they can derive from their drafts, quickwrites, short-answer essays, warm-up exercises, or writing they're doing for other classes. One day a week, set aside ten minutes for partners to quiz each other on their personal spelling lists. Once a student has spelled a word correctly three weeks in a row, have him or her cross it off the list.

Key Quality: Punctuating Effectively and Paragraphing Accurately

When it comes to teaching punctuation, the best advice I can give you is to start with the basics and move to more-complex issues over time. For instance, you might want to start by reminding students to *always* place a punctuation mark at the end of a sentence—either a period, question mark, or exclamation point. As they progress, introduce them to internal marks such as dashes, ellipses, colons, semicolons, and quotation marks. Tell them that these punctuation marks will not only make their sentences correct, but also make them more interesting and comprehensible to the reader, because they provide natural stopping and starting points that help the reader construct meaning.

Invite students to examine books and magazines for creative uses of punctuation and other conventions. In Gary Paulsen's picture book *Dogteam*, for instance, they'll find ellipses, hyphens, series commas, series semicolons, and even invented words such as *dogdance*, *dogmoon*, and *dognight*. And the book ends with a question mark. Interesting. As readers, we appreciate writers who take time to make conventions work hand in hand with the other traits to create clear, fluent writing. Grammarian and author Lynne Truss puts it perfectly: "On the page, punctuation performs its grammatical function, but in the mind of the reader it does more than that. It tells the reader how to hum the tune" (2005, p. 71).

Another skill to teach early on is paragraphing. You might want to start by showing students a continuous piece of writing and indicating where one thought ends and another begins by breaking those thoughts into separate paragraphs. From there, teach them more-sophisticated skills, such as paragraphing of dialogue. As with punctuation, the key is showing them how paragraphing can help to guide the reader through the text. Use the following Think About to expand students' notions about punctuating effectively and paragraphing accurately.

THINK ABOUT:

- Did I place quotation marks around dialogue and direct quotes?
- Did I punctuate complex sentences correctly?
- Did I use apostrophes to show possessives and contractions?
- Did I begin new paragraphs in the appropriate places?

WARM-UP Punctuating Effectively and Paragraphing Accurately

Distribute copies of the Think About and the Rules to Remember for Punctuation and Paragraphing reproducible on the CD that accompanies this book. Write the following piece on the chart or project it and ask students to find and correct 25 punctuation errors in it. From there, have them identify a logical place for a paragraph break.

> Its snowing outside screamed Dino when he woke up and looked outside Its snowing in June He was ecstatic his essay on the life cycle of the dung beetle was due that day and it wasnt finished He still had to write the conclusion make a title page and add two more references to the bibliography Would he be lucky enough to get a snow day and more time Dino get up he heard his mother say School is two hours late but Ill drop you off on my way to work

Corrected version:

> "It's snowing outside!" screamed Dino when he woke up and looked outside. "It's snowing in June!" He was ecstatic; his essay on the life cycle of the dung beetle was due that day and it wasn't finished. He still had to write the conclusion, make a title page, and add two more references to the bibliography. Would he be lucky enough to get a snow day and more time?
>
>   "Dino, get up," he heard his mother say. "School is two hours late but I'll drop you off on my way to work."

Then ask students to examine a piece of their own to ensure they've followed the rules. If they edit the piece, have them share it with a partner for an accuracy check.

Punctuating Effectively
and Paragraphing Accurately

The Semicolon

It's fun to collect professional writers' controversial, often hilarious opinions about different punctuation marks and share them with the class. In my experience, students find them fascinating. Who knew? The semicolon is my personal favorite. I've been collecting opinions about it for years. Like most internal punctuation marks, it has had its fair share of admirers and critics. Here's the proof:

The Triggering Town, by Richard Hugo

No Semicolons. Semicolons indicate relationships that only idiots need defined by punctuation. Besides, they are ugly. (1979, p. 40)

The Medusa and the Snail, by Lewis Thomas

It is almost always a greater pleasure to come across a semicolon than a period. The period tells you that that is that; if you didn't get all the meaning you wanted or expected, anyway you got all the writer intended to parcel out and now you have to move along. But with the semicolon there you get a pleasant little feeling of expectancy; there is more to come; to read on; it will get clearer. (1979, p. 126)

Fumblerules, by William Safire, "Rule #13"

In some cases, you will want a burst of short sentences to make your declaration punchy; at other times, you will use a string of commas, rhythmically, repetitiously, to make your point; though, when the moment comes, to link ideas without fully merging them, to engage in the trial marriage of thought—make a dash for the semicolon. (1990, p. 39)

Eats, Shoots and Leaves, by Lynne Truss

The semicolon has been rightly called "a compliment from the writer to the reader." And a mighty compliment it is, too. The sub-text of a semicolon is, "Now this is a hint. The elements of this sentence, although grammatically distinct, are actually elements of a single notion. I can make it plainer for you—but hey! You're a reader! I don't need to draw you a map!" (2005, p. 124)

Introduce students to the semicolon by sharing these opinions. After giving them a chance to talk about the pros and cons of its use, send them on a hunt for opinions about other punctuation marks, such as the dash, the colon, the hyphen, the ellipses, or the comma, and write them down on note cards. Then bind the cards together with a loose-leaf ring. As students edit their work, invite them to read the opinions of professional writers when a particular mark is giving them trouble.

Air Quotes

To get students thinking about how to punctuate and paragraph dialogue, put them into groups of three and have them browse their favorite novels. When they find an exchange between two characters that is at least a page long, have two students from each group read the lines of dialogue aloud, with each student assuming the role of one of the characters. As they read, have students use "air quotes" with their index and middle fingers to indicate where the quotation marks go. Tell them to snap their finger at each paragraph break, when the speaker changes. Ask the third student to read the narrative—lines that are not part of the dialogue. Allow students time to practice and then have them read their dialogues to the class, using air quotes for punctuation and finger snaps for new paragraphs.

When all groups have finished reading, talk about the importance of punctuating and paragraphing dialogue correctly. Ask students to share ideas about why air quotes are often used in real conversations. If time allows, have them search the Internet for more information about air quotes, such as when they first came into use and what experts say about their role in oral communication.

Proofreading for Paragraphs

To get students into the habit of looking over their drafts and using a paragraph symbol (¶) to mark spots where new paragraphs might begin, try this activity. Tell students there are three main methods writers and editors use to indicate the beginning of a paragraph. Ask students to name them. If they can't, ask them to look in books, magazines, newspapers, and print sources for the answer. On the board, record paragraphing methods and examples as students discover them:

Indented first line
Examples: handwritten stories, textbooks, newspapers, some forms of published literature

Left-justified or block style
Examples: business letters, memos

Left-justified (block) first paragraph and others within that section indented.
Examples: professional books, some textbooks, some forms of published literature

Post examples of paragraphing methods and ask students to consult them when writing. If you have a preference for how students should paragraph their papers, show them that method and remind them to use it. If you don't have a preference, ask students to decide which method best fits their writing. Remind them that, regardless of their method, they must start a new paragraph when an idea shifts within their piece.

Key Quality: Capitalizing Correctly

Capitalization rules are like amusement park rides. There are ones that everyone knows, loves, and jumps upon without pause: "Always capitalize *I* and the first word in a sentence." Then there are the less familiar but still approachable ones: "Always capitalize acronyms, proper nouns, and important words in titles." And, finally, there are the ones for true thrill-seekers: "Always capitalize geographical regions ('I've always wanted to visit the South') but not directions ('I've been driving south for three hours and still can't find the Grand Canyon')." To write well, students need the confidence to go on all the rides—even those that make their heart race. Use the following Think About to expand students' notions about capitalizing correctly.

THINK ABOUT:

- Did I capitalize proper nouns for people, places, and things?
- Did I capitalize dialogue correctly?
- Did I capitalize abbreviations, acronyms, and people's titles correctly?
- Did I capitalize the title and/or other headings?

Reproducible
on **CD**

WARM-UP Capitalizing Correctly

Distribute copies of the Think About and the Rules to Remember for Capitalization reproducible on the CD that accompanies this book. Write the following paragraph on the chart or project it, and ask students to find and correct 15 capitalization errors in it.

> on inauguration day we went to washington, d.c., and waited in the cold to see president obama and his family. "here he comes," i cried when i spotted his presidential limousine rounding the southeast corner of pennsylvania avenue and head toward the national mall.

Corrected version:

> On Inauguration Day we went to Washington, D.C., and waited in the cold to see President Obama and his family. "Here he comes," I cried when I spotted his presidential limousine rounding the southeast corner of Pennsylvania Avenue and head toward the National Mall.

Then ask students to examine a piece of their own to ensure they've followed the rules. If they edit the piece, have them share it with a partner for an accuracy check.

ACTIVITIES Capitalizing Correctly

People, Places, and Things

Ask students to get into pairs and write a short story that includes two characters from column #1 in the chart below, a setting from column #2, and as many things as they'd like from column #3. Tell them their story must contain at least six lines of dialogue between the two characters.

Characters	Settings	Things
a doctor	a famous landmark	jewelry
a foreign dignitary	a road or highway	designer socks
a plumber	an art museum	a pen
a movie theater cashier	a movie theater	an SUV
a purebred dog	a favorite restaurant	a cell phone

When students finish, have the writers read their stories aloud. Then project the stories and have the class check the use of capitals. If any capitals need correcting, discuss why and make the change on the draft copy, using the appropriate editor's marks, listed on page 298 and the CD that accompanies this book.

Capital Collection

Put students into pairs and ask them to search print and nonprint sources to find three examples of each of the four capitalization rules from the Think About on page 289. Then have them gather their findings in a chart like the one on page 291. Tell students they can use each source only one time. So, for example, if they find a proper noun in Cornelia Funke's *Inkheart*, they may not use that book for titles. If they find an example that breaks one of the four rules, record it in the "Other" row for later discussion.

Traits of Writing: The Complete Guide for Middle School

Capital Collection

Proper Nouns	Example: Page 19, paragraph 3 of *The Hunger Games* by Suzanne Collins (2008): The Treaty of Treason gave us the new laws to guarantee peace, and as our yearly reminder that the Dark Day must never be repeated, it gave us the Hunger Games.
First Word of Dialogue	Example: Page 25, paragraph 1 of *Fahrenheit 451* by Ray Bradbury (1951): "Give me a pencil and some paper, quick," I said, and wrote it down.
Abbreviations, Acronyms, and People's Titles	Example: Page 88, paragraph 1 of *People* magazine, February 9, 2009: Myeia Bautista sobbed with joy when she heard the Blue Eagles of South Cobb High School in Austell, GA, were one of the 103 groups picked to march in the Inauguration Day parade.
Publication Titles and Other Headings	Example: From the summer reading list on the librarian's desk *Holes*, *Hatchet*, *Harriet the Spy*
Other	Example: From a flyer to parents about school attendance zones Southwest region

Texting With Conventions

Without question, text messaging, or "texting," is the latest craze among middle schoolers—and I couldn't be more delighted. Our students are writing because they want to, not because they have to. When students text, however, they write very quickly in a language that doesn't even come close to standard English, particularly rules of capitalization.

To see what I mean, take a look at the "Dear Abby" letter on page 293 written in standard English and the response written in standard text messaging language. To read the response, trust me, you'll need the accompanying "texting key."

Share the letter and response with your students. Give them a copy of the texting key and ask them to star the items they use most frequently when they text and add any others they use.

Invite students to write their own "Dear Abby" letters about a problem associated with texting and standard English, such as convincing a teacher to allow them to text notes in class rather than write them out the traditional way. Assign partners and ask students to write a question in standard English to "Abby," asking for advice about something related to text messaging. Ask the partner to answer the message using text-messaging language. If time allows, have students write a follow-up question and answer. Encourage students to be creative and have fun.

If you're concerned that using texting language will hinder students' use of standard English, don't be. I've found that when they're given the opportunity and expectation to use both languages, students rise to the challenge. They show amazing facility in writing, particularly in conventions, because they must think deeply about when it's okay to break rules—and when it isn't.

Key Quality: Applying Grammar and Usage

Explicit grammar instruction is back. It fell out of favor over the past several decades as many educators came to believe that students would pick up grammar rules as they read and wrote on a daily basis. Unfortunately, those educators were wrong. That approach did not help students produce writing with strong syntax: the grammatical organization of words in a sentence. Students need to know the parts of speech. They need to know how to use verb tenses consistently within a piece. They need to know how to create agreement between subjects and verbs. They need to know how words work together so they can create strong phrases, clauses, and sentences.

Now for the good news. During this hiatus, we learned that teaching grammar is not an all-or-nothing proposition. It is not just about tired instructional practices like drills and diagramming. It's about taking an interest in how language works. It's about noticing problems students have with writing and showing them how to improve it by applying rules that govern language. It's about giving all students background and experience with grammar (the study of words and their syntactical relations and functions) and usage (the

Dear Abby,

I am writing you today because I have tried to talk to my mom so many times about this text messaging deal and every time I do she always changes the subject or she just says, "No." This is really frustrating me because all my friends have unlimited texting and I don't. So a lot of times when they keep texting me I can't text back because I don't have unlimited texting like they do. I am asking you today if you have any advice or suggestions on what I should ask my mom. I have tried a lot of things, but nothing seems to work. I would appreciate a response back. Thank you,

Textless in Topeka

4U txlss ;)

FWIW i know where ur comin frm. LOL wn i wz a kid my mom dnt gt unlmtd txtng ethr & it mde me rely rely mad & :-(!!!! but 1 day i srchd the net 4 a deal LOL and i fnd 1 :-D so I pt it on my tbl and sd yo mom it wud mn alot to me if u jst tok a lk at ths & consdr it sh did & sd TYVM 4 duin ths so i wll set it. LOL I waz so :-D!!!! ROFL. FWIW my advs to u dont B mad and B patnt u nvr no she cld say ya mabe SWIM? THX for kpin patnt evn tho UR mom sys no. jst remember dnt B X-(& hpe 4 +++.

PWB abby :)

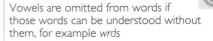

Texting Key

Vowels are omitted from words if those words can be understood without them, for example *wrds*
Unnecessary words, such as *an*, *and*, and *the*, are often omitted.
Capital letters and punctuation marks are used only when necessary.
Paragraphing is unnecessary.
4U means *for you*.
;) is a wink to show you understand.
Numerals often stand for words, such as 1/won and 4/for.
:-D means very pleased.
↑ means *up*.
+++ means a big yes.
yo means *dear* or *hello*.
duin means *doing*.
FWIW means *for what it's worth*.
LOL means *laugh out loud* or that something is funny.
wz means *was*.
& means *and*.
rely means *really*.
:-(means unhappy.
!!!! shows emphasis.
TYVM means *thank you very much*.
ROFL means rolling on the floor laughing.
B means *be*.
SWIM means *see what I mean?*
THX means *thanks* or *thank you*.
UR means *your* or *you're*.
X-(means crabby.
PWB means *please write back*.

customary manner in which a language is written), so when they write, everyone can read it and understand what is being said.

But grammar and usage have to be taught—they are not learned by osmosis. We can teach students how to diagram a sentence, for instance, but only if that skill helps them solve a problem with the grammar of their own sentences, not as a mindless, repetitive exercise. We want our students to use these conventions, along with the others, with accuracy, style, and confidence, in order to improve their writing. Use the following Think About to expand student's notions about applying grammar and usage.

Reproducible on CD

THINK ABOUT:

- Did I use special words such as homophones, synonyms, and antonyms correctly?
- Did I check my sentences for subject-verb agreement?
- Did I use verb tense (past, present, future) consistently throughout my piece?
- Did I make sure pronouns and their antecedents (the words they stand for) agree?

WARM-UP   Applying Grammar and Usage

Distribute copies of the Think About and the Rules to Remember for Grammar and Usage reproducible on the CD that accompanies this book. Write the following bulleted list on a chart or project it, and discuss the differences in meaning between *all together* and *altogether* and *all ready* and *already* with the class.

All together: *everything at the same time or place* as in "You'll find your homework all together in your backpack." Or "If we are all together on this, we might change Dad's mind about driving us to the concert." Or "All together now, breathe!" (a phrase)

Altogether: *entirely or completely* as in "I lost cell phone reception altogether." Or "Altogether, there were ten of us trying out for one spot on the hockey team." (adverb)

All ready: *completely prepared* as in "Are you all ready for soccer camp tomorrow?" (a phrase)

Already: *previously or has happened* as in "Did you already pack everything for soccer camp tomorrow?" (adverb)

Ask students to work with a partner to use *all together, altogether, all ready*, and *already* in an original piece of writing, using the fewest words and sentences possible. Here's an example: "With my supplies all together, I was all ready to go camping. I knew that my friends were already at the site, waiting. But when the rain started falling, I lost my enthusiasm altogether."

ACTIVITIES   Applying Grammar and Usage

Preposition Song

Just as the planet Earth is made up mostly of water, sentences are typically made up mostly of prepositional phrases that contain important information. A prepositional phrase can answer the question "Which one?"—for example, "The boy *with the brownish black hair* and *in the green sweatshirt* is signing up for soccer, too." Both prepositional phrases describe the boy and, therefore, serve as adjectives. A prepositional phrase can also answer the questions *how, when,* and *where*—for example, "*In the bottom of my locker,* you'll find the sneakers you loaned me" (where). Or "*Before class,* I realized Janelle had my sneakers" (when). Or "I'm worn out *from running during practice*" (how and when). These prepositional phrases describe the action and, therefore, serve as adverbs. So when teaching parts of speech, it makes sense to cover prepositions first. Once students learn the meaning and function of prepositions, and can identify prepositional phrases in sentences, they find it easier to add details that answer *which one, how, when,* and *where* questions. They also find it easier to move phrases around until the sentence is clear and is working as well as possible.

There are so many prepositions, however. Where do you begin? Try "The Preposition Song" in the box at right, which is sung to the tune of "Yankee Doodle Dandy." Give students a copy of the song, allow them to practice it, and then have them sing it to make sure they've learned the bounty of prepositions it contains. Start by singing along with the whole class to familiarize students with the lyrics and make them feel comfortable singing. From there, have them sing the song in small groups. Allow reluctant students to sing it in private or at home. Or simply let them write the words down instead of singing at all. If you have students who can use sign language, ask them to "give you a hand" leading a sing-along with the class. Do whatever it takes to help students remember the lyrics' prepositions for use in their own writing.

> ### The Preposition Song
>
> (Sung to the tune of "Yankee Doodle Dandy")
>
> About, above, across, after,
> Along, among, around, at,
> Before, beside, between, against,
> Within, without, beneath, through,
> During, under, in, into,
> Over, of, off, to, toward,
> Up, on, near, for, from, except,
> By, with, behind, below, down.

Beware the Adverb

Don Emblen, Sonoma County's first poet laureate and my late uncle, wrote this poem for me a few years ago to share with teachers. I hope you enjoy it as much as I do.

```
THE ADVERB

     . . . Came whiffling through the tulgey wood
     And burbled as it came.    -- Lewis Carroll

Beware the frumious adverb, son!
Opportunistically, he slips in, hit or miss,
and galumphing, grossly swells the leanest prose
to something vaguely poem-like (like this).
The bandersnatch is nothing, friend, to fear
compared to one hyperbolically, inflatably,
wonderfully redundant adverb__debatably
employed, the writer says, for meter's sake,
or on the principle that extra syllables
do make of hamburger, a steak.

#
DLE   2/8/05
```

Share the poem with students and discuss the role of adverbs in sentences—how they can help the reader see the action more clearly, but only when used sparingly. Too many adverbs can bog down a piece of writing. Brainstorm a list of 20 verbs and post them. Ask students to get into pairs and, on a separate sheet of paper, write down the verbs and add an adverb to each one. For example, if the verb is *run*, they might add *swiftly* or *quickly*. Then, ask students to think of a synonym for each phrase they create—one strong verb that means the same thing—such as *scamper* or *zoom*. When students have finished, ask them which is more powerful, the adverb/verb phrases or the one-word synonyms? They will likely respond that the one-word synonyms are stronger. Invite students to search a book, magazine, newspaper, or other print resource for adverbial phrases and replace them with more powerful, unmodified verbs.

ACTIVITY Working With Multiple Conventions

Challenge: Before and After

The seventh-grade piece on page 297 is titled perfectly because it not only tells the story of a challenge, but it's also a challenge to read. Give students a copy of the original draft, and ask them to read it aloud to a partner. Then ask partners to edit the piece, using the editor's marks on page 298. When they've finished, show the final version to the class and ask students to note the edits they caught and edits they missed. Discuss whether the editing process not only helped them "correct" the piece, but also invited revision to make the piece more readable and engaging. (Both versions of "Challenge" and the editor's marks chart are on the CD that accompanies this book.)

Original Draft

Challenge

A Warm sunmer day in June. the slight breiz was comferting. we sat like stunps in the grassey feald whating Four Someone to do the dare. No one Had the courage to do the dare even if it was eating the worm that sat in the middle Circle. Tonya sat in a grin looking everyone and then looking at the worm. Her Thoughts were She Did the dare So She didnt half to eat the slimy worm. The circle was still realy quite no one moved no one Brehed. There eyes were looking at the worm with discust. The Chalenge between the worm and the Kids was vary grate there mouths were were gawked open and there eyos were upend as wide as could be. The gigel from Tonya was so agreating that I couldnt let Her get away with Calling me a chicken. By the tine I thought about eating the worm it Had mangeled over to me. I felt myself say out loud "I will do it. I will eat that worm!" every one looked at me in anaznent I picked up the worm and I about stuck it in my mouth and Tonya yelled "tear it in Half." I took the worm pout 4 Fingers around it and polled it in 2 parts. One part I stuck in my mouth and gulped it and the other Half Went Down write after and From then on when we played truth or dare they never called me a chiken

Editor's Marks

ℒ	Delete material.	The writing is is good.
ⓢⓟ	Correct the spelling or spell it out.	We are learning ②traits this week
◯	Close space.	To day is publishing day.
∧	Insert a letter, word, or phrase.	My teacher has books. wonderful
ℒ/∧	Change a letter.	She is a great writer.
⚠/#	Add a space.	Don't forget agood introduction. #
∿	Transpose letters or words.	She raed the piece with flair!
≡	Change to a capital letter.	We have j. k. Rowling to thank for Harry Potter's magic.
/	Change to a lowercase letter.	"The Proof is in the Pudding" was his favorite saying.
¶	Start a new paragraph.	"What day is it?" he inquired. "It's Groundhog Day," she replied.
⊙	Add a period.	Use all the traits as you write⊙

Challenge

It was a warm summer day in June; the slight breeze was comforting. We sat like stumps in the grassy field, waiting for someone to do the dare. No one had the courage to do the dare since it was eating the worm that sat in the middle of the circle!

Tanya sat with a grin, looking at everyone and then looking at the worm. Her thoughts were that she had done the dare, so now she didn't have to eat the slimy worm.

The circle was still really quiet. No one moved; no one breathed. Their eyes were looking at the worm with disgust. The challenge between the worm and the kids was very great. Their mouths gawked open and their eyes opened as wide as could be.

The giggle from Tanya was so aggravating that I couldn't let her get away with calling me a chicken. By the time I thought about eating the worm, it had mangled its way over to me. I felt myself say out loud, "I will do it! I will eat the worm!" Everyone looked at me in amazement.

I picked up the worm, and I had just about stuck it in my mouth when Tanya yelled, "Tear it in half!" I took the worm, put four fingers around it and pulled it into two parts. One part I stuck into my mouth and I gulped it down— the other half went down right after it!

From then on, whenever we played truth or dare, they never called ME a chicken.

The "Editing and a Bit o' Revision" Checklist

When professional editors proofread, they usually review the text for all conventions simultaneously. But as I said, they're professionals. One way to get students started is to have them focus on one convention and add others over the course of the year. The form on page 301 will help you do that. In addition to providing a logical sequence of proofreading skills, beginning with checking spelling, it also prompts students to check revision-related matters so they produce the best papers they can. You can use this form in order, or use one, two, or more of the editing and revision prompts in the order that you teach them.

Here are some suggestions for how to phase in the form, one convention at a time:

1. Give each student a color copy of the form, if possible. (You'll find a color master of the form on the CD that accompanies this book.) Otherwise, use the black-and-white version on page 301.

2. Have students use a draft that is ready for editing and work with a partner to carry out step 1 on the list: check spelling.

3. When students have checked spelling and are ready to turn in their draft, ask them to attach the form and check off the skill(s) for which they edited.

4. As students learn a new skill in punctuation, have them carry out step 2 on one of their drafts.

5. As students learn new editing skills, continue the process for steps 3 to 6.

6. Once they have a handle on sentence fluency and voice, have students apply steps 7 and 8 to their work.

7. Once they have a handle on all the traits, have students apply step 9 to their work.

Editing and a Bit o' Revision Checklist

Writer: _____ Title of Work: _____

Got your pens ready? Here we go!

☐ 1. Read the paper backward, one word at a time. Circle all possible spelling errors in BLUE, BLUE, BLUE. Check your word list, ask a fellow writer, or check the dictionary for correct spellings.

☐ 2. Use RED, RED, RED to show how you used punctuation. Circle the mark you used at the end of each sentence and any other punctuation you tried.

☐ 3. Use GREEN, GREEN, GREEN to show how you used capitals on the beginning of each sentence and for proper nouns. Circle "I" when used as a personal pronoun.

☐ 4. Trace the first word of each sentence in GREEN, GREEN, GREEN and the end punctuation of each sentence in RED, RED, RED. This will give you a color-coded image of your sentence lengths. Make sure no more than FOUR sentences begin with the same word in your whole paper.

☐ 5. Use ORANGE, ORANGE, ORANGE to mark the beginning of each paragraph using the paragraph symbol: ¶. Think about how long your paragraphs are and if they need more sentences.

☐ 6. Use PURPLE, PURPLE, PURPLE to mark any places in your text where there are grammar and usage problems. Correct the problems later by working with a partner and/or using a print or online resource.

☐ 7. Highlight your favorite sentence in YELLOW, YELLOW, YELLOW. Write a quick note next to it that says why it is your favorite. I'll write back and tell you which one was mine.

☐ 8. Read your piece aloud with VOICE, VOICE, VOICE. If it doesn't grab your attention or make sense, back up, add in what is missing, clean up what is confusing, and then read it again. Listen to your text for grammar. See? Editing makes a difference!

☐ 9. Look at your paper one more time. Have you found EVERYTHING that you can to get it ready for a reader to enjoy?

Final Thoughts

On the surface, conventions may appear to be only about following rules. But in reality, they are about something much more important. When students apply everything they know about spelling, punctuation, paragraphing, capitalization, and grammar and usage to their writing, using that knowledge to make their writing easy to read, they have accomplished something that is every bit as important as drafting and revising. The editing process can turn a toad into one good-lookin' prince.

Students need all the traits to make their writing work. They need conventions for editing just as much as they need ideas, organization, voice, word choice, and sentence fluency for drafting and revision. And they need to learn them in the context of their own writing. No other context will do.

After they've revised and edited a piece of writing, and they feel it's ready to go public, the writer must consider how it will ultimately look. That's where presentation comes in. It's the final stop on the middle school writing express. All aboard!

CHAPTER 10

Presentation:

Lookin' Good!

The sixth-grade students from Michigan who made the posters on page 304 understand the importance of creating eye-appealing work. They took great care to combine text, illustration, and color to create posters that capture the essence of every trait—including the trait that this final chapter is all about: presentation. Their work is clear, readable, and, most important, well suited for their audience, which makes viewing them a pleasure. (Color versions can be found on the CD that accompanies this book.)

Unfortunately, middle school writers don't always produce work so carefully. Throughout my nearly 20 years of teaching English, I would somehow find myself avoiding students' papers simply because of how they looked. I had two options: (1) plunge in and try to read them while I had the strength and will, or (2) put them at the bottom of the stack, hoping that the presentation fairy would clean them up before they reemerged.

Since fairies don't exist, no matter how strongly Peter Pan wants us to believe they do, it's up to us to teach students how to create writing that is readable. We must teach them that it's important to slow down and make their work visibly appealing, since readers don't want to and shouldn't have to decipher their work. Readers are busy. Puzzling out what the writer is trying to say because the handwriting is messy or the margins are nonexistent is frustrating. And if the reader is a teacher, this sloppiness can make assessing the piece nearly impossible, which never works in the student's favor. Students need to take pride in their work. They need to make their ideas, organization, voice, word choice, sentence fluency, and use of conventions shine by applying good presentation skills.

The Presentation Trait: A Definition

Presentation is about the look of the piece—its physical appearance, plain and simple. A visually appealing piece is a welcome mat. It invites the reader in. Presentation isn't as much a writing skill as a visual or even a fine-motor skill because, when applying it, the writer is focusing not on what he is saying, but rather on how he is presenting what he is saying. Bad handwriting, uneven margins, poorly chosen typefaces, improper word and line spacing, and too much or too little white space can be the kiss of death for an otherwise great piece of writing because they do nothing but distract the reader. Middle school students don't know this intuitively. We must teach them how to make their pens dance, their keyboards sing.

There was a time when the presentation trait was not an acknowledged part of the trait model. But, in 1995, while working with a researcher at the Northwest Regional Educational Laboratory, I noticed that raters were consistently more discrepant scoring in conventions than in any other trait. In interviews, many of the raters revealed that they factored in appearance and neatness, even though the scoring guide for conventions did not mention those issues, while other raters said they stuck to the scoring guide, point by point.

When I created the presentation trait to address a piece of writing's appearance, conventions scores fell back into line. A new trait was born—not a full-blown one like the other six, but a more minor one based on visual aspects of the writing and fine-motor skills of the writer. As such, it is best applied after the writer has edited a piece and is truly ready for it to go public. Editing a piece for conventions and publishing it for its intended audience are two different matters that need to be addressed at two different points in the writing process. Each one requires different skills. The key qualities of presentation are:

* Applying Handwriting Skills
* Using Word Processing Effectively
* Making Good Use of White Space
* Refining Text Features

Why Students Struggle With Presentation

Not all papers go through multiple drafts in preparation for a wide audience. But for those papers that do—papers that have been drafted, revised, and edited—time spent on presentation is time well spent. However, making their work neat and attractive can be challenging for some students. Here are three reasons why.

We Aren't Sure of the Best Ways to Teach Handwriting and Keyboarding

Handwriting is really hard for many students. There are students who can write neatly, but don't take time to do so. And then there are those who can't, no matter how much time they take. Their handwriting is deplorable—their letters are haphazardly formed, their spacing between letters and words is uneven, their margins are razor thin or downright nonexistent. And if you tell them their work is hard to read, they usually respond, "I know. I really try, but this is the best I can do."

I'm often asked by teachers if poor penmanship in middle school is a result of scattershot handwriting instruction and/or too much freedom on the keyboard in elementary school. While it's safe to say that printing is taught almost exclusively in the primary grades, teachers typically shift their focus in the intermediate grades. Some begin to teach cursive, while others choose D'Nealian (a stylized form of printing that incorporates elements of cursive). And, of course, many don't teach handwriting at all. Since experts do not agree which method is the best, it's doubtful there will be consensus in the research community any time soon. The best you can do is discuss handwriting with your colleagues and agree on a reasonable standard that may boil down to simple legibility. Then hold kids accountable to that standard, across the board in every class.

There's also no consensus on how and when to teach keyboarding skills. In fact, most students are self-taught from a very early age, using the hunt-and-peck method. Some teachers feel this instills bad habits and makes it difficult to teach standard keyboarding later. Others say just the opposite: students who start by hunting and pecking pick up standard keyboarding as soon as their hands are big enough to span the keyboard. Whatever the case, by middle school, students should be keyboarding well. After all, using the keyboard is a lot faster and more efficient than using a pen. And corrections are easier to make. I find that when I sit down to write thank-you notes, for instance, I have a hard time pushing my thoughts through a pen. But when I write those same notes on the computer, my fingers fly. All middle school students should be given a choice—especially those with weak fine-motor skills who find handwriting a challenge.

> **"** If you ask me, and you did, I'd say I like presentation the most of all the traits because it's where you get to make your writing look good. Even if it's not written very well, you can make it look good, and teachers like that. **"**
>
> —Serena, grade 7

They're Trying to Express Who They Are by How They Write

The middle school years are all about searching for and establishing identity. To that end, for better or worse, students experiment. Whether they're focusing on clothes, music, or friends, they like to dabble until they find a fit that's just right for them. Handwriting is no exception. Sometimes girls will dot there i's with hearts. Sometimes boys adopt a blocky, architectural style of printing. Some students use big and swoopy letters, leaving no space between lines, whereas others write so small you need a magnifying glass to read the piece. I had a student once who wrote everything backward. Seriously. And she was good at it.

During the middle school years, students also begin to mess around with type styles on the computer. They may avoid using standard, easy-to-read fonts just because less common, more-difficult-to-read fonts "look cool." It's also not unusual to see a student revise his or her signature multiple times during a school year. As an eighth grader, I remember spending hours perfecting the *R* in *Ruth*. When I look at my work from that time, so many years later, I can see early indications of the handwriting that I would settle on for the rest of my life.

Don't be too concerned with handwriting and word processing in middle school. Allow plenty of room for experimentation. If you must have a rule, try this: "Your work needs to be readable!" And put it on the "No Excuses" list. (See pages 263–264 for details.)

They Don't Consider the Whole Page as They Write

During your career, how many papers have you received with a left-hand margin that starts out just fine at the top, but gradually shifts to the right, until, by the end of paper, a virtual ski slope has been created? My guess is a lot. You'd think the student would notice the problem herself and correct it. But, no, it's usually not on her presentation radar, so it's up to you to put it there.

Making the pen do what you want, such as creating uniform margins, requires visual skills and fine-motor skills, which, as I've said before, need to be taught. So don't be afraid to ask students to keep an eye on the top margin line, not just the one above the line where they are writing. Gradual sloping results from lining up writing one line after the last. By cuing students to see the whole page, you'll teach them to spot sagging margins and avoid them on the next draft. Over time, they will take the whole page into consideration as they write and self-correct as necessary.

Considering the whole page relates to spacing as well. We want students to develop an eye for the right amount of space before and after titles, around text features, and between letters, words, and lines. So we must teach them those skills and give them opportunities to practice them, without losing sight of our primary goal: to help students create papers that are readable.

Another option, of course, is allowing students to use the computer to compose. Letters are formed perfectly with every keystroke and margins are preset and easy to change. Given technology's current and future impact on our students' lives, we simply can't rule out this option.

Assessing Student Work for Presentation

The following papers, written by students in grades 6, 7, and 8, represent a wide range of presentation skills. Review the scoring guide on page 309 and read each paper carefully. If the paper is handwritten, assess it for "Applying Handwriting Skills," "Making Good Use of White Space," and "Refining Text Features" by following the steps on pages 50–51 under "Assessing Writing Using the Trait Scoring Guides." If the paper is word processed, assess it for "Using Word Processing Effectively," "Making Good Use of White Space," and "Refining Text Features." Then read my assessment to see if we agree. Use your own students' writing for further practice.

Time to Assess for Presentation

Making the piece readable is the final stage of the writing process. It allows the reader to take in the ideas, without getting bogged down by aggravating, surface-level issues. In this section, papers #1, #2, and #3 are handwritten and, therefore, assessed for "Applying Handwriting Skills," "Making Good Use of White Space," and "Refining Text Features." Papers #4, #5, and #6 are word processed and, therefore, assessed for "Using Word Processing Effectively," "Making Good Use of White Space," and "Refining Text Features."

Scoring Guide: Presentation

The physical appearance of the piece. A visually appealing text provides a welcome mat. It invites the reader in.

6 **HIGH**

EXCEPTIONAL

A. **Applying Handwriting Skills:** The writer uses handwriting that is clear and legible. Whether he or she prints or uses cursive, letters are uniform and slant evenly throughout the piece. Spacing between words is consistent.

B. **Using Word Processing Effectively:** The writer uses a font style and size that are easy to read and a good match for the piece's purpose. If he or she uses color, it enhances the piece's readability.

C. **Making Good Use of White Space:** The writer frames the text with appropriately sized margins. Artful spacing between letters, words, and lines makes reading a breeze. There are no cross-outs, smudges, or tears on the paper.

D. **Refining Text Features:** The writer effectively places text features such as headings, page numbers, titles, and bullets on the page and aligns them clearly with the text they support.

5

STRONG

4 **MIDDLE**

REFINING

A. **Applying Handwriting Skills:** The writer has readable handwriting, but his or her inconsistent letter slanting, spacing, and formation distract from the central theme or story line.

B. **Using Word Processing Effectively:** The writer uses an easy-to-read font, but formats it in a way that makes the piece cluttered and distracting. His or her choice of font style and/or size may not match the writing's purpose. He or she may use color with varying degrees of success.

C. **Making Good Use of White Space:** The writer creates margins but they are inconsistent or ineffective as a frame for the piece. Spacing between letters, words, and lines makes reading difficult at times. An occasional cross-out or smudge blemishes the piece.

D. **Refining Text Features:** The writer includes complex text features, such as charts, graphs, maps, and tables, but not clearly or consistently. However, he or she does a good job with less complex features such as the size and placement of the title, bullets, sidebars, subheadings, illustrations, and page numbers.

3

DEVELOPING

2 **LOW**

EMERGING

A. **Applying Handwriting Skills:** The writer forms letters and uses space in a way that makes the piece virtually illegible. The handwriting is a visual barrier.

B. **Using Word Processing Effectively:** The writer creates a dizzying display of different font styles and sizes, making the piece virtually unreadable. The misuse of color also detracts.

C. **Making Good Use of White Space:** The writer formats margins inconsistently and uses white space ineffectively, making the piece hard to read. Space between letters, words, and lines is nonexistent, or there is so much space it's distracting.

D. **Refining Text Features:** The writer does not include features or includes features that are confusing or indecipherable rather than useful to the reader. The paper is seriously marred with cross-outs, smudges, and/or tears.

1

RUDIMENTARY

some people have advantages and some is advantages. I am the youngest child in my family. One advantage in my family is that I get more thing then my sisters on holidays. Also I get more atenshen from my dad more, because we do more thing together. Another advantage is that I see my dad more than my sisters. These were the avantage that I had in my family. One disavantage that I have is that my sister that live w... ster gets to see my big sister because she has ger ucar and I don't. The next disadvantage that I have is... wh... my... an... fr... go... ho...

If there is 1 food I could eat for a whole year it would be RAISEN BRAND. I would eat it with nice cold milk in a large bowl with lots of raisens. I would eat this everyday because it is the best food made to man in my opinion and you could eat it for breakfast lunch or dinner. You can make it into raisenbrand muffins or Raisenbrand cookies. You can eat it with milk and on the side you can drink it with anything from ice tea to soda or orange juice to lemonade. The perfect bowl of raisenbrand in my opinion would be lots of raisens, extremely cold milk which just enough amount to not sog the flakes.

PAPER #1

Score	**1: Rudimentary**
Range	**Low**

Oh, my! This piece is hard to read. The handwriting is practically illegible, and the poorly formed margins, haphazard spacing between words, and many cross-outs are distracting. I'd definitely ask this student for a cleaner copy—one that isn't perfect, just readable. Here's a rule of thumb: It shouldn't take you longer to read the paper than it took the student to write it.

PAPER #2

Score	**4: Refining**
Range	**Middle**

Ah, this is more like it. The letters, for the most part, are sized and formed consistently. However, I'd ask the writer to make her letters smaller to fit more words on each line and create more space between each line. The writer's margins are excellent—they surround the text nicely.

PAPER #3

Score	6: Exceptional
Range	High

Before you accuse me of including a word-processed paper in this section, let me assure you that this paper is, indeed, handwritten. The writer is in such strict control of her penmanship that virtually every like letter is identical throughout. Notice the clear and precise margins that neatly frame the piece. The spacing between letters and words is just right, making it easy to isolate each letter and word, while moving from line to line. Not many writers of any age can handle a pen so well. A beautifully presented piece.

PAPER #4

Score	1: Rudimentary
Range	Low

It's a font love-fest! The writer has chosen to use three different, oversized fonts for the title, and another, almost illegible one for the text. He underlines and boldfaces a few words within the text, but the purpose for doing so is unclear. The text is centered, which makes reading difficult because the lines stretch to varying degrees into the left and right margins. Bottom line: this piece needs to be cleared of formatting and given a "presentation makeover."

> We arrived at the hamlet by the road from Saigon. The humidity was intense and the land was cloaked in dense fog. Certainly miserable weather to conduct an expedition in, but we were already a day behind schedule because the monsoon rains had turned the road from Saigon into a sludgy track more water than mud. Our automobile proved unequal to the task, so Jacques and I had to drive (push) it back to Saigon and pick up some mules. We were soaking wet when we reached the hamlet and so mud-caked we could barely carry its weight. The colonial officer cleaned us up at headquarters but warned us about the perils of an expedition up the Mekong during the monsoon season. I politely explained it could not get much wetter than it was here. I thanked him and we excused ourselves. We waded to a large boat stocked with crates and camping supplies.
>
> Our rowing crew made excellent time. By the first day of rowing against the current we covered thirty-two kilometers. Jacques helped the rowers make camp on the bank in the rain while I trudged inland and explored. I chanced upon a new variety of jungle ivy and netted several exotic indigo butterflies. The expedition was engrossing, and I returned only as darkness

Brothers
and *Sisters*

Yes I would like to have brothers and sisters. I like to have someone to talk to. I also like someone to play with when I'm *bord*. I also like someone to have my back.

The first reson I would like to have brothers and sisters is because I like to have someone to talk to. I feel I can trust my brothers and sisters to lisen. I also think they help a lot. That is a reson my would like to have brothers and sisters. The **second reason** is that I like to play with them. I play videogames with them. I go outside with them and play football and others sports. I also play bordgames with them. That is why I like to play with them. **The last reson I would like to have brothers and sisters is because they always have my back. They always have my back when I'm mad sad or down and they always help. Another way they have my back is help me if I'm going to get in troble the tell me what to do. These are some reasons I feel they have my back.**

Vacation

It's typical to see a family take a vacation to some place like Florida or **Calorado**. Well my family decided to take a vacation to some place different. We left in the summer for a vacation that wasn't quite like any others. I experienced a lot of things that no other vacation has ever shown me.

It all began with delayed flights and stale airplane food. We were on our way to Africa, my mother and I. A few delayed flights were slowing us down, but once we arrived the long hours were worth it. The African sun was just setting over the horizon.

The airport in Africa was different then ones I had ever been to. But here almost everything was different. Once we spotted my Dad and brother I was happy to see them. They had been here days before climbing Mt. Killmanjaro. We had a taxi take us to a hotel for the night. The hotel was different then the ones back in the U.S. There were canopies of Itchy Misquito nets that draped over or tan twin beds. When we woke up we hurried to get to our safari. When we got to the van we met or driver and guide. They were our new friends for the week.

Later on during vacation:

My family and I rode in that van everyday for a week, finding animals hidden in the savanah and watching elephants bathe in a cool spring. At night we camped under the starry African sky. When our safari was over we left for one more adventure. I was going to dance with a Mossian tribe and eat in their village. The tribe members acted very honored to have us there. We were treated like royalty. I was having lots of fun until dinner came. I almost got sick having to eat goat cooked on a fire, exspecially after seeing it alive an hour ago. That vacation is hopefully something I can look back on when I'm older and remember every detail. It's not that common when you have the chance to go on a safari in Africa or tribal dance in a real Mossian village!

It was a bitter cold winter afternoon. I had been skipping happily

through the Rochester Onyx parking lot. I had just won my hockey

game and couldn't be more pleased with the way I played. Suddenly, I

felt my stomach roar up at me...........

"Ughhh, Mom I'm starved", I cried

"Okay, how about we stop at a restaurant on the way home", Mom

replied

"Fine by me, Lets go!"

So we drove off into the parking lot debating on where to go.......

"Mmmmm..... , how about.....??? PIZZA!", I shouted

"Great, Shields?", Mom asked

"Awesome", I answered

About 15 minutes later we glided into the Shields parking lot in

my moms monstrous red ride. But enough about that all I could think

about then was pizza. CHEESY, GREASY, SAUCY! My mouth was

watering as a I dashed into Shields as fast as I could. I seriously could

not take it! I needed pizza! FAST!!!!

My mom and I were next to be seated. We stepped up to the

PAPER #5

Score	**3: Developing**
Range	**Middle**

Styling the title to this degree was fun, I'm sure, but it draws too much attention away from the text. There is a disproportionate amount of space between the title and the text as well. The font used for the body is too small and flowery, making the words and sentences hard to read. The header in the middle of the paper is as distracting as the title at the start. Justifying the text was a smart move, though the left and right margins are too narrow. The writer would fill the space at the bottom if she set the side margins to a standard size. This piece is readable, but needs work in presentation.

PAPER #6

Score	**6: Exceptional**
Range	**High**

I love the simplicity of this piece. It's easy on the eye from beginning to end. The writer has chosen a simple, sans serif font that is a breeze to read in both uppercase and lowercase. The margins are balanced side to side and top to bottom. The lines are double-spaced, which allows the eye to focus on the words. The paper is neat, clean, and welcoming to the reader.

Why Handwriting Is an Issue—But Not the Main Issue

If you compare the two papers below by the same sixth-grade writer, you'll find it much easier to read the finished, word-processed version than the handwritten draft. However, the ideas, organization, word choice, and sentence fluency were already working pretty well in the draft. The writer tightened up his thinking to create the final product, but that's about it. When the two pieces are put side by side, however, one is a real challenge to read, the other is not. Proof positive that presentation is important.

It's important for writers to welcome readers, and handwriting is a big part of that, but it's not the only part. After all, there are many ways to help students with poor penmanship, as you'll see in the next section. Handwriting shouldn't determine how students identify themselves as writers, nor should it affect how we assess their writing for traits other than presentation. It can be hard to keep presentation in its place, but we must try. Writing is about much more than being neat. Oh, so much more.

Magical Train Ride

"Magical Train Ride"—handwritten

MAGICAL TRAIN RIDE

One day I was sleeping in the middle of the night when I heard a noise a rumbling sound followed by a whistle? I thought I knew what it was it was a train. I knew trains didn't run this late or on my street for that matter. I went outside and there it was right before my eyes despite my knowledge of trains needing tracks to ride on. But there it was a train. There was a man in the window. I couldn't make out his face but he has as short as my 4 year old cousin. He yelled to me "you coming". I nodded my head and got on.

The inside was bright and comfortable. The man told me to sit turned and looked out the window and within a couple minutes he yelled "stop!" the train stopped. Two people got on it were my friends Matt and Bozz. The gloomy man in the window turned and said "congratulations you just boarded an unmarked train to the moon." Bozz laughed and told him

"Magical Train Ride"—typed

Teaching Writing With the Presentation Trait

The time to be concerned about presentation is *after* a piece has had a chance to develop and improve over time, whether it's a research report and poster created by a small group, a PowerPoint presentation created by two students, or a handwritten or word-processed essay created by one student. Regardless of format, students will appreciate learning about how to make their final product as appealing as possible to the eye of the reader. So make sure students learn over time your expectations for presentation—specifically, its key qualities:

* Applying Handwriting Skills
* Using Word Processing Effectively
* Making Good Use of White Space
* Refining Text Features

To make teaching presentation more manageable, I've organized the remainder of this chapter into sections that correspond to those qualities. Within each section, you'll find a Think About—a list of important questions students should ask themselves as they prepare their work to go public—and a focus lesson. (The key qualities and Think Abouts are also included on the CD that accompanies this book.) The point of each section is to make students more conscious of the appearance of their finished work; encourage them to explore the appearance of writing in books, magazines, and other publications; and use what they learn in their own work.

At the end of the chapter, I've included a cover sheet that helps students check to make sure they've covered all bases when finishing up and turning in work. I've also included presentation posters created by a sixth and a seventh grader to use as models in your class. Give your students a list of key qualities for a trait, and have them design posters to show what they know about that trait—which can be a lot, as these middle school students from Missouri prove.

Key Quality: Applying Handwriting Skills

Handwriting wields more power than it probably deserves given that, really, it has very little to do with the primary goal of writing: capturing ideas on paper. But poor handwriting can serve as a roadblock, preventing the reader from engaging in those ideas. Conversely, good handwriting can serve as a smoke screen, seducing the reader into believing that a terrible piece of writing is better than it actually is. Students need to know that. They need to know that handwriting is more than something teachers and parents nag them about. It's the reader's first impression of them as writers. Use the following Think About to expand students' notions about applying handwriting skills.

THINK ABOUT:

- Is my handwriting neat and legible?
- Did I take time to form each letter clearly?
- Do my letters slant in the same direction throughout?
- Does my spacing between words enhance readability?

FOCUS LESSON Applying Handwriting Skills

In this lesson, students examine three versions of one seventh-grade piece entitled "My Favorite Place" and learn why it's important to use clear and readable handwriting.

Materials:

- copies of the three student papers (pages 316, 318, and 319, and CD)
- three copies of the scoring grid (page 317 and CD) to project
- copies of the student-friendly scoring guides for all the traits (on the CD)
- pens, pencils

What to Do:

1. Distribute copies of the original, handwritten version of "My Favorite Place" and read it with your students. If you struggle to get through it, don't feel alone. It took me quite a while to read it. The piece clearly needs editing for presentation. Puzzle it out with your students.

2. Distribute copies of the student-friendly scoring guides. Project the scoring grid. Call out the traits one at a time and have students use the guides to negotiate a score for each one. Once they've reached a consensus, write the score in the spot provided on the grid.

3. Ask students in which traits the paper scored the highest and lowest. If time allows, talk about why the paper scored higher in some traits than others, using language from the student-friendly scoring guides.

4. Hand out the typed version of "My Favorite Place," have students read it, and have them score it for each trait, as they did for the original, handwritten version. Then record the scores on a fresh grid. Compare the scores by asking questions such as Did both versions receive the same scores? Or did the handwritten version get lower or higher ones? Was this version easier to read than the original, handwritten piece?

5. Discuss any discrepancies between scores for the handwritten and typed versions.

6. Give students a copy of the edited version of "My Favorite Place." Ask students to score it one more time. Record their scores on a fresh grid.

7. Compare their scores for all three versions of the paper. Invite a discussion about the importance of presentation, emphasizing its impact on the other six traits.

Original Handwritten Version

Favorite Place

early morning The birds chirping, the wormth of
the sun beatting dawn on me, well I sit in my tent
and Poot on my close for a long day of fun. I open the
tents door, good moring my granpo woodsun to me,
gist siring Ther looking at him he reminded me of a bruther and
dad. the fresh swect smell of baken and agos, like the
first smell of a stake you instintle now wut it is. Anuther
butefol morning at the lake. after we eat well
go dawn to the lake and go fishing, to my
fishing and the water is like leting a kid loos
in a candy store   you now he will never want to leve.
Ones I got dun with brekfist we wint dawn to the
lake, scare the bluesh green worers and The reflecshin
like a meat win you fase it at the sun. we got in to

The bote and pushed of the shore and paduld
to the mittel. We casted are lines awt and it
remindid me of win hu dropsh anker of of a ship
it kceps qowing and gowing intell it hits the
botum, gist siting ther in the boat like a kid
looking at all the candy. looking in the woter I saw
3 or 4 inch objccts that hit moving, I new we
wr in a good spot Tab the kwik jult otmb
red I now it wus tine for me Tio prepare for
the big hit. Uank the end of my red wiht dawn
I yanked it vp the bind made me think I wus
gowing to brake my pole the fite like your
mom puling yev abrof the condy ile and not leting you git
ing candy. ones I got him to the top he larg
and fat. It tack me and my grandpo to gft him
in.   that is why that lake is my faver it plase
it has the bigist fish   and I wus oluas with
my grandpo win we go to that favret spot

Scoring Grid

PAPER:	Score 6	Score 5	Score 4	Score 3	Score 2	Score 1
Ideas						
Organization						
Voice						
Word Choice						
Sentence Fluency						
Conventions						
Presentation						

Favorite Place

early morning the birds chirping, the wormth of the sun beatting down on me,

well I sit in my tent and poot on my close for a long day of fun. I open the tents

door, good moning my granpa wood sah to me, gist siting ther looking at him he

reminded me of a bruther and dad. the fresh sweet smell of baken and ages, like

the first smell of a stake you instintle now wut it is. Anuther butefol morning at the

lake. after we eat well go dawn to the lake and go fishing, to me, fishing and the

water is like leting a kid loos in a candy store you now he will never want to leve.

Ones I got dun with brekfist we wint dawn to the lake, seanig the bluesh green

waters and the reflecshin like a mear win you fase it at the sun. we got in to the

bote and pushed of the shore and paduld to the mittel. We casted are lines awt

and it remindid me of win you drop an anker of of a ship it keeps gowing and

gowing intell it hits the botum, gist siting ther in the boat like a kid looking at all the

candy. looking in the water I saw 3 or 4 inch objects that wir moving, I new we wir

in a good spot tab the kwick jult ot my rod I now it was time for me to prepare

for the big hit. Uank the end of my rod wint dawn I yanked it up the bind made

me think I was gowing to brake my pole the fite like your mom puling you out of

the candy ile and not leting you git inny candy. ones I set him to the top he larg

and fat. It tack me and my grandpo to git him in. That is wy that lake is my faveret

plase it has the bigist fish and I wus olwas with my grandpa win we go to that

faveret spot

Edited Version

Favorite Place

Early morning, the birds chirping, the warmth of the sun beating down on me. Well I sit in my tent and put on my clothes for a long day of fun. I open the tent's door, "Good morning," my grandpa would say to me. Just sitting there looking at him, he reminded me of a brother and dad. The fresh sweet smell of bacon and eggs, like the first smell of a steak. You instantly know what it is: Another beautiful morning at the lake.

After we eat we'll go down to the lake and go fishing. To me, fishing and the water is like letting a kid loose in a candy store. You know he will never want to leave. Once I got done with breakfast we went down to the lake. Seeing the bluish green waters and the reflection like a mirror when you face it at the sun. We got in to the boat and pushed off the shore and paddled to the middle. We cast our lines out it reminded me of when you drop anchor off of a ship it keeps going and going until it hits the bottom.

Just sitting there in the boat like a kid looking at all the candy, looking in the water I saw three or four inch objects that were moving. I knew we were in a good spot to be. The quick jolt of my rod; I know it was time for me to prepare for the big hit. *Yank*, the end of my rod went down. I yanked it up. The bind made me think I was going to break my pole; the fight like your mom pulling you out of the candy aisle and not letting you get any candy. Once I got him to the top he was large and fat. It took me and my grandpa to get him in. That is why that lake is my favorite place. It has the biggest fish and I was always with my grandpa when we go to that favorite spot.

Key Quality: Using Word Processing Effectively

I couldn't live without my computers. Whether I'm writing on my desktop at home or on my trusty laptop when I travel, I've come to rely on them to draft, revise, and edit. In fact, about a year ago, my editor stopped making edits using a red pencil and mailing them to me, and started making them using Microsoft Word's "track changes" function and e-mailing them to me. So I'm more tied to the computer than ever.

I know many writers who write their first drafts by hand and then move to the computer to revise and edit, but that intimidates me. I find starting with a blank screen, rather than a blank page, far less threatening. And, of course, being able to revise and edit as I go is a big bonus. Cutting and moving elements is so much easier than literally crossing them out and rewriting them. My computer's editing features, such as spell check, grammar check, and the online thesaurus and dictionary, are a great help, too. And I know so many middle school students who feel the same way. The computer should be a tool for your students to use freely in the writing classroom. The following Think About will expand their notions about using word processing.

Reproducible on CD

THINK ABOUT:

- Is my choice of font style easy to read and appropriate for the audience?
- Is the font size appropriate?
- Did I use formatting such as boldfacing, underlining, and italicizing effectively?
- Does color enhance the look and feel of my piece—or does it weaken them?

FOCUS LESSON   Using Word Processing Effectively

I highly recommend allowing your students to use word processing because of its many benefits: it's fun, it's motivating, and it's faster than handwriting. It's also good for kids. Since the 1970s, research on the effectiveness of using word processing to improve student writing has been well documented. Students not only make their writing more readable using a computer, but also make the content stronger (MacArthur, 2006). This lesson encourages students to tap the computer's full potential as they use it to draft, revise, and edit a handbook of basic word-processing functions. The handbook can be shared with other students and teachers in your school to provide answers to questions as they arise during computer time.

Materials:
- computers with word-processing software, ideally one for every two students
- the paper or online user manual for the software
- paper, pens, markers

What to Do:

1. With the class, brainstorm word-processing software functions and write them on a chart or overhead—font style, font size, margin size, location of page numbers, text alignment, formatting options (italics, underscore, boldface), charts, bulleted lists, numbered lists, and so on.

2. Put students into pairs, assign them a software function, and ask them to go to a computer. Have them familiarize themselves with the function by finding it on the computer and reading about it in the user manual. For example, if two students are assigned font style, they might locate the different font choices on the screen, count them, and read in the manual about how to select them.

3. Tell the class that it is going to create a handbook of basic word-processing functions, which will contain tips for writers. Each pair of students is responsible for creating the page about the function they were assigned. Since the handbook is intended for writers who have never used word-processing software before, they need to be extremely clear about the purpose of the function and how to use it.

4. Ask students to keep their guidelines simple and easy to follow. For instance, if they are writing about font style, they may wish to select two or three styles they recommend for school papers and two or three styles for more-creative forms of writing. They should also suggest the size of margins and amount of spacing between lines.

5. Ask each pair to give a class presentation about their software function—what they found out about it, why it is useful and important, and what they included on their page.

6. As a class, discuss the design and number of pages for a handbook. Also, decide whether the handbook will be photocopied onto paper or, if it's an option, posted online so students and teachers throughout the school can access it.

7. Share a draft of the handbook with other teachers and classes to make sure the writing is clear and that your students have included all the most important information. Then have students revise, edit, and publish the handbook. Make the final version available to everyone in the school community.

Lesson Extension

Share the handbook with parents at back-to-school night. Send a copy home with parents or give them the link to find it online. Parents will appreciate having easy-to-follow guidelines for helping their middle school writers. They may also appreciate having them for use in their own professional and personal writing.

Key Quality: Making Good Use of White Space

When we look at a piece of writing, our eyes are drawn to its text and illustrations. But we see that text and those illustrations clearly because of the white space that surrounds them—specifically, the margins and the area between letters, words, lines, and text features. As writers who care about our work, we seek to create the right amount of balance on the page. And we make sure no cross-outs, smudges, and tears mar the final product. Use the following Think About to expand students' notions about utilizing white space.

Reproducible on CD

THINK ABOUT:

- Do my margins frame the text evenly on all four sides?
- Did I leave enough white space between letters, words, and lines to make the piece easy to read?
- Did I avoid cross-outs, smudges, and tears?
- Did I create a nice balance of text, text features, illustrations, photographs, and white space?

FOCUS LESSON   Making Good Use of White Space

Forms are a daily part of life. As your students progress through school and into the workplace, they will be barraged by them. Whether a form is filled out online or by hand, it's important for the writer to pay attention to the amount of space provided in order to fill it out neatly. In this lesson, students get to practice not only completing forms, but also leaving enough white space to ensure what they've written is readable.

Materials:

- a dozen or more everyday blank forms
- pens, pencils
- computers (optional)

What to Do:

1. Collect forms that students typically fill out or will fill out someday soon:
   - health records for school
   - school registration forms
   - job applications (fast-food restaurant employee or store clerk, for instance)
   - registration for a sports team
   - driver's license application
2. Give each student two copies of one of the forms, one to use as a rough draft and the other for the final copy. Tell them to fill in the rough-draft form in pen since that is how they would complete it in real life.

3. Tell students to plan what they are going to write before they start writing. In other words, tell them to use the blank space provided without going into the margins or writing on the back of the form, unless the directions invite them to do so.

4. Ask students to show their rough drafts to a classmate and discuss how they used the space, noting any improvements they need to make in the final copy.

5. Have students complete the final copy and turn it in to you. Group the forms by type (such as school records, job applications, and activity registrations). Then ask students to flip through the groups to find the forms that are the most appealing to the eye.

6. Ask students to discuss how difficult it was to fill in information in the spaces provided. Also discuss how handwriting affects the look of the final copies.

7. Discuss how handwriting might influence a coach's, potential employer's, or school secretary's first impression of you. Then discuss how handwriting might color a teacher's first impression of their writing. Could poor presentation serve as a roadblock to seeing skills in other traits—ideas, organization, voice, word choice, sentence fluency, and conventions?

Lesson Extension

Ask students to find an age-appropriate Web site for an organization that interests them, such as the Chamber of Commerce for a city they'd like to visit or the headquarters of a volunteer project for teens. Then have them fill out the form necessary to get more information about the organization.

Key Quality: Refining Text Features

Students may find it effective to incorporate different kinds of text features into their writing, to guide and enlighten the reader. Illustrations, photographs, captions, timelines, subheads, charts, graphs, tables, and bulleted lists are only a few of the features a writer can employ to break up the running text to emphasize a point, section, or key idea. Typically, writers create these features as they draft and revise a piece. But they refine them in the final stages of writing. Use the following Think About to expand students' notions about refining text features.

THINK ABOUT:

- Do my illustrations and photographs help to make the piece easy to understand?
- Did I include my name, date, title, page numbers, and headers and footers?
- Are text features such as bulleted lists, sidebars, and timelines clear, well positioned, and effective in guiding the reader and enhancing meaning?
- Are charts, graphs, and tables easy to read and understand?

FOCUS LESSON   Refining Text Features

Text features make it easier to navigate and add interest to a piece of writing. In this lesson, students explore books, magazines, and resources they're using in their academic work for good and bad examples of text features—the dos and don'ts of text features, in other words. In the process, they learn how professional writers use text features and apply what they learn to their own writing.

Materials:
- print resources such as textbooks, age-appropriate magazines, and advertising
- pamphlets, high-quality picture books, chapter books, and young adult books
- poster paper
- pens, pencils, markers

What to Do:
1. Choose a print resource and ask students to examine it for different kinds of text features, such as title page, page numbers, chapter titles, section or part numbers, charts, and captioned photographs and illustrations.
2. With the class, make a list of the different kinds of text features and display it so students can see it easily.
3. Invite students to browse another resource of their choice to find more text features. Then have them add those features to the master list, noting which ones were most useful in helping them understand and enjoy the author's overall message.

4. Once the list is complete, have students discuss what makes a text feature work—and what doesn't. They may comment, for instance, on the color, the type size, and the quality of photographs or charts.

5. Ask students to work with a partner and choose four text features. Hand out a sheet of poster paper to each pair. Have pairs divide the poster paper into four sections, one for each feature, and divide each section into three parts:
   - the name of the text feature
   - a bad example
   - a good example

6. Ask students to title their chart "The Dos and Don'ts of Text Features," fill it in, and share their finished products with the class.

7. Display the charts so students can consult them when they write.

Lesson Extension

Tell your students that they have become your "Text Feature Posse." Ask them to search print and online sources for examples of two kinds of writing:
- writing that is in dire need of text features to enhance its clarity
- writing that contains text features that clearly need work

Choose the ten best examples, post them on a bulletin board entitled "Top 10 Text-Feature Scoundrels," and refresh them periodically.

ACTIVITIES   All Key Qualities of the Presentation Trait

A Cover Sheet

Create a cover sheet that students will fill out and turn in with assignments to help them determine whether they've done everything necessary to score high in the presentation. A boilerplate version appears on page 326 as well as on the CD that accompanies this book. You may wish to customize it for each assignment.

Cover Sheet for _____

Name _____ Date _____

Teacher's Name _____ Class _____

Please review your final paper carefully and answer each of the following questions.

1. Applying Handwriting Skills *[If you wrote your paper on the computer, skip to #2.]*
- ☐ Is my handwriting neat and legible?
- ☐ Did I take time to form each letter clearly?
- ☐ Do my letters slant in the same direction throughout?
- ☐ Does my spacing between words enhance readability?

2. Using Word Processing Effectively *[If you wrote your paper by hand, skip to #3.]*
- ☐ Is my choice of font style easy to read and appropriate for the audience?
- ☐ Is the font size appropriate?
- ☐ Did I use formatting such as boldfacing, underlining, and italicizing effectively?
- ☐ Does color enhance the look and feel of my piece—or does it weaken them?

3. Making Good Use of White Space
- ☐ Do my margins frame the text evenly on all four sides?
- ☐ Did I leave enough white space between letters, words, and lines to make the piece easy to read?
- ☐ Did I avoid cross-outs, smudges, and tears?
- ☐ Did I create a nice balance of text, text features, illustrations, photographs, and white space?

4. Refining Text Features
- ☐ Do my illustrations and photographs help to make the piece easy to understand?
- ☐ Did I include my name, date, title, page numbers, and other headers and footers?
- ☐ Are text features such as bulleted lists, sidebars, and timelines clear, well positioned, and effective in guiding the reader and enhancing meaning?
- ☐ Are charts, graphs, and tables easy to read and understand?

The information here is complete and accurate.

_____
(your signature)

I checked the paper for presentation and found the information here to be complete and accurate.

_____
(a classmate's, parent's, or other reader's signature)

Once your paper has been checked for presentation, attach this sheet to the final version and turn it in. Congratulations on a job well done!

Presentation Posters

Ask your students to create presentation posters that contain the four key qualities explained on page 34 and a symbol that stands for presentation. While they're creating their posters, remind students to capture what the presentation trait is all about: appealing text and visuals that welcome the reader. When they're finished, hang the posters for students to use as reference when they're finishing up pieces from their writing folders.

Student-made posters of the presentation trait, from Blue Springs, Missouri. Color versions can be found on the CD that accompanies this book.

Final Thoughts

Presentation significantly affects the reader's perception of a piece of writing. Applying it well requires writers to employ a set of skills beyond the ones needed to set down their ideas on paper. It requires writers to use good strategies to make their work visually appealing. From first draft to final copy, the traits support middle school writers at each step in the writing process, including the final step: creating a finished product that they're proud to share.

Epilogue

One of the hardest things about writing is knowing when to stop. But for me, right now, it's easy. I've shared all I know to date about the traits and middle school writers, and it's been the best experience of my life. I've reviewed research on writing and middle school; I've read fabulous new young adult books; I've met wonderful middle school teachers who generously shared their best ideas—and, like me, their hopes and dreams that this book will help them get results; I've tested lessons and activities in middle school classrooms and seen the traits work their magic; I've gathered and assessed student papers to provide you with an abundance of models; I've rewritten the scoring guide for each trait so it's clearer and more useful than ever; I've organized all of these materials around each trait's key qualities to build a bridge between assessment and instruction. And here are all those materials—waiting for you to try.

And, of course, I met Melanie and Ryann, the two girls you met in the prologue, who reminded me of how important this work is to middle school students everywhere. So, who better to wrap up this book than they?

At the end of their eighth-grade year, their teacher, Linda Brock, asked Melanie, Ryann, and their classmates to write a reflection on what they had learned about themselves as writers. Some of those reflections are scattered throughout this book. But Linda asked Melanie and Ryann to go one step further and write a letter to me, explaining how the traits helped them. Here's that letter:

April 23, 2008

Dear Ruth,

Sup Ruth. These are the steps we took to writing our book. We used the six traits that Mrs. Brock taught us this year we were taught throughout our middle school education. We learned that the six traits are conventions, sentence fluency, word choice, ideas, organization, and voice.

One of the easier things for us to do was conventions and sentence fluency. They both come naturally to us. Now that we are eighth graders, we make few grammatical and spelling errors. The mistakes we do make you fix for us. We reread what we've written to make sure our sentences flow together well.

When we choose our words, we imagined what we wanted in our story. Then we choose the words that help describe the image we saw in our heads. In class we did exercises on showing not telling which helped us make better descriptions. One example is when we had different topics to write about but couldn't use the words from the topic to describe what the topic was about. Also we did fluency practices where we chose a topic and wrote about it for five minutes. This helped us choose our words at a faster pace.

We got our ideas by visualization. To get started, we liked making graphic organizers to help us see what we wanted to put in our book. We made little cartoon pictures to go with our ideas. As we write the actual story, we kick ideas off each other and write them down on paper. Then we add details to it to make a new graphic organizer. We also use real life experiences and modify them to add it to our book. Like the character Mrs. Brock. She is based off our English teacher and our social studies teacher. They are both funny in their own way during class, and we made them into our own wacky teacher in the book.

For organization, we put the events in chronological order. We then went back and added logic to the story. We put ourselves in the situation and thought what we would do and how and added it to our graphic organizer. In the graphic organizer, we put in all the things we could think of. When we get ready to write another chapter, we brainstorm out loud and ask questions to each other. We give possibilities and talk it out. After we get an answer and we put it on our graphic organizer, then we then added details. We also put some rejected ideas into the graphic organizer as part of future chapters.

We make the characters sound the way we talk to each other in real life to add voice. We also use the way kids in our area talk to each other. We just try to make it sound natural to us. We were very inspired by Psych, the fake psychic detective show. The humor in Psych and the cases in Psych are inspirational. We listen to how the characters in Psych talk to each other and try to put in their sarcastic tone into our characters. Another inspiration to us is Cheez-Its. It was a funny joke during MAP (Missouri Assessment Profile) testing. Mrs. Brock said we could have extra Cheez-Its if we finished typing chapters 3 and 4. We finished typing the chapters. You delivered 12 boxes of Shrek Cheez-Its to the school as a bribe to finish the book. We each got to keep 6 boxes. We had a Cheez-Its party that night while we started the next chapter. We also watched Psych while we ate and wrote.

From Your Next Big Authors,

Ryann (Tang)

Melanie (Mango)

The year ended on such a high note. I am so proud to be even a small part of the writing success that Melanie and Ryann experienced during their middle school years. But just like writing, it didn't stop there.

On July 4, 2008, Ryann wrote this e-mail:

Hey. Sorry we haven't written in a while. We've been busy since school's been out. We barely wrote anymore in our book but we're starting it up again. Guess What?!?! Since you used us at the beginning of your book, we're doing a prologue (or however you spell it), too. It's when the girls are eight and it's their very first assignment!! Cool huh. There's only one problem. I'm not exactly sure what the assignment is going to be. But I got every thing else planned out. What do you think the assignment should be? I guess it's going to take longer to finish this book than we thought!

Ryann and Melonhead (but mostly Ryann!!!)

Ah, yes, dear Ryann and Melanie, it always takes longer to finish a book than you plan because you keep thinking—which is definitely the best part! I hope you keep writing; I hope you publish your wonderful detective novel; I hope the joy you've felt as writers this year never fades.

Professional Books and Articles Cited

Alliance for Excellent Education. (2007, April). *Making writing instruction a priority in America's middle and high schools.* (policy brief). Washington, DC: Author. Retrieved November 11, 2008, from http://www.all4ed.org/files/WritPrior.pdf

Anderson, N. (2006, December 15). Are iPods shrinking the British vocabulary? *Ars Technica.* Retrieved November 14, 2008, from http://arstechnica.com/news.ars/post/20061215-8431.html

Applebee. A. (1986). Problems in process approaches: Towards reconceptualization of process instruction. In A. Petrosky & D. Bartholomae (Eds.), *The teaching of writing. Eighty-fifth yearbook of the National Society for the Study of Education, Part II* (pp. 95–113). Chicago: University of Chicago Press.

Applebee, A., Langer, J., Nystrand, M., & Gamoran, A. (2003). Discussion-based approaches to developing understanding: Classroom instruction and student performance in middle and high school English. *American Educational Research Journal, 40,* 685–730.

Arter, J., Spandel, V., Culham, R., & Pollard, J. (1994). *Study findings on the integration of writing assessment & instruction: School centers for classroom assessment final report, 1992–93.* Portland, OR: Northwest Regional Educational Laboratory.

Atwell. N. (1987). *In the middle: New understanding about writing, reading, and learning.* Portsmouth, NH: Boynton/Cook.

Atwell, N. (1990). *Coming to know.* Portsmouth, NH: Heinemann.

Bangert-Downs, R. L. (1993). The word processor as an instruction tool: A meta-analysis of word processing in writing instruction. *Review of Educational Research, 63*(1), 69–93.

Beal, G. (Program Coordinator). (2008). A few notes on formatting. Academy of motion pictures and sciences: Nicholl fellowship in screenwriting. Beverly Hills, CA. Retrieved October 20, 2008, from http://www.oscars.org/nicholl/format.html

Beers, K., Probst, R., & Rief, L. (2007). *Adolescent literacy: Turning promise into practice,* Portsmouth, NH: Heinemann.

Braddock, R., Lloyd-Jones, R., & Schoer, L. (1963). *Research in written composition.* Urbana, IL: National Council of Teachers of English.

Brenner, D., Pearson, P. D., & Rief, L. (2007). Thinking through assessment. In K. Beers, R. Probst, & L. Rief (Eds.), *Adolescent literacy: Turning promise into practice* (pp. 257–272). Portsmouth, NH: Heinemann.

Brooks, B. (1990). Bruce Brooks. In D. Gallo (Ed.), *Speaking for ourselves: Autobiographical sketches by notable authors of books for young adults* (pp. 33–35). Urbana, IL: National Council Teachers of English.

Calkins, L. (1986). *The art of teaching writing.* Portsmouth, NH: Heinemann.

Calkins, L. (1994). *The art of teaching writing* (new edition). Portsmouth, NH: Heinemann.

Coe, M. T., Hanita, M., Nave, G. R., Nishioka, V. M., & Smiley, R. H. (est. 2011). *Experimental study on the impact of the 6+1 Trait Writing Model on student achievement in writing.* Portland, OR: Northwest Regional Educational Laboratory.

Corbett, S. (2007). Baseball for life. In D. Marannis (Ed.), *The best American sports writing 2007* (pp. 225–239). Boston: Houghton Mifflin.

Cramer. R. (2001). *Creative power: The nature and nurture of children's writing.* New York: Longman.

Culham. R. (2003). *6+1 traits of writing: The complete guide for grades 3 and up.* New York: Scholastic.

DeFoe, M. C. (2000). *Using directed writing strategies to teach students writing skills in middle grades language arts.* (ERIC Document Reproduction Service No. ED444186)

Diederich, P. B., French, J., & Carlton, S. (1961). Factors in judgment of writing quality (Research Bulletin No. 61-15). Princeton, NJ: Educational Testing Service.

Diederich. P. B. (1974). *Measuring growth in English.* Urbana, IL: National Council of Teachers of English.

Einstein, A. (1930, November 9). What I believe. *The New York Times Magazine,* 1–4.

Elbow, P. (1998a). *Writing with power: Techniques for mastering the writing process.* New York: Oxford University Press.

Elbow, P. (1998b). *Writing without teachers.* New York: Oxford University Press.

Emig. J. (1971). *The composing processes of twelfth graders.* Urbana, IL: National Council of Teachers of English.

Ezarik, M. (2004). Beware the writing assessment: Q & A with George Hillocks Jr. (Curriculum update: the latest developments in math, science, language arts and social studies). *District Administration Journal, 40,* 66.

Fletcher, R. (1992). *What a writer needs.* Portsmouth, NH: Heinemann.

Gallagher, C., & Lee, A. (2008). *Teaching writing that matters.* New York: Scholastic.

Gallo, D. (Ed.). (1990). *Speaking for ourselves: autobiographical sketches by notable authors of books for young adults.* Urbana, IL: National Council Teachers of English.

Garg, Anu. (2007). *The dord, the diglot, and an avocado or two: The hidden lives and strange origins of the common and not-so-common words.* New York: Plume.

Goldstein, A., & Carr, P. G. (1996, April) Can students benefit from process writing? *NAEPfacts, 1*(3), Washington, DC: National Center for Educational Statistics. Retrieved June 14, 2008, from nces.ed.gov/pubs96/web/96845.asp

Graham, S. (2006). Strategy instruction and the teaching of writing. In C. MacArthur, S. Graham, & J. Fitzgerald (Eds.), *Handbook of writing research* (pp. 187–207). New York: Guilford.

Graham S., & Perin, D. (2007). *Writing next: Effective strategies to improve writing of adolescents in middle and high schools: A report to Carnegie Corporation of New York.* Washington, DC: Alliance for Excellent Education.

Graves, D. H. (1975, Winter). An examination of the writing processes of seven-year-old children. *Research in the teaching of English 9,* 227–241.

Graves, D. H. (1983). *Writing: Teachers and children at work.* Portsmouth, NH: Heinemann.

Graves, D. H. (1994). *A fresh look at writing.* Portsmouth, NH: Heinemann.

Hall, D., & Emblen, D. L. (2002). *A writer's reader* (9th ed.). New York: Addison-Wesley.

Harvey, S. *Nonfiction matters.* (1998). Portland, ME: Stenhouse.

Hillocks, G., Jr. (1986). *Research on written composition: New directions for teaching.* Urbana, IL: National Conference on Research in English.

Hillocks, G., Jr. (2002). *The testing trap.* New York: Teachers College Press.

Hugo, R. (1979). *The triggering town.* New York: Norton.

International Reading Association (IRA) and National Council Teachers of English (NCTE). (1996). *Standards for the English Language Arts.* Urbana, IL, and Newark, DE: NCTE and IRA.

Jaschik, S. (2007, March 26). Fooling the college board. *Inside Higher Ed.* Retrieved October 23, 2008, from http://www.insidehighered.com/news/2007/03/26/writing

Jefferson, T. (1776). *A rough draught: Declaration of Independence.* Retrieved September 16, 2008, from http://www.princeton.edu/~tjpapers/declaration/declaration

Killion, J. (1999). *What works in the middle: Results-based staff development.* Oxford, OH: National Staff Development Council.

King. S. (2000). *On writing.* New York: Scribner.

Lamott, A. (1994). *Bird by bird: Some instructions on writing and life.* New York: Random House.

Langer, J., & Applebee, A. (2003). Balancing the curriculum in the English language arts: Exploring the components of effective teaching and learning. In J. Flood, D. Lapp, J. R. Squire, & J. Jensen (Eds.), *Handbook of research on teaching the English language arts* (2nd ed., pp. 676–684). Urbana, IL, and Newark, DE: NCTE and IRA.

Lederer, R. (1991). Small words. *Weekly reader: Writing, 16*(7) 3–5 (adapted from *The miracle of language,* Pocket Books).

Legislative Analyst's Office. (2002). *Analysis of the 2001-02 budget bill.* Retrieved September 18, 2008, from http://www.lao.ca.gov/analysis_2001/educational/ed_11_Assessments_anl01.htm

Lenhart, A., Arafeh, S., Smith, A., & Macgill, A. R. (2008). *Writing, technology, and teens.* College Board, National Commission on Writing. Cover.

Lewis, M. (2007). What keeps Bill Parcells awake at night. In D. Marannis (Ed.). *The best American sports writing* (pp. 159–180). Boston: Houghton Miflin.

Lewis, W. H. (Ed.). (1966). *Letters of C. S. Lewis.* London: Geoffrey Bles.

Lyon, E. (2003). *A writer's guide to nonfiction.* New York: Perigee.

MacArthur, C. (2006). The effects of new technologies on writing and writing processes. In C. MacArthur, S. Graham, & J. Fitzgerald (Eds.), *Handbook of writing research* (pp. 248–262). New York: Guilford.

Mouland, B. (2007, February 1). Global warming sees polar bears stranded on melting ice. *Mail Online.* Retrieved October 22, 2008, from http://www.dailymail.co.uk/news/article-433170/Global-warming-sees-polar-bears-stranded-melting-ice.html

Murphy, C. (2000). Lulu, queen of the camels. In D. Quammen (Ed.), *The best American science and nature writing* (pp. 135–149). Boston: Houghton Mifflin.

Murray, D. (1985). *A writer teaches writing.* Boston: Houghton Mifflin.

Murray, D. (1998). *Write to learn.* San Diego, CA: Harcourt Brace.

National Assessment of Educational Progress. (2007). *The nation's report card: Writing 2007.* Retrieved May 21, 2008, from http://nces.ed.gov/nationsreprtcard/pubs/main2007/2008468.asp

National Commission on Writing. (2003). *The neglected "R": The need for a writing revolution.* Retrieved January 10, 2008, from http://www.writingcommission.org/report.html

National Commission on Writing. (2008). *Writing, technology and teens.* Retrieved July 19, 2008, from http://www.pewinternet.org/

National Writing Project (NWP) & Nagin, C. (2003). *Because writing matters.* San Francisco: Jossey-Bass.

O'Connor, P. T. (1996). *Woe is I.* New York: Penguin.

Perl, S. (1979). The composing processes of unskilled college writers. *Research in the Teaching of English, 13,* 317–333.

Persky, H., Deane M., & Jin, Y. (2003). *The nation's report card: Writing 2002* (NCES 2003-529). Washington, DC: U.S. Government Printing Office.

Popham, W. J. (1995). *Classroom assessment: What teachers need to know.* Needham Heights, MA: Allyn and Bacon.

Prensky, M. (2001). Digital natives, digital immigrants. *On the horizon, 9*(5). Retrieved May 21, 2008, from marcprensky.com/writing/

Prior, P. (2006). A sociocultural theory of writing. *Handbook of writing research.* New York: Guilford.

Pritchard, R., & Honeycutt, R. (2006). The process approach to writing instruction. In MacArthur, C., Graham, S. & Fitzgerald, J. (Eds.), *Handbook of writing research* (pp. 275–290). New York: Guilford

Purves, A. C. (1992). Reflections on research and assessment and written composition. *Research in the Teaching of English, 26,* 108–122.

Quammen, D. (Ed.). (2000). *The best American science and nature writing.* Boston: Houghton Mifflin.

Rhoden, W. C. (2007). An unknown filly dies, and the crowd just shrugs. In D. Marannis (Ed.), *The best American sports writing 2007* (pp. 81–83). Boston: Houghton Mifflin.

Safire, W. (1990). *Fumblerules: A lighthearted guide to grammar and good usage.* New York: Doubleday.

Scott, C. (2008). *How to create a strong ending in fiction.* eHow. Retrieved October 24, 2008, from http://www.ehow.com/how_4556278_creat-strong-ending-fictional.html

Siera, S. (2005, April). *Study findings on the integration of writing assessment and instruction.* Professional Development: Research on Quality Effectiveness. AERA, Montreal, Quebec, Canada.

Smith, G. (2001). *Beyond the game: The collected sportswriting of Gary Smith*. New York: Grove.

Sommers, N. (1982). *Revision strategies of student writers and experienced adults*. Washington, DC: National Institute of Education. (ERIC Document Reproduction Services No. ED220839)

Stiggins, R. (1994). *Student-centered classroom assessment*. New York: Macmillan College Press.

Strunk, W. Jr., & White, E. B. (2000). *The elements of style* (4th ed.). New York: Longman.

Templeton. S. (1986). Synthesis of research on the learning and teaching of spelling. *Educational Leadership, 43,* 73–78.

Texas Education Agency. (2007). *TAKS study guide: grade 7*. Retrieved October 18, 2008, from http://www.etesttx.com/studyguides/G7WritingE.SGPDF

Thomas, L. (1979). *The Medusa and the snail*. New York: Viking.

Thomason, T., & York, C. (2000). *Write on target: Preparing young writers to succeed on state writing achievement tests*. Norwood, MA: Christopher-Gordon.

Torrence, M., & Galbraith, D. (2006). The processing demands of writing. In C. MacArthur, S. Graham, & J. Fitzgerald (Eds.), *Handbook of writing research* (pp. 67–80). New York: Guilford.

Truss, L. (2004). *Eats, shoots and leaves*. New York: Gotham Books.

Truss, L. (2005). *Talk to the hand*. New York: Gotham Books.

Wiggins, G. (1998). *Educative assessment: Designing assessments to inform and improve student performance*. San Francisco: Jossey-Bass.

Zinsser, W. (1976). *On writing well*. New York: HarperCollins.

Books for Children and Young Adults Cited

Alexie, S. (2007). *The absolutely true diary of a part-time Indian*. New York. Little, Brown.

Barakat, I. (2007). *Tasting the sky: A Palestinian childhood*. New York: Farrar, Straus and Giroux.

Bradbury, R. (1951). *Fahrenheit 451*. New York: Simon & Schuster.

Canales, V. (2005). *The tequila worm*. New York: Wendy Lamb.

Cisneros, S. (1991). *Woman hollering creek*. New York: Vintage.

Collins, S. (2008). *The hunger games*. New York: Scholastic.

David. L., & Gordon, C. (2007). *The down-to-earth guide to global warming*. New York: Scholastic.

Davies, N. (2001). *Bat loves the night*. Cambridge, MA: Candlewick.

Earley, T. (2000). *Jim the boy*. New York: Little, Brown.

Earley, T. (2008). *The blue star*. New York: Little, Brown.

Ferraro, T. (2007). *Top ten uses for an unworn prom dress*. New York: Delacorte.

Flake, S. G. (1998). *The skin I'm in*. New York: Hyperion.

Funke. C. (2003). *Inkheart*. New York: Scholastic.

Jinks, C. (2008). *Genius squad*. San Diego, CA: Harcourt.

Johnson, M. (2008). *Suite Scarlett*. New York: Scholastic.

Joseph, L. (2000). *The color of my words*. New York: HarperCollins.

Jurmain, S. (2005). *The forbidden schoolhouse*. Boston: Houghton Mifflin.

Kadohata, C. (2004). *Kira-kira*. New York: Atheneum Books/Simon & Schuster.

Klise, K. (2005). *Regarding the trees*. San Diego, CA: Harcourt.

Konigsberg, B. (2008). *Out of the pocket*. New York: Dutton.

Macaulay, D. (1979). *Motel of the mysteries*. Boston: Houghton Mifflin.

McCormick, P. (2006). *Sold*. New York: Hyperion.

McLerran, A. (1995). *The ghost dance*. New York. Clarion.

Mosley, W. (2003). *What next: A memoir toward world peace*. Baltimore: Black Classic Press.

Paulsen, G. (1983). *Dogteam*. New York: Delacorte.

Paulsen, G. (1994). *Winterdance: The fine madness of running the Iditarod*. San Diego, CA: Harcourt.

Paulsen, G. (1998). *My life in dog years*. New York: Random House.

Paulsen, G. (2001). *Guts: The true stories behind the Hatchet and Brian books*. New York: Random House.

Paulsen, G. (2003). *How Angel Petersen got his name*. New York: Wendy Lamb.

Perkins, L. R. (2005). *Criss cross*. New York: Greenwillow.

Ritter, J. (2006). *Under the baseball moon*. New York: Philomel.

Salinger, J. D. (1951). *The catcher in the rye*. New York: Little, Brown.

Schmidt, G. D. (2007). *The Wednesday wars*. New York: Clarion.

Scieszka, J. (1989). *The true story of the 3 little pigs*. New York: Viking.

Scieszka, J. (1995). *Math curse*. New York: Viking.

Scieszka, J. (2002). *The stinky cheese man and other fairly stupid tales*. New York: Viking.

Scieszka, J. (2007). *Science verse*. New York: Viking.

Scieszka, J. (2008). *Knucklehead*. New York: Viking.

Selznick, B. (2007). *The invention of Hugo Cabret*. New York: Scholastic.

Sonnenblick, J. (2006). *Notes from the midnight driver*. New York: Scholastic.

TenNapel, D. (2006). *Iron west*. Berkeley, CA: Image Comics.

Yang, G. L. (2006). *American born Chinese*. New York: First Second Books.

Index